HOW TO PRICE AND TRADE OPTIONS

Since 1996, Bloomberg Press has published books for financial professionals on investing, economics, and policy affecting investors. Titles are written by leading practitioners and authorities, and have been translated into more than 20 languages.

The Bloomberg Financial Series provides both core reference knowledge and actionable information for financial professionals. The books are written by experts familiar with the work flows, challenges, and demands of investment professionals who trade the markets, manage money, and analyze investments in their capacity of growing and protecting wealth, hedging risk, and generating revenue.

For a list of available titles, please visit our Web site at www.wiley.com/go/bloombergpress.

HOW TO PRICE AND TRADE OPTIONS

Identify, Analyze, and
Execute the Best Trade Probabilities

Al Sherbin

WILEY | **Bloomberg**
PRESS

Published by John Wiley & Sons, Inc., Hoboken, New Jersey.
Published simultaneously in Canada.

For general information on our other products and services or for technical support, please contact our Customer Care Department within the United States at (800) 762-2974, outside the United States at (317) 572-3993 or fax (317) 572-4002.

Wiley publishes in a variety of print and electronic formats and by print-on-demand. Some material included with standard print versions of this book may not be included in e-books or in print-on-demand. If this book refers to media such as a CD or DVD that is not included in the version you purchased, you may download this material at http://booksupport.wiley.com. For more information about Wiley products, visit www.wiley.com.

Library of Congress Cataloging-in-Publication Data:

Sherbin, Al, 1956–
    How to price and trade options : identify, analyze, and execute the best trade probabilities / Al Sherbin.
        pages   cm. — (Bloomberg financial series)
    Includes index.
    ISBN 978-1-118-87114-0 (paper/website); ISBN 978-1-118-87103-4 (ePDF); ISBN 978-1-118-87122-5 (ePub)
    1. Options (Finance)   2. Investments.   I. Title.
HG6024.A3S5145   2015
332.63'2283—dc23   2014041593

Printed in the United States of America
10 9 8 7 6 5 4 3 2 1

As I always teach my children, any project worth doing is worth doing well. With respect to this book, if in the end it is judged to be done well, it is only through the efforts of many whose names do not appear on the cover.

First, I would like to thank my friend and fellow author, Larry Shover, for both encouraging and inspiring me to write this book and for introducing me to Pamela Van Giessen of John Wiley & Sons and Stephen Isaacs of Bloomberg Press. Pamela, Stephen, and I conceived this book over some good coffee and excellent pastries. Stephen continued on as my support system throughout the process of writing the book, fielding (too) many confused phone calls and setting me back on the right path.

Special thanks to Judy Howarth, my developmental editor, who always had a quick, concise answer to my questions and who took a rough, raw manuscript from me and somehow returned a book.

I am quite sure this book would not have come to be without the strong, even-handed guidance I received from Kathy Graham, founder of the HQ Companies Group. Kathy's influence far exceeded this project. She was, and continues to be, a light in the storm of my career. When I am unsure of my path, I turn to her for help. Thank you for bringing me to, and through, this project.

To my many friends, colleagues, fellow traders, and students, I thank you for teaching me my trade. I find that you often learn the most valuable lessons from the most unexpected people. Only some of you fall into this category, as I knew I would learn much from those close to me. Thank you for sharing your knowledge, support, and encouragement with me even when I continued to whine that I would never get this done.

Nothing I could say would do justice to what the love and support of my family have meant to me. To my beautiful wife, Kathleen, this is every bit as much your book as mine. As always, you went through every second of sweat, pain, fears, and turmoil as I did. Only, somehow, you managed not to complain! You encouraged me, prodded me, supported me, and loved me until it was complete. To my wonderful children, Mark, Emily, Kevin, Ted, and Kerry, I know for the past many months you could see me, but, at least mentally, I was not always there. Or as one of you so tactfully put it, "Dad, the lights are on, but nobody's home!" Thank you for the love and support and the thousands of "it will be great" e-mails, texts, phone calls, and discussions.

Contents

Introduction

Options are one of the most powerful money making asset classes ever devised. Yet they were not devised as a money making tool. Rather, their "purpose for being" is to limit portfolio risk. Whether you are talking about a portfolio of one stock, a hundred stocks, stocks mixed with commodities, or a myriad of other combinations, options can be used to either enhance your portfolio's return on capital, take advantage of leverage to enhance yield, or limit your risk by exchanging a bit of profit potential for the "insurance" a long option provides. But if you are looking to buy an option to limit your risk, someone has to be on the other side of the trade. In years past, the other side of the trade was usually taken by professional options traders. The professional options trader was a mythical creature who made thousands of dollars every day by "picking the pocket" of the poor individual investor. I want to emphasize the word *mythical*. The professional options trader was merely someone who understood that options trading is nothing more than an exercise in simple probability theory. And this probability theory is easy enough to learn; with a bit of time and effort, most people can master it and use it for their own benefit. Furthermore, today options markets are, for the most part, so efficient that you can trade either side of a narrowly quoted market. Thus, there is no one out there picking anyone's pockets. Options provide the fairest, most level playing field one can hope for.

When most investors hear the words *options trading*, they think "too much risk," they think "calculus . . . too complex," they think "too time-consuming," and they think "the professionals will clean my clock." However, none of these thoughts are accurate. I am not purporting that options trading is easy and that anyone can do it. In fact, I am purporting only half of that statement! If you are a motivated learner, trading options is not that difficult to learn. Though it is not easy, virtually anyone can learn to trade options with a little effort. Let's illustrate my point by addressing each of the foregoing excuses individually.

If options trading has a bad rap, it got it as a result of the Crash of 1987. In fact, that single event has, to date, changed the way people price options.

(More on that in a later chapter.) During the crash, there were stories of traders losing everything as a result of being short "naked puts." Does that mean there is truth to the statement that options are too risky? Let me answer that question with a question. Most people are comfortable owning stocks. Which trade carries more risk, owning 100 shares of XYZ stock or being short an XYZ put (which commands 100 shares of stock)? Would you be surprised to know that owning stock is actually riskier? And would you be surprised to know that you have better odds of making money being short an out of the money put than being long stock? The difference in the odds can be considerable and quite surprising to many.

Maybe you have done your homework and have discovered that option pricing models are generally based on either some form of the Black-Scholes model, which is a partial differential equation, or the binomial model, which is a decision tree–style model. Your eyes have glazed over already! Calculus! Complex math! Time to find another book to read? Well, hold on a minute. As a retail options trader, you have no need to understand the calculus behind the models. In fact, your (carefully chosen) broker should provide you with all the calculus-induced models you need to trade effectively and profitably! And some do so at no charge to you! Before you think, "No math? Awesome," I need to burst your bubble. I did not claim there would be no math. I said there would be no complex math. For you to be effective at options trading, instead of the calculus behind the pricing models, you need to understand the odds, or probability theory, behind options. You do not need to become a statistician. You merely need to understand a few basics, which I will address in this book. In fact, it is the probability basis of options that makes trading so much fun (and profitable) for me. I am, and have always been, enamored of games. Games can keep me interested for many hours, days, weeks, and months on end. And when they put money in my pocket, all the better!

You may be thinking, "I do not have a lot of time to devote to this." While it will take some time and effort to learn to trade options effectively, once you get the hang of it you can trade by devoting 10 minutes per day to it. As I write this book, I am teaching individuals and groups how to trade, I am teaching college finance classes, I am commentating on TV every week, I am speaking at conferences, I am preparing research, I am attempting to be a good father and husband, and, yes, I am trading around 10 minutes per day. My return on capital year-to-date far exceeds the market's return, which is in turn having a nice year! In fact, my trading has been profitable for each and every one of the 26 years I have traded. I am certainly no trading savant. I have just learned how to effectively take advantage of the probabilities that options provide any investor. We will explore this in detail.

Is it worth the trouble to learn to trade options? Well, that is a personal decision. While there are some people who I believe should stay away from the options markets, they are few and far between. If you like games of chance (in which you have the odds in your favor) and you like to earn money, you might want to put a bit of time into learning to trade options. I believe you will find it fun and rewarding! But be prepared. In my experience, you cannot take the training wheels off until you have been trading for around 18 months, on average. Of course, some people catch on much quicker, and I have coached traders who had never made a trade before to be consistently profitable after only three months of effort. And I recall one person in that group who was simultaneously working 60 hours per week at their systems development job.

As for the fear that the professionals will "clean your clock," know that options trading is a much less personal experience. It is not "us against them." I find that retail traders often make money because of the professionals, and not despite the professionals. We talk more about that later.

With all this being said, there are a plethora of books written on the mathematics of options. And there are many people who trade options full-time who are struggling to make money. In this book, I will subscribe to the K.I.S.S. (keep it simple. . .) method and stick to only the things you must know to trade effectively and profitably. I hope you will stay with me as we explore the world of options.

CHAPTER 1

Why Trade Options?

I am frequently asked, "With so many places to invest and with the complexity of the markets, wouldn't I be better off letting a professional manage my money rather than trying to trade options myself?" Couple that with money managers asking, "You wouldn't do your own brain surgery, would you, so why manage your own money?" I understand one's reluctance to enter the world of self-directed investing. But after 33 years in the business world and over 26 years in trading, I can assure you that no one cares for your money like you do. Many money managers go through a three- to six-month training program and they are off and running trading your hard-earned savings. Compound that with the fact few managers beat the S&P 500 returns (after fees and commissions) on a consistent basis, and you should begin to wonder why you have not been investing your own capital all along.

The next questions that arise are "But options are so complex, am I not better off just trading stocks?" and "How could I possibly compete with the options professionals?" As a long-time professional options trader who now trades "retail" right along with self-directed investors, I have much to say on this topic. So, let's begin by looking at the nature of options.

Strategic without Being Directional

If you put three or more market professionals in the room and ask, "Which of you can predict market and individual stock direction the best?" you better be ready for the heated argument that will ensue. The economist will explain that she can, because she understands the mechanisms that drive the market in the long term. The fundamental analyst will tell you that everyone knows the market goes up in the long run but he can differentiate which stocks will go up the most. The technical analyst will say, "Hey, people, the market moves in two directions. And I can tell you when you will be near support or resistance levels, and when the Fibonaccis have retraced."

Though always a hot topic of debate, research shows that market movement is mostly random in the long run. And this premise of random (Brownian) motion is actually at the heart of every option pricing model. If markets move randomly, then how does anyone make money in the markets? Well, markets actually move randomly, but with a "positive drift." This means that in the long run almost everyone who owns a diversified stock portfolio should make money. And that amount should be around what is known as the "risk-free rate of return." Over the past 50 years, that has amounted to a bit over 6.2 percent per year. Now, that's a fair bit of change, so you could do worse with your money. But you can also do better—a lot better, actually.

As the technical analyst said, the market moves in two directions. In fact, over the past 50 years, the market (as represented by the S&P 500 index) has gone up on 52.89 percent of the days and down on 47.11 percent of the days. So why try to make money by guessing which stock will go up the most? Options allow you to profit from movement in either direction or from no movement at all! In other words, options are strategic without being directional. You can make money from virtually any scenario if you craft your trade properly.

A Word about Leverage

Leverage is a concept that is often vilified. Yet when leverage is used appropriately, it is one of the most powerful means of enhancing portfolio returns available. Why are we talking about leverage and how does it relate to options?

Leverage is when you use borrowed money to enhance the return on your investment. And before you ask, yes, leverage increases risk to your portfolio. But if you are to be successful at trading, you must understand that risk can be a positive concept. All financial instruments are merely means of transferring risk. (Even the "risk-free rate of return" causes the bond purchaser to incur the risk that our federal government cannot pay its debt. And that risk seems to be a bit higher of late.) As long as you are "paid" more than you perceive your additional risk to be, risk becomes your means of making money. In other words, you need to stop thinking of risk as something to be avoided and start embracing risk as your means of making money. It is half of the risk versus return trade-off that should play a part in every trade you make. By means of illustration, let's look at the prospect of selling hurricane insurance. If I offered to pay you $4,000 to insure my $1,000,000 condominium on the coast of Florida when a hurricane is bearing down on it, would you do it? If you answered "Yes," you may want to rethink your answer, or rethink taking up trading. But if I offered you the same $4,000 to insure my Chicago area home against hurricanes, you should jump all over the deal. In this case, the return was the same, but the risk differed. Now, if I offered you $900,000 to insure my Florida condo and $4,000 to insure my Chicago home, we have a different picture. Here we have differing risks for differing returns. Each of those insurance policies is different. Which is better? I would consider the Chicago home "free money," or as close to free as could be. Chicago has never seen a hurricane to the best of my knowledge. But if I believe the chances of the condo being damaged are 50 percent and the amount of any damage exceeding $900,000 as being very slim, the condo might be the better "trade." Even though the risk is higher, the return may be more than commensurate with the risk. The increased risk led the insurance buyer to pay too high a price, in your eyes. Of course, all risk is not good risk. The types and amounts of risk you take on in your portfolio should depend on your particular situation. Inputs to this decision include how old you are, how capable you are of withstanding drawdowns (and replacing those lost funds), how well you understand riskier trades, how much edge you perceive in the trade, and on and on. One powerful piece of information options tell you is how much risk the options market participants as a whole perceive in a given trade. So, you have millions of investors' collective opinion at your disposal to aid you.

Getting back to leverage, you don't remember saying you wanted to borrow any money, do you? Maybe your credit rating is not up to snuff. Or maybe you just do not want to make those monthly payments. No worries! You have two means of achieving leverage with options without having to submit yourself to a credit check each time you borrow and without receiving those fat coupon books in the mail. First, when you open a margin or portfolio margin account, you are in fact setting up a mechanism for borrowing money. You do not even need to ask to borrow from then on. If you exceed the capital in the account, your broker will automatically lend you additional funds and charge your account only for interest on the amount utilized. How much can you borrow? You can borrow quite a bit, actually. We will look in more detail at that later.

More to the point is that options are levered instruments in and of themselves. If you want to purchase 100 shares of GOOGL (Google) stock ($590) in your IRA (no leverage), you would currently have to come up with around $59,000. But for a mere $3,300, you could command the same 100 shares for the next 189 days, by purchasing a Mar 15 600 Call option. Sure, the option has a different risk profile and profit and loss profile, but above a certain price ($633), you will fully participate in the stock's upside. After those 189 days, you will either need to cough up the remainder of the money to hold the stock, or sell out your options to lock in your profit without ever having to come up with the additional money. Now, that's leverage! Where else can you borrow that kind of money without a credit check? And have you tried to borrow money lately? Even my sister requires fingerprints and a full financial statement for me to borrow $20.

Going a bit deeper into what options leverage means to your returns, let's say GOOGL stock moves up to $650 at expiration of the options. While it is true you will make more money with stock in this example, let's examine the ROC (return on capital) for each trade (see Table 1.1).

As you can see, the nonannualized ROCs for the two strategies are 10.17 percent for the stock purchase and 51.52 percent for the purchase of the call options. Quite a difference! And one that may make a trade in GOOGL possible, considering not everyone has $59,000 to plunk down for 100 shares of stock! This is the power of leverage that options provide. Multiply that power by the loan you automatically receive in your margin or portfolio margin account and you have the framework for some handsome returns!

TABLE 1.1 Return on Capital for Google Stock versus Call Options

	Price	Cost	"Strike"	Breakeven	PnL at $650	ROC
Stock	$590	$59,000	$590	$590	$6,000	10.17%
Options	$33	$3,300	$600	$633	$1,700	51.52%

Options Are a Decaying Asset

You know the old saying that a new car loses 30 percent of its value the second you drive it off the lot? Though that might be exaggerated a bit, the concept is clear. Options are much like cars, though an at the money option's depreciation starts out slow and accelerates the closer it gets to the end of its "life." At least you can make use of cars while they depreciate, but you can't drive your option to the store to buy a gallon of milk or a cup of yogurt. So, what good are options? To the owner of an option, its decay leads to a bit of impatience in hope of seeing your option grow in price before the decay "gets you." But to the seller of the option who took on the risk of the short option, decay is their friend. So why would you ever purchase an option if you know it will decay away over time and serve no useful purpose while doing so? Well, options are not quite that simple. There are two parts to the value of an option, and they are called intrinsic value and extrinsic value. We will discuss this in more detail later, but for now, you need to know only that extrinsic value decays, whereas intrinsic value does not. So, back to the car analogy: Sometimes your option ends up in the junkyard and other times it becomes a collector's item! It all depends on the option's intrinsic value at expiration.

One other point needs to be made about the decaying nature of an option. When you purchase an option, you are paying more than the option is (intrinsically) worth at that time. In other words, you are paying some premium (often called time premium or insurance premium) for the right the option provides. Let's look at an example. Let's say XYZ stock is trading for $48.50 and the $47 call is trading for $2.25. If you bought the call, exercised it immediately and sold the stock out you received from the exercise, you would receive $1.50 for your trouble, exclusive of fees. Let's walk through this. When you exercise the $47 calls, you get to buy the stock for $47 and sell it out at the market price of $48.50. That means you keep $1.50. This is your intrinsic value. But you paid $2.25 for that call, so you are still out $0.75. This is the extrinsic value, or time premium, which you paid for. It is this amount of $0.75 that will decay away unless the stock rallies. And if you purchase an out of the money option, it is all extrinsic value by definition. This means that if you buy an option, your probability of profiting from it is less than 50 percent. So, why purchase it? A long option has limited loss (what you pay for it) and unlimited profit potential. Does that make it worth the money or should you be selling options instead? For the first part of that discussion, we will examine the nature of long and short options in a bit more detail. But there will be much more of this discussion to come later in the book!

Insurer or Insured?

Have you ever wished you could make money like insurance companies do? Rather than paying for insurance each month, you could figure out how to collect enough premiums over time to pay for the catastrophic events that might occur plus a bit extra (or a lot extra) as profit? Or are you content to pay those premiums so you do not have to worry about things, even if it proves to be a bad financial decision? Once again, as we have discussed, every trade is about transference of risk. When you buy an option, someone is taking on your risk and collecting a fee for their trouble (much like you buying insurance). More often than not, that seller will be the one profiting from the transaction (much like an insurance company). And that profit maxes out at the premium you paid (and they collected). But at times, you get to cash in on your policy in a big way. So, over time, who comes out ahead? The answer is a definite, unqualified "It depends!" Wouldn't it be nice if you could figure out the probabilities of an event occurring and its cost beforehand? Just like an insurance company utilizes actuaries to calculate the probabilities and costs of losses and sets premiums accordingly, option sellers do the same thing! But you may feel like you will never be able to figure that out. The math is daunting and the concepts beyond reach. Thanks to some incredibly powerful and easy-to-use software provided free of charge by a good broker, it is actually pretty easy! Thus, if a trader feels the option is too cheap and that the expected value of the trade over time gives her a profit, she can buy it. And if she feels it is too expensive, she can sell it, take on someone else's risk, and hope to profit from it (just like an insurance company). In essence, you can choose to be the insurance company or the insured, and switch roles at any time, based on your assessment at the time.

Probability of Making Money

One of the most amazing qualities of options is that you can quantify the probability you have of making money on any given trade before you make it! That sure makes things easier, don't you think? Although it is definitely a huge advantage, making money trading options is a bit more complicated than that. In fact there are at least three more major moving parts that we need to discuss. We will introduce the concepts here and drill down much deeper later.

If you are able to make money on 60 percent of your trades, does that guarantee you will make a profit? What if you lose twice as much on your losing trades as you make on your winners? Using a quick example, let's assume you make

10 trades and you make a profit of $1 on 6 of them, giving you a probability of profit of 60 percent. That gives you a total of $6 in winnings. But on each of the four losing trades, you lose $2. You now have $8 of losses, giving you an overall loss of $2 on your 10 trades. So, we can see it is not just the probability that leads to profitability. It is also the ratio of our average winner to our average loser.

The first thing you learn in a beginning statistics class is that probabilities have merit only if there is a large sample size. In other words, if I flip a (fair) coin 1,000 times, I can expect to get about 500 heads and 500 tails. I will not be off by much because I have a 50/50 chance of achieving either result. But if I flip the coin twice, I have only a 50 percent chance of achieving one head and one tail. In 25 percent of the cases, I will flip two heads and 25 percent of the time I will flip two tails. In other words, the probabilities have little hold over my results when the number of occurrences is few.

Probabilities also have something to add to the discussion of how large your trades should be. Trade size, in fact, is one of the most frequently overlooked subjects when learning to trade. Let's look at an example. Let's say you have $1,000 and bet $250 on each of four successive flips of a coin. What is the probability that you will lose all four flips and be completely out of money? The math is "p^x," where "p" is the probability of the event occurring and "x" is the number of sequential times you are testing for the event to occur. Thus, in a coin flip, where you have a 50 percent probability of losing, the probability of losing four times in a row is $.50^4$, or 6.25 percent. If your probability of losing each individual event were 30 percent (you win 70 percent of the time), you would go broke after four occurrences $.30^4$, or 0.81 percent of the time. If your probability of losing each event were 70 percent (you win 30 percent of the time), you would go broke after four occurrences $.70^4$, or 24 percent of the time. Based on these results, betting $250 is too large a bet for my comfort, especially if my odds are less than 50 percent. Translating this to trading, if 25 percent of my account size is too much to risk on each trade, what size is optimal?

Once again, the answer is "it depends." Since there is not a simple answer and because the answer hinges on a number of inputs, we will save that discussion for later also.

Market Efficiency

You may be asking yourself, "Even if I can learn all this, how can I possibly hope to compete against professional traders?" I have good news for you on that front! Though professional traders and retail traders are "watching the same picture" and trying to profit from the same theoretical edge, the types of strategies employed differ greatly. As such, the retail trader is actually in a better position to profit thanks to the existence of the professional trader. Let me explain.

We will start by looking at a few of the more common professional trading strategies. First, we look at options market makers. Market makers are traders who get better treatment in several ways due to the fact they provide liquid, two-sided markets in all options for all stocks they are assigned, or choose. There are rules for how far apart the bid and offer can be placed based on the price of the option. So, when a retail trader wants to buy or sell an option, the market maker is out there providing liquidity to facilitate the trade. The market maker can "skew" his quotes so the trader is more likely to buy or sell, based on his opinion. But the market maker has to take whichever trade accepts his market. That is, if someone wants to buy the market maker's offer or sell his or her bid, the market maker is obligated to make the trade. The retail trader, on the other hand, has the advantage of choosing his trades! We can shop for the best bid or best offer for the exact trade we choose to make. Do not underestimate the advantage that gives us!

The same liquidity argument can be made for HFT (high-frequency trading) scalpers. HFT scalpers are persons or firms who quote markets at hyper-speed using complex computer algorithms. All you really need to know about them is they make tight, deep markets of which retail traders can take advantage, but trade only in the stocks they choose. This is in sharp contrast to market makers, who have an obligation to always make markets in all their stocks.

Another professional strategy is that of volatility arbitrage. Proprietary traders, who buy volatility they deem cheap and sell that which they feel is expensive, typically use this strategy. Of course, for "vol arbs," most stocks' options are typically cheap or expensive at the same time. For example, if VIX is 12.50, most equity options trade for a relatively low implied volatility (IV). When VIX is 40, most equity options are expensive, as their implied volatilities are rich also. So, the operative word for vol arbs is "relative." They will always be long option premium they deem cheap compared to the rest and will be short option premium they consider rich compared to the rest. Though they will run a short premium or long premium book (portfolio) based on their opinion of the overall volatility in the market, they will often be on the other side of trades the retail trader wants to make, thus facilitating our trades.

Though there are many other strategies employed by the professional trader that often finds him on the other side of the retail trade, there are two points I would make about each and every strategy:

1. This does not mean the professional is right and the retail trader is wrong. In fact, since each trader could be doing something different with a trade, both could be wrong or both correct.

2. The most important point to be made is that the professional trader supplies liquidity to the marketplace that the retail trader must have in order to be profitable. Without the professionals, the retail traders would be out of business! It is a symbiotic relationship that is to be nurtured, not feared! The professionals keep markets tight and deep. We term this "liquidity" and it means you can buy or sell any liquid option with very little slippage in price. If you think the offer for a particular SPY call is too expensive at $1.78, you can probably sell it for $1.77. This is the sign of an efficient marketplace, without which this book would have been one sentence that stated, "Do not trade options." Instead, I have yet to figure out why everyone who has the capital and the desire to learn does not trade options. It is perhaps the most efficient, level playing field the financial markets have ever known.

Tired, Worn-Out Metaphors

It is time for two tired, worn-out metaphors to make their appearance. Why? We will discuss them because they are accurate and illustrative. The first one we just discussed. But I want to reiterate it because it holds the key to successful, profitable options trading. Let's think about an insurance company and how they price their products. An insurance company takes in (relatively) small amounts of premium from each customer on a regular basis in order to cover large amounts of risk for the customer. They hire a staff of actuaries, highly trained in math and probability theory, to look at the probabilities of disaster occurring, amount of average loss, and so on. They determine the amount of premium they need to charge to give the firm a certain percentage profit in the long run while protecting the firm from catastrophe in the short and long run. They know that a certain number of their customers will make large claims (meaning occasional large costs for the insurer). These are the same things we do as options traders. If we are premium buyers, we are the insured, buying a policy from our insurance company. We generally pay more than the option is worth for the protection or, in the case of options, unlimited profit potential it provides. If we are a premium seller, we are the insurance company. We sell options for more than they are worth, win on a high percentage of trades, but have an occasional larger loss as part of our trading life. In general, short premium is the winning strategy for options trading, just as most insurance companies make money. The small amounts of premium consistently collected more than make up for the occasional large loss.

The other metaphor is one I hesitate to use as it can easily be misconstrued. I will try to make it clear. If you go to the casino every month for the next 10 years and play craps, roulette, or the slots, you will almost certainly come up a loser. The term "gambler" in my mind points to a person who is playing "against the odds." That is, they do not have the odds in their favor but are nevertheless hoping to overcome them. Though this can be done in the short run, it is highly unlikely you will do so in the long run. Using this definition, casinos do not gamble. Rather, they have the probabilities working for them and they know if they do one thing correctly, they will be profitable. What is that one thing? Sizing bets made in their casino properly. My guess is if you were to walk into a casino and slap $1 billion on the pass line of a craps table, the casino would not take the bet. If they have the odds on their side, why wouldn't they take the bet? Odds work only if you have a high enough number of occurrences. So, for a single bet, the casino would not risk losing that amount of money. Now, if the same gambler came in and wanted to bet that same $1 billion in $100,000 chunks, that would be a different story entirely. The casino would take all 10,000 $100,000 bets. In fact, the pit boss would probably be looking at a nice bonus if he got you to split up your bets that way and stay at his casino. Why the difference? He is not gambling. He is going to win because the odds are in his favor *and* the number of occurrences facilitates the odds getting to work their magic. Also, the casino is now able to withstand the maximum drawdown it might incur while the odds have time to "do their thing."

CHAPTER 2

What to Look for in a Broker

Before you trade any financial instrument, you must open a brokerage account. Yes, more paperwork! But for many, that is not the worst part. There are many terms and concepts embedded in the paperwork that are foreign to most new investors. And there are many warnings as to the risks of various types of investments. In fact, there are additional risk disclosures specific to options you must read and sign when you open an account that allows options trading. But what brokers do not warn you about are the risks that are inherent in choosing the right brokerage firm. What do I mean by that? Let's explore the topic in more depth.

Brokerages versus Banks

Most people are comfortable putting their money into banks. They are sure that when they drive to their local branch and ask for $300 to do some shopping, the bank will comply. They are also comfortable that when they choose to withdraw large percentages of their accounts, the bank will not have a problem coming up with the funds. This is particularly true for larger banks. Despite some times of distress, such as our most recent financial crisis of 2008–2009, the fact that the government-run FDIC (Federal Deposit Insurance Corporation) insures accounts for up to a total of $250,000 for each deposit ownership category in each insured bank lends further security to the depositor. But what do banks do with your money when you deposit it? If you are to be truly comfortable, shouldn't you know what happens with it when you drop it off? Well, very soon after you drop your money off, the bank is out loaning it to someone else or to some other business. Of course, everyone who has heard George Bailey in *It's a Wonderful Life* proclaim, "I don't have your money. It's in Tom's house . . . and Fred's house" knows that! It is what banks do. That is their business. And it is for this exact reason that 2008 and 2009 were such terrible years to be a bank. The real estate crisis put tremendous stress on banks' balance sheets as many loans became uncollectable. And it is for this reason that the government insures bank accounts. So, why am I convincing you of the safety of your bank account when we are talking about brokerages? Well, in my opinion, if you choose the proper brokerage, your money is even safer there. When you deposit funds in a brokerage account, your financial institution has a legal obligation to segregate your funds into a separate account for your benefit. In other words, your funds will not be at risk if Tom or Fred loses his job and cannot pay back his loans. Furthermore, though the FDIC does not cover your account, it is in fact covered by SIPC (Securities Investor Protection Corporation). And it is covered for $500,000, $250,000 of which can be in cash. In total, it is covered for twice that of your bank account. Of course, this protection does not extend to trading losses or fraud. (We will get back to this point.) Rather, it covers you against your brokerage firm going bankrupt due to less nefarious reasons. But SIPC is not a government-run (or funded) corporation. It is funded by the member firms that are covered by SIPC. So, though SIPC is there to protect you, just as when you choose a bank, there is no reason to tempt fate. You do not want to rely on the "safety net" under your account. So, let's look at further steps you should explore to protect your money.

Depth of a Broker's Pockets

Just as the small, local bank down the street is enticing, but fails to have as much "room for error" as the large bank in town, a large brokerage firm is generally a safer bet with less risk of losing your funds. Though I suppose that statement can be subject to debate, let me explain my reasoning. First, large brokerages, by definition, have deeper pockets. Thus, just as JP Morgan Chase was able to easily withstand losses from the "London Whale's" trading as a result of its deep pockets, a large brokerage can likewise withstand losses caused by errors. Furthermore, large brokerages do not start out as large institutions. They have paid their dues and are usually run by experienced industry professionals with expertise far beyond those of most small firms. They have generally also "vetted" their policies and procedures to be sure they are proper and safe and work in all (or virtually all) market conditions. Larger firms also generally have instituted what we call "enterprise risk management policies and procedures." These are designed to add safety against all known risks to the firm. But the risks that I pay closest attention to and that I have the most exposure to are those related to trading.

Trading Risk Management

If you have been around floor traders for any length of time, one comment you might have heard is, "My clearing firm's risk managers are pains in my behind!" I cleaned up the language (more than a little), but you get the point. This is one area in which I believe professional traders are misguided. For me, I am happy when the risk manager calls. In fact, before I open an account, most of my questions for the sales team center around their trading risk management policies and procedures. And once my account is open at a firm that I have little experience with or knowledge of, the first thing I do is run up my risk just beyond my limit. Why? I want to be sure the trading risk managers are on the ball. If they do not call me, I do not consider it a courtesy or a blessing. Quite the opposite! If they are not calling me concerning my risk, they are not calling others about their risk either. A market breakdown could then put the firm at risk of losses beyond their ability to cover, thereby putting everyone's money at risk. After a phone conversation and a quick covering of my risk, I will try the process over again. If they fail the second test, I close my account and move my money elsewhere. This has happened twice to me in my career. And if you are a less experienced trader, you should take comfort in the fact that a seasoned, knowledgeable professional who understands your risk better than you do is watching your back.

Of course, there are other considerations. One brokerage firm I have dealt with has a very quick "trigger finger" and will cover your risk for you without even a single phone call. Though this is preferable to not calling at all, it can subject you to losses you might not need to incur. There is a commonsense balance I want my brokerage risk managers to maintain. I want them to let me know when my risk is too large, but I want to have the opportunity to cover my own risk, providing I do so quickly.

Learning from Recent Events

Previously, I mentioned that brokerages are not insured against trading losses or fraud. We have had two recent examples of this, and they have shaken the faith of some investors with respect to brokerages. First, there was the bankruptcy of MF Global on October 31, 2011. MF Global was known in the trading world as a large futures clearing firm, though it had a multifaceted business. Ultimately, MF Global violated the segregation of funds law we discussed earlier and dipped into customer funds to cover its own obligations. What led to their shortfall? Purportedly, they had lost hundreds of millions of dollars purchasing sovereign debt from some of the countries mired in the European debt crisis (Spain, Italy, Portugal, Belgium, and Ireland). So, not only are you not insured against your own losses, but also you are not insured against losses incurred by your brokerage firm. This is why I stress getting a firm with deep pockets and good trading (and enterprise) risk management experience and procedures. Ultimately, investors recouped around 93 percent of their money from the firm.

On July 10, 2012, Peregrine Financial (also known as PFGBest) filed for bankruptcy. Unlike MF Global, Peregrine went bankrupt for a much more nefarious reason. Their CEO, Russell R. Wasendorf Sr., admitted to embezzling money from customer accounts over a period of 20 years. How did he get away with it for so long? He became very adept at forging bank statements, and he set up a false address for a bank so that NFA (National Futures Association) regulators thought they were receiving "proof" of his accounts. In truth, he was forging inflated bank statements to hide his embezzlement and was fraudulently creating false statements on a daily basis for regulators. For his efforts, after a failed suicide attempt and a guilty plea, Wasendorf received a 50-year jail sentence, the maximum allowed by law.

Once again, my goal here is not to frighten you, but rather to make you aware that you need to do your due diligence when choosing a brokerage firm. Fortunately, with each "failure," regulators learn more and become more adept at their jobs. Personally, I have not lost one second of sleep about the safety of my funds in the brokerages with which I currently have accounts.

Account Types

Though there are various ways to break down account types, I will stick with the three types that are applicable to options trading. So, for our purposes, we will categorize accounts as the following:

1. Cash
2. Reg-T Margin
3. Portfolio Margin

Cash Accounts

Perhaps the most common type of cash account is an IRA. You can get permission from your broker (after signing all those risk disclosures we discussed) to trade options with the following restrictions:

- All option purchases must be paid in full.
- You can never be short stock or short naked calls.
- When you trade a covered call, your stock is immediately restricted.
- All option sales must be backed in cash up to the maximum loss possible.

Of course, since options are levered instruments in and of themselves, the ability to trade options in a cash account vaults your account type into the category of a "partial margin account." This is just semantics, so do not get confused. Your IRA is still tax-deferred.

Reg-T Margin Accounts

Unlike a cash account, where all securities must be paid for in full, a margin account allows an investor to borrow money from his broker to cover the cost of the security (for long options) or to cover the risk of the security (for short options). Regulation T limits the amount borrowed toward the trade to no more than 50 percent.

I am often asked, "Doesn't that increase your risk?" Margin can increase your risk by allowing you to put on more trades than you would otherwise be able to make without a loan. But if you diversify your portfolio properly, it does not necessarily have to increase your risk. The act of levering will increase your return on capital, as long as you are profitable.

Portfolio Margin Accounts

In April 2007, the SEC began allowing portfolio margining in retail accounts. For portfolio margin accounts, the margin is calculated based on the overall risk in the portfolio. This means if trades have offsetting risk, margin can actually drop as you add trades. The margin is calculated each night by the OCC (Options Clearing Corp.), using a system known as the "Theoretical

Intermarket Margining System" (TIMS). This system calculates the largest potential loss for all positions (in aggregate) in a product class across a range of underlying prices and volatilities. That margin amount is generally less than that calculated by the Reg-T margin system. And again, position margin is not additive but rather calculated as a total portfolio, thus giving the account type its name.

One note about portfolio margin accounts you should know. Most portfolio margin accounts have much higher minimum capital requirements than do margin accounts. At my broker, you can open a Reg-T margin account with as little as $2,000, while a portfolio margin account requires a minimum of $125,000. Furthermore, some brokers will require you to pass an exam exhibiting your knowledge of margining and trading prior to allowing you access to a portfolio margin account. So though there are advantages to a portfolio margin account, they are not for everyone and are controlled for the greater good of the broker's clients.

Overall, newer options traders should be looking to open a margin account, while experienced traders that qualify should look to open a portfolio margin account. You do not always have to utilize the increased leverage available, but it is nice to have access to it when a situation for which it is advantageous arises.

Commissions

Commissions of all kinds are a cost of doing business. Many traders will shop brokerages based on fees alone. I believe this is a bit shortsighted for a number of reasons. First, we will discuss the types of commissions that brokerages charge, and then we will discuss their ramifications for our trading and our choice of brokers.

Commissions are generally charged in one of three ways:

1. A per transaction fee (often) up to a certain number of contracts
2. A ticket charge plus a per contract fee
3. Per contract fee alone

The first type, a fixed price, per transaction fee, is actually rare in the options world. It is much more prevalent with stocks where you might be able to trade up to 1,000 shares of stock for a set fee, or even unlimited shares per transaction for a set fee. These types of setups might be great for someone who trades stock in large chunks. But for a newer trader who is trading in a small account, I would highly recommend staying away from this type of structure. Let's look at an example where you are charged $7 per transaction and you generally trade 100 shares of stock per trade. That would work out to $.07 per share in and $.07 out, which means you need to make $.14 per trade just to break even.

Moving back to the options world, the equivalent of this type of structure is the "ticket charge plus transaction fee" setup. Using an example, you might be offered a $7.95 ticket charge plus $0.75 per contract fee. This means that for every options transaction you make you will be charged $7.95, plus $0.75 times the number of contracts executed in your order. If you trade one contract, your fee is $8.70 (($7.95 + (1 * $0.75)). For 10 contracts, your commissions would be $15.45 (($7.95 + (10 * $0.75)), or $1.545 per contract. If you trade 50 contracts in your order, your charge would be $45.45 (($7.95 + (50 * 0.75)), or $0.909 per contract.

An alternative might be to incur a per contract fee only. That fee, for new accounts, might be $1.50 per contract. As you can see, if you are trading one contract per trade, you would be much better off with this structure as you will be paying $1.50 per trade instead of $8.70 per trade. As a 50-contract trader, you might be better off with the mixed structure, but my guess is that if your average contract size is 50 contracts, you could get your per transaction charge down low enough to still want to avoid ticket charges.

One of the interesting points to note is that brokerages will often try to force new traders to have a ticket charge. This insures the brokerage will make money on each transaction, even if you don't! This is backwards, as a new trader will certainly cease to be an options trader at all with those types of fees. After all, if you are starting to trade and are selling a $1 wide credit spread for $0.35, and your commissions are $8.70 to put it on and $8.70 to close the trade, your maximum profit is now ($0.35 − (2 * $8.70)) or $0.176, while your potential loss is ($0.65 + (2 * $8.70)) or $0.824. With your probability of profiting at around 65 percent, these trades are virtually guarantees you will lose money over time. So, I suggest not opening an account at a brokerage that insists on a ticket charge. Most brokerages, but not all, will negotiate this. If the one you are looking at will not, it is time to look at another firm.

Assuming you have opened an account and settled on a fixed commission schedule, I just want to put commissions in perspective. Though they are variable costs (i.e., costs you incur only when you actually make a trade) that can certainly affect your profitability, there are other considerations that offset and, in my opinion, far outweigh the commission schedule's importance.

We will deal with many of them in more detail later in the book, but for your consideration:

- Trading liquid options with tight bid/ask spreads has a much greater effect on your profitability than commissions. Here is an example. Let's say you are trading a fairly illiquid stock called XYZ. The option you want to sell is quoted $3.40 bid at $3.70 offer. If you need to give up $0.30 getting in and out because of the bid/ask spread, you are really giving up $30 per contract, due to the options "100 share" multiplier. Contrast this with the difference between a $1.50 versus a $1.00 commission structure per share, and you will quickly see the bid/ask spread in this example is 60 times larger.
- Of course, your choice of which options you choose to trade, and thus the width of the bid/ask spread, is relatively unaffected by your choice of brokers. But your broker's ability to get your orders filled somewhere in the middle of the spread is of huge importance. I recently had an account with a broker who gave me excellent rates, very strong front-end trading software, and decent support, but whose execution was abysmal. After two months, I felt I had given up more money in missed trades and poor executions than their cheap commissions could have saved me in several years.
- Back to that strong front-end system: Having a trading system that helps in finding and managing your trades is also of huge importance. After all, what good are cheap commissions if you cannot find a way to make money trading?
- Data feeds can be very expensive. Many brokers charge a monthly fee to their customers as a means of recuperating their costs of data acquisition. Others will absorb those fees as a cost of doing business. Depending on how frequently you trade, this may be a very important consideration for you. If you get lower commissions but have to pay data-feed fees, you may be paying more in the long run. You are exchanging variable costs for fixed costs.
- There is nothing more frustrating than trading in a slow market for years and then, when you finally have an active market, your broker's systems cannot keep up and you fail to take advantage of a golden opportunity. This reliability, once again, can be far more important than a 25- or 50-cent reduction in commissions.

Interest Rates

We spoke earlier about margin accounts. With those accounts, your broker will automatically loan you money when you have exceeded the amount of cash available in your account. That privilege does not come free of charge.

Your broker will charge you interest on the funds you borrow. Though all brokers disclose this to you, it seems to surprise many newer traders when they suddenly have an interest charge hit their accounts at the end of a month. And similar to our discussion on commissions, the rates charged are usually less significant than other issues, but should still be considered in the mix nonetheless. Personally, I trade in a portfolio margin account and rarely incur an interest charge. Only when the market heats up and opportunities grow do I use enough of my capital to need to borrow funds. At that point, the difference between a 3 percent and a 4 percent interest rate is the least of my concerns. If you are always borrowing, then the interest rate will be more important to you. But if you are always borrowing when the market is slow and volatility is low, we have more important things to discuss first!

Stock Borrow and Loan

If you are always trading highly liquid stocks and options, stock borrow and loan may not be a very important topic for you most of the time. But sometimes (like after certain corporate actions) a stock in which you have a position may become hard, or impossible, to borrow. Let's discuss a few terms and then examine how choosing a good broker might make your life easier.

Shorting Stock

People new to trading are often confused and surprised by the concept of "shorting stock." Shorting stock is when you sell stock you do not presently own. How can you sell something you don't own? By borrowing it from someone else, of course. It is not like you are borrowing your next-door neighbor's lawnmower and selling it to a guy across town. That might make your neighbor a bit angry. Stocks are more generic in nature. That is, one share of XYZ stock is the same as any other share of XYZ stock (provided we are speaking of the same class of stock). Your broker finds someone to borrow the stock from on your behalf and allows you to sell it. Thus, the term *stock borrow and loan*. Why would you do that? You would do that if you think the price of the stock is too high and want to profit from its returning to a more "reasonable" price. You "sell" it now and you must purchase it back at a later day and time in order to "return" it to the lender of the stock. Again, the borrowing and returning are all done by your broker and are transparent to you. So, what could go wrong if this is all done behind the scenes? Why talk about it at all, other than to say it is a normal part of stock trading? We are getting to that!

Easy to Borrow

In normal circumstances, everything goes smoothly with the stock borrow and loan activity. Every trading day, your broker finds each and every stock that it can for you to borrow in anticipation that you, or another customer, might have the desire to do so. When the stock is readily available, we term the stock *easy to borrow*. That means you can short the stock with no problems . . . for now. Generally, this is reflected via your broker's trading software by a lack of any tagging. Some brokers might explicitly tell you it is easy to borrow (ETB), but generally it is a lack of notification that tells you all is well.

Hard to Borrow

There are times when many people, all watching the same picture, come to the same conclusion. If that conclusion is that the stock is overpriced, people who are long the stock might sell their stock (and might even go short the stock). By selling their stock, they no longer have stock to lend. People who have no position might choose to short also. The availability of stock to borrow starts to dwindle and the stock becomes "hard to borrow." When a stock is hard to borrow, it will be reflected on your trading software, and if you want to short the stock, you will probably need to have direct communication with your broker. The broker will search further for you to find stock. At times, they may offer to lock up stock for you for a fee. This fee is reflected by an interest rate you must pay to hold the stock aside for you to borrow against. Your trade now takes on a new risk/return ratio for you to consider before moving forward.

Impossible to Borrow

When there is no stock available to borrow at (virtually) any price, we term this stock "impossible to borrow." You cannot short this stock. Your trading software will stop you. Furthermore, your broker, somewhere on their website, publishes a list of impossible-to-borrow stocks for your perusal each and every day.

Buy-Ins

What happens if you short a stock when it is easy to borrow that later becomes impossible to borrow? By law, your broker cannot allow you to remain short the stock if the stock that your broker borrowed on your behalf gets pulled away (either sold or the owner just refuses to lend any more). Your broker looks around for new sources of stock to borrow and comes up empty. You are now subject to what we call a "buy in." This means that late in the trading day, the broker will buy some or all of your stock back on your behalf and place it in your account. Your short position will be reduced or eliminated at the price your broker chooses to pay. Though your broker "cares" what happens to you, they do not have a lot of time to spend on buy-ins and (especially in illiquid stocks) the prices they pay will usually be "top dollar." In other words, it is in your best interest to avoid buy-ins whenever possible. How do you do that if it was easy to borrow at the time of the trade? Here are a couple of tips on seeing the freight train when it is a bit further down the track, so to speak.

Short Interest

One way to predict the difficulty you might have in borrowing stock is to keep track of a stock's short interest. "Short interest" is defined as the number of shares sold short and not yet repurchased. If you sell shares you own, this does not affect the short interest. But if you sell shares you do not own (short the stock), this sale gets reflected in the short interest number. How are you to interpret the short interest number? There are two ways, either of which can be used to raise a red flag.

Let's say XXX stock has a short interest of 6 million shares and ZZZ stock has a short interest of 24 million. Does this mean shorting ZZZ stock has more risk than shorting XXX stock? Not necessarily. There are two different factors to which we can compare the short interest number to assess our risk.

First, we can compare this number to the stock's float. A stock's float refers to how many shares are actually available to be bought and sold by the general investing public. By dividing the short interest into the float, we get a reading as to the percentage of available shares that are currently sold short. We can get a stock's float from a variety of financial websites (such as yahoo.finance.com), as it is a widely known and distributed number.

Going back to our example, if XXX stock has a float of 24 million shares, its short interest is 25 percent. If ZZZ has a float of 480 million shares, its short interest is 5 percent. So, XXX would have the greater buy-in risk, all other things being equal.

We can also look up the stock's "days to cover" number. *Days to cover* refers to the stock's short interest divided by the average daily volume of the stock. This gives you an idea of how difficult it might be for short sellers to buy back their stock should they want to (or need to!). When the days to cover starts to creep up near double digits (10), I get concerned and will often look to start paring back my short position.

Both the short interest and the days to cover numbers are published every two weeks by the NASDAQ on its website. If you do a search on your stock ticker followed by the words *short interest*, the NASDAQ page should be one of the first choices you see.

No matter which method you use, a growing short interest can add risk to your short position by increasing your buy-in risk. It can also add to the chance of a real, old-fashioned short squeeze occurring. We will look at that in more detail when we start looking at trading strategies.

Where Your Broker Matters

Why discuss all this in a section called "Stock Borrow and Loan"? Once you have gone through a buy-in, you will probably say you would rather have a root canal. You will do everything you can to avoid another. A large, reputable broker will have a large inventory and many relationships forged that will give it better access to stock availability for borrowing. While traders at smaller, less connected firms are getting bought in, traders at the better firms might get to borrow stock out of the broker's inventory. Though size is not the only consideration, size and reputation often play key roles in your broker's ability to borrow stock on your behalf. Though I trade mostly highly liquid stocks and rarely run into buy-ins, I find no reason to tempt fate. Even liquid Exchange Traded Funds ("ETFs" are securities that track an index, or basket of assets, that trades like a stock) will occasionally have borrowing issues, particularly when involved in a corporate action, such as a rights offering.

Trading Platforms

One of the often-underestimated pieces of the "which broker do I choose" decision is the strength of their trading platforms. Some brokers have multiple platforms, one for frequent traders (and professionals) and another for the average retail trader. If you do not fall into the first category, I would be leery of accepting the "dumbed down" platform. Unless the broker can convince you that they are simplifying your life by shielding you from unneeded information, it seems they are telling you you're a second-class citizen who could not make use of and learn the tools other "smarter" traders use. This does not begin the broker/trader relationship in a very positive manner. If they take the time and money necessary to build the tools, you should be able to assess for yourself the value, or lack thereof, that the tool could provide to your trading. A good front-end trading system should do four things at a minimum:

1. Be easy to use and/or provide excellent means to learn the platform
2. Allow you to see historical options and stock data
3. Have a mobile platform available
4. Show trade "probabilities of profit" clearly, accurately, and readily. After all, it is the use of these probabilities that can help make us consistently profitable traders.

Easy to Use

Once you have traded options for a period of time, you will see how easy they really are to learn. Yet options are derivatives of an underlying instrument and therefore have several levels of complexities you can learn. Though it is not necessary to learn all the complexities, they are there and you probably will find certain areas that "speak to you." So, the platform should be simple enough to personalize and use in whatever way makes sense to you. No two traders see things identically. That is what makes a market. Your platform should support you in your endeavor without you needing to spend exorbitant hours of time learning and working with it.

Historical Data

Almost all traders, once they are proficient, will find the need to look backward in time to see what the market has done. Whether it is a simple three-year stock chart, implied volatility data going back two years, or actual option quotes from a year ago, this data will allow you to back-test strategies, make trade assumptions, and gain confidence in your trading. This data does not come cheaply, however. To capture complete option data and store it for your perusal requires approximately a terabyte of data per day! That's a lot of floppy disks! A broker who provides this service "free of charge" is probably passing on costs elsewhere. And why shouldn't they? It is your job to ascertain how much the data is worth and add it into your decision-making process. And the more experience you gain, I believe the more you will value this data.

Mobile Platform

Not only are most applications going mobile, but also desktop operating systems are slowly morphing to look and function more like mobile operating systems. Unfortunately, handheld devices, though growing rapidly in power, are still unable to handle all the functionality built into a good trading platform. But we cannot live in front of our computer screen all day long. Even full-time traders need to be away from their screens from time to time. Your broker should provide a mobile application for use in monitoring and closing trades, at a minimum. Being able to open trades is nice also, but is not nearly as essential as being able to take profits or cut losses while on the road. If your broker does not provide this, I suggest you get mobile and find a new broker.

Trade Probabilities

Now we touch on a topic we will speak about again (and again and again) in this book. All option pricing models are based on probability theory. If your platform does not allow you to determine your trade probabilities before placing a trade, it is derelict in its duties. This is an essential piece of the puzzle you need so you can create an effective trading plan that has a positive expectancy of making money. We will get into how to accomplish this throughout most of the rest of the book. Without a platform that provides these trade probabilities, you will have a difficult time transforming much of what we discuss from theory into reality.

Conclusion

When shopping for a broker, you need to consider so much more than just commissions. Think of your broker as your partner in business. When looking for a partner, do you look for the cheapest choice or do you find the one who adds the most value? I would argue the latter. Fight for the best commission structure you can get, but only after considering all the other value propositions offered by each broker. In my opinion 25 or 50 cents per contract differential in commissions, while it can be significant, is not the key consideration when choosing between brokers. As many of the traders I coach often say, "You don't know what you don't know." Until you have worked with many platforms, had to deal with different firms on buy-ins, or had your trading platform shut down during busy market conditions, you have little conceptual basis for these decisions. I hope you at least now have a better idea of the questions you should ask and what value you need to get from your broker.

CHAPTER 3

Building the Foundation

Though some may find this chapter a bit technical, I believe it is the most important chapter in the book. If you do not know what a call or put is, or are not aware of the Greeks and what they tell us, you may want to do a little (free) research on the Internet before digging in.

I will begin with a short history of option pricing models, but will stay away from the math, for the most part. My goal here is to explain the inputs that go into the pricing of options, which might affect your decision-making process. We will also discuss the probabilistic nature of options. It is this nature that allows us to be "consistently" profitable over long periods of time with our options trading. But so there is no misunderstanding, "consistently" does not equate to "always." Probability dictates we will have periods of drawdown (loss). But if we learn a proper mechanical trading style that takes advantage of the probabilities inherent in option pricing, we should be able to be profitable virtually every year in our trading. This includes periods when the overall market has negative returns, both small and large. We will also begin our journey into a discussion of options volatility, both implied and historical, and discuss their essential role in trading probabilities and in trading profitability.

Option Pricing Models

The first commonly recognized option pricing model was published in 1973 by Fischer Black and Myron Scholes as a result of their attempt to eliminate risk in portfolios. Their formula was a simple, elegant partial differential equation that birthed the current era of options trading. However, there are many assumptions and limitations associated with the Black-Scholes model that later pricing models handle more effectively. Though there are six commonly recognized limitations, we will address only one at this point, as it is a critical part of our ongoing quest to trade profitably.

The technical terminology for this limitation reads, "The instantaneous log returns of the stock price is a random walk with drift; more precisely, it is a geometric Brownian motion, and it is assumed its drift and volatility are constant." What this means (in English) is that the model assumes that the price of the underlying (meaning the stock, future, commodity, or currency on which the option is based or "derived") moves randomly. So there is a (mostly) normal distribution curve of stock prices, without which all of our current option pricing models could not exist.

But you are probably wondering how stock price movement could be considered random! Don't stocks "trend"? Don't they have momentum? Well, over the long haul, their movement has been shown to be mostly random in nature. In fact, just as flipping five heads in a row when using a fair coin is predicted by probability theory and has an assigned probability, or instance of occurrence, random movement predicts our short-term "trends" in prices. And though this discussion on random movement has many dissenters, I want to be clear that all option pricing models must assume this premise as fact for their math to make sense. We will get back to the accuracy or inaccuracy of this statement in more detail later.

Shortly after Black and Scholes published their formula, Robert Merton came along and refined their model further. One of the early changes is that the distribution curve is considered to be lognormally, rather than normally, distributed. Why the change? While the price of an underlying can rise (theoretically) forever, it can fall only to zero. Thus, our curve cannot be normal, but rather must be lognormal in nature. Furthermore, after the crash of 1987, the distribution curve changed shapes yet again, at least with respect to equities and equity indices. A different shape of skew entered into the distribution curve, which we will discuss in more detail later. The point you should be getting is that much time and money has been, and continues to be, spent defining the proper distribution curve of the instruments underlying our options. Why? It is because every option is priced today using a model that depends on this distribution curve. Which option pricing model you use is of far less importance than the distribution curve you utilize. And the upshot for you and me is that these distribution curves allow us to define probabilities of occurrence, or confidence intervals, for any and every event that could occur in the marketplace. Let me repeat that, as this is the key to options trading!! It is the very reason options trading is not guesswork. It is not gambling. If done correctly, over the long haul, each and every options trader can be profitable. This is because options trading is nothing more than a probability game. A thorough understanding of this nature of options will set you up to be successful.

Before we dig deeper into this area, let's examine the inputs that drive option pricing models. Not only is this important to our understanding of the probability calculation, but also it is essential for our understanding of the risks inherent in options trading.

Option Pricing Model Inputs

There are six inputs that drive the pricing of options. Some people will combine the "cost of carry" and "the dividend" into one input and call it "basis." They will then say there are only five inputs. Do not be confused. Regardless of whether we call it five or six inputs, we are talking about apples and apples. It is just semantics. We will choose the five-input method for our discussion and examine each input with a short explanation of how it individually affects option prices. In reality, it is the interplay of all of them that make options trading so much fun and so challenging at the same time.

1. Stock price: This is the most obvious of the inputs. Since options are derivatives of their underlying, it makes sense that the price of the underlying instrument would have a major effect on the price of all its options. And when we speak of the "distribution curve," it is the distribution of the stock's price to which we refer. As the stock price moves, so do option prices. The Greeks will tell you by how much, with "delta" describing the price change based on stock movement alone.

2. Strike price: As a retail trader, you get to choose your trades. This is in sharp contrast to market makers, who have to accept whatever trades come their way and "lift their offer" or "hit their bid." Strike price is one of the choices we get to make on each and every trade. Obviously, the further out of the money the strike price, the lower the price of the option. By how much is partially defined by the distribution curve. Each strike price will generally have a different implied volatility (we are getting

to that!). This volatility is driven by the distribution curve, which in turn drives our probability calculation. So, the bottom line is we can choose our strike price to give us whatever probability of profit we are looking for. Of course, the greater the probability of profit, the fewer credits we receive if we sell the option. The lower the probability of profit, the more we receive or the less we pay (if we buy). Again, this is in keeping with the risk versus return decision we must make on every trade.

3. Expiration date (or days to expiration): As we discussed before, the price of an option is made up of two parts—intrinsic value and extrinsic value. Extrinsic value is often called time value. All options, except possibly far deep in the money options or far out of the money options, have extrinsic value. It is this value that decays. So, the more time left on the option, the more extrinsic value there is to decay, all other inputs being equal.

4. Basis: Basis is defined as the cost of carry minus the dividends due to be paid between now and the expiration of the option. Of course, in nonequity instruments, there are generally no dividends. Also, different asset classes may have different types of carrying costs. For equities, the cost of carry is dependent on the cost to carry the stock and options. But for commodities, it may include storage costs and transportation costs, among other things. The higher the basis, the more the call is worth relative to the put and vice versa. If our "at the money" (ATM) straddle is worth $3 and the basis is zero, the call and put are each worth $1.50 (if the stock price and the strike price are exactly the same). If the basis rises either as a result of a rise in carry or a reduction in dividend, the call value goes up and the put value goes down, but our straddle continues to trade very close to its $3 price.

Cost of carry: This is the cost of holding your stock and options between now and expiration. In equities, it is the cost of the stock times the annual interest rate times the time to expiration in years. It can also include a component for the carry on the cost of the option if the option is in the money (ITM) and trades for a substantial price. But if the option is American, it will never trade below parity. As interest rates rise, the cost of carry rises and thus more of the straddle value is assigned to the call and less to the put. This makes sense as if you remember our discussion of leverage: the higher the interest rate, the larger the difference in cost there is between owning stock and owning a call option. So, the higher the interest rate, the more you might be willing to pay to own a call option instead of owning stock.

Dividends: As the amount of the dividend increases, the basis is reduced. This causes the value of a call to decrease and the value of the put to increase. This makes sense since when you own stock, you get paid the value of the dividend, but when you own a call option, you do not. So, the higher a dividend paid to shareholders, the less you would pay for a call option as the stock holds the advantage of receiving the dividend amount.

5. Implied volatility: Perhaps the most mysterious (and important) input into the value of an option is the implied volatility. If you listen to or read anything about options, much will be made of implied volatility. Simply stated, implied volatility is defined as the predicted measurement of a one standard deviation move in the underlying instrument for a one-year period. So, for example, if a $100 stock has an implied volatility of 20 percent, we would expect that in one year's time, the price of that stock would close between $80 and $120 approximately 68 percent of the time. The 68 percent comes from the statistical definition of one standard deviation in a normal distribution, and is more accurately 68.2 percent, which we rounded down to make it easier.

Note: In reality, this statement is a little simplistic as it assumes a normal distribution of stock prices. Though the stock price distribution often resembles a normal distribution, it is generally lognormal with a skew and/or kurtosis. Also, some underlyings are not as normally distributed as others, with much larger tails than expected. We will look at some examples later.

Implied volatility is a forward-looking indicator that "predicts" (or is the market's best guess of) the future movement of the underlying. It is also known as the "fear indicator" as the implied volatility of a stock generally rises when the price of the stock falls. This is especially true for stock indices like SPX, NDX, and RUT. Furthermore, implied volatility is the one input that many people describe as "guessed at." That is, the market "discerns" what it believes the proper implied volatility should be and prices options, both calls and puts, from this guess. So, how does the market arrive at these guesses? Though many traders dismiss the role of "historical volatility" in pricing options, I believe it has a very real impact on the implied volatility of an option.

Historical Data as Input into the Implied Volatility of an Underlying

If I ask you to give me your best estimate of the implied volatility I should use when pricing the "at the money" (ATM) options of XYZ stock, what would be your response? Certainly, you would need more information about XYZ. You may want to know what the company does. After all, biotechnology stocks, for example, are known to be particularly volatile. They seem to have a lot of large gaps in their stock prices. If it were a biotech stock, wouldn't we want to know so we could build more buffer into our pricing? Is the stock a new issue, which has had very little time for the price of the stock to shake out? Is the stock a large cap or is it a micro cap? Is there some important news coming soon (prior to expiration) that might significantly affect the stock price? There are dozens of questions that might come to mind. But three of the most important questions you might ask would be the following:

1. How has the market priced the stock's implied volatility in the past?
2. How has the underlying moved in the past? That is, what is the stock's historical volatility?
3. What does the distribution curve for the stock's movement look like? Is it reasonably normally distributed or are the tails particularly large?

We will look at each of these questions and how we utilize this information in Chapter 5, "Choosing Your Trades." For now, it is important to grasp the concept that an option's implied volatility is not just a guess. Yes, it is a prediction and therefore might be considered a "guess" of sorts. But it is a prediction borne of some past data, thereby elevating it from a guess to an educated guess, at a minimum.

Implied Volatility as a Predictor of Stock Movement and Probabilities

We introduced the concept of implied volatility as a predictor of future stock movement. We used XYZ's 20 percent implied volatility to predict that the stock will close within a range bounded by up 20 percent or down 20 percent one year from now with a probability of 68.2 percent. That is, if the stock is trading for $100, we expect the stock to close between $80 and $120 one year from now approximately 68.2 percent of the time. This represents, by definition, an annualized one standard deviation move. But what if we make a trade whose options expire in a time frame other than one year? How do we decide the one standard deviation move for XYZ if we sell a $100 straddle with 90 days to expiration? To determine this, we factor the annualized volatility by multiplying by the square root of the time to expiration on an annualized basis:

(Stock price) × (Annualized implied volatility) × (Square root of (Days to expiration / 365)) = 1 Standard deviation expected move

So, using the foregoing example, XYZ's expected one standard deviation range for an option expiring in 90 days is $100 × .20 × (Square root of (90/365)) = 9.93.$100 +/− $9.93 gives us a one standard deviation range of $90.07 to $109.93. In a similar manner, if the option expired in 30 days, the expected range would be $100 +/− ($100 × .20 × (Square root of (30/365)), which gives us a one standard deviation range of $94.27 to $105.73.

As is true for much of what we will discuss with regard to options probabilities, one of the major inputs into the formula is the implied volatility. And since implied volatility changes almost constantly, the probabilities and the expected range are really based on a snapshot in time. That is, it is based on the then current implied volatility. Recognition of what your expectations are for implied volatility in the future is therefore a necessary part of assessing the confidence and validity you place in the probability at which you arrive. Though this seemingly adds to the complexity of using probabilities for determining success with options trading, I believe this actually provides us a key to our decision-making process when lining up trades, because if we can predict the direction of the movement in implied volatility during the life of our trade, we can gain an extra edge. We will spend a great deal of time on this in our discussion of how to choose an underlying.

The Distribution Curve

As we discussed, all option models have the underlying's distribution curve at its heart. Let's dig a bit deeper into the distribution curve, what various assets' distribution curves generally look like, and how probability and statistics answer that key question for you of "What is the probability of a given trade making a profit?" before you even make it.

Let's be clear at which distribution curve we are looking. Just as implied volatility is an option's predictive, forward-looking guess at movement in the underlying, and historical volatility is a backward-looking view of movement in the underlying, we can also look at two distribution curves. The distribution curve that feeds our pricing model and probability assumptions when trading options is the curve defined by the implied volatility of the options in an option chain. This distribution curve allows us, through the use of statistics, to quantify the probability of any strike's price being breached either before expiration or at expiration. These are the curves that were originally considered to be normally distributed, then lognormally distributed,

FIGURE 3.1 Normal Distribution

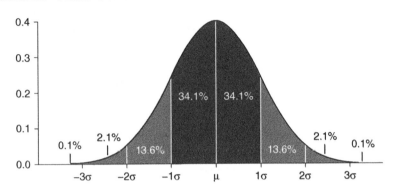

and finally thought to be skewed and leptokurtic, at least with respect to equity options and equity index options. Many traders do not even look at the historical distribution curve at all, and I think that is a huge mistake. We will talk more about that later, but for now, we will concentrate on our forward-looking distribution curve as defined by the implied volatility of the options.

As I have stated several times, the original Black-Scholes model assumed that underlying assets moved randomly. What this means is that the distribution of the movement of the asset is described by a bell curve (see Figure 3.1).

After Merton got involved in the process, it was recognized that the curve was actually lognormal in shape as an asset's value can theoretically go up infinitely but can never go to a negative value. Thus, our curve changed shapes slightly (see Figure 3.2).

Another assumption of the original Black-Scholes model was that the underlying's movement was random but with a positive drift. This led to another modification to the distribution curve that added a positive skewness, as shown in Figure 3.3. The distribution is skewed to the right, or positively skewed. Although the "mound" of values occurs in the left portion of the distribution, it is the tail of the distribution, extending to the right and containing extremely large values, that determines the skewness of the distribution. Those large extremes pull the mean of the distribution toward that tail, while the median of the distribution remains more firmly anchored in the center of the distribution. For those mathematically inclined, the skew can be calculated as follows:

$$\text{Skew} = \frac{3 * (\text{Mean} - \text{Median})}{\text{Standard deviation}}$$

FIGURE 3.2 Lognormal Distribution

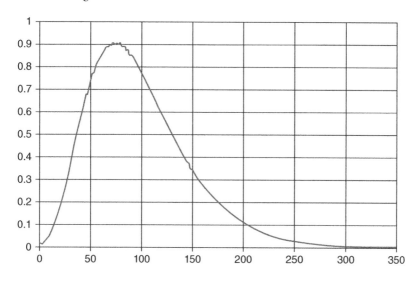

FIGURE 3.3 Skewed Lognormal Distribution

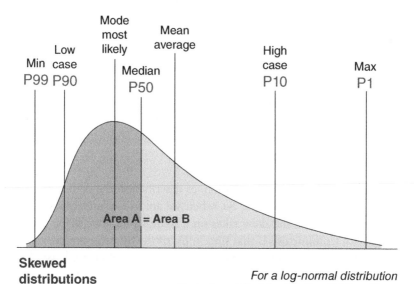

FIGURE 3.4 Kurtosis

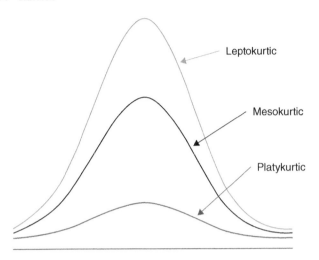

Source: http://whatilearned.wikia.com/.

One last facet of the distribution curve is its level of kurtosis. Kurtosis is, statistically speaking, a measure of the peakedness of the distribution curve. There are three basic shapes of peakedness, as described in Figure 3.4.

As you can see, there are names assigned to each level of peakedness. Typically, equity index distribution curves are categorized as leptokurtic. Investopedia defines leptokurtic skewness as follows:

> A statistical distribution where the points along the X-axis are clustered, resulting in a higher peak (higher kurtosis) than the curvature found in a normal distribution. This high peak and corresponding fat tails means the distribution is more clustered around the mean than in a mesokurtic or platykurtic distribution, and will have a relatively smaller standard deviation.

As we know, the standard deviation, as described in the definition, is synonymous with implied volatility. So, when we are in a relatively low implied volatility environment, the skew takes on a more leptokurtic shape. The biggest issue with leptokurtosis is that since most of the observations are bunched around the mean, by definition, we have fatter tails. Therefore, we have a higher probability of an outlier event occurring. As a result, the more leptokurtic our distribution curves become, the greater the risk that premium sellers will get caught with their pants down when the underlying has a tail risk–style event.

The opposite level of skewness is when the distribution curve gets very wide and flat. This is termed a *platykurtic distribution* and occurs when the implied volatility (or standard deviation) gets relatively high for that underlying. In this instance, the implied volatility, and therefore the option price, is accounting for a wide distribution of prices. Therefore, there are fewer tails (surprises) and selling premium takes on less risk. (Of course these events happen when risk feels the highest and you want to pull in your horns.)

How does all this affect our trading from a more practical perspective? How do we see this relatively complex probability theory in the pricing of the options we trade? To explain this, we now look at a typical equity option chain in Figure 3.5. The embedded graphic depicts the option chain for QQQ after the close of trading on June 20, 2014.

What I want you to take note of is the pattern taken on by the implied volatility of each strike. As you can see, the further the price of QQQ drops (or the lower the strike price goes), the higher is the implied volatility. Looking at the 93 puts on the right side of the option chain, the implied volatility of the bid-ask midpoint is 10.69 percent. The implied volatility of the 92 puts is 11.50 percent, the 91 puts is 12.31 percent, and so on in an ascending pattern. The upside calls (meaning strike prices above the price of the underlying) show the opposite volatility pattern, with each ascending strike showing a lower and lower implied volatility, up to a point. The option chain shows that with the 93 calls trading for an implied volatility of 10.84 percent, the 94 calls having an implied volatility of 10.10 percent, the 95 calls trading for a 9.51 percent implied volatility, and so forth. At some point in time, the implied volatility of the upside calls will usually turn back upward, either when the implied volatility gets to an abnormally low absolute level or when the options get down to a low absolute price at which traders are simply willing to either purchase back short calls or make cheap speculative purchases.

With these patterns in mind, we now look at a different graphical representation of the same skewness" phenomenon in Figure 3.6.

As you can see, this view does not look like a normal distribution, or even a skewed distribution that we might see in a statistics book. Yet this does indeed show the same thing, and in a much clearer manner for our purposes, as this view shows us the real effect of the distribution curve's skewness. It is the skew in the distribution curve that shows the change in implied volatility per strike. And it is the absolute level of implied volatility that signals what type of kurtosis exists in our distribution curve. The takeaway from all this is that all these technical and scary-sounding terms that describe our distribution curve are accounted for in our option chain in a way that is more readily visualized and understood.

FIGURE 3.5 QQQ Option Chain

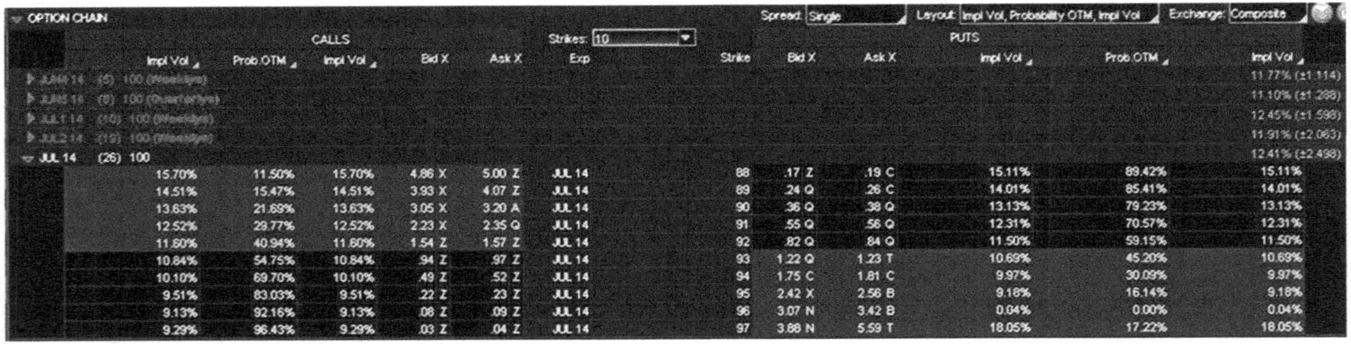

Spread: Single   Strikes: 10 ▶   Layout: Impl Vol, Probability OTM, Impl Vol   Exchange: Composite

		CALLS					Strike			PUTS			
Impl Vol	Prob OTM	Impl Vol	Bid X	Ask X	Exp			Bid X	Ask X	Impl Vol	Prob OTM	Impl Vol	
JUN 14 (5) 100 (Weeklys)												11.77% (±1.114)	
JUN 14 (9) 100 (Quarterlys)												11.10% (±1.296)	
JUL 14 (12) 100 (Weeklys)												12.45% (±1.598)	
JUL 14 (19) 100 (Weeklys)												11.91% (±2.063)	
(26) 100												12.41% (±2.458)	
JUL 14													
15.70%	11.50%	15.70%	4.96 X	5.00 Z	JUL 14		88	.17 Z	.19 C	15.11%	89.42%	15.11%
14.51%	15.47%	14.51%	3.93 X	4.07 Z	JUL 14		89	.24 Q	.26 C	14.01%	85.41%	14.01%
13.63%	21.69%	13.63%	3.05 X	3.20 A	JUL 14		90	.36 Q	.38 Q	13.13%	79.23%	13.13%
12.52%	29.77%	12.52%	2.23 X	2.35 Q	JUL 14		91	.55 Q	.56 Q	12.31%	70.57%	12.31%
11.60%	40.94%	11.60%	1.54 Z	1.57 Z	JUL 14		92	.82 Q	.84 Q	11.50%	59.15%	11.50%
10.84%	54.75%	10.84%	.94 Z	.97 Z	JUL 14		93	1.22 Q	1.23 T	10.69%	45.20%	10.69%
10.10%	69.70%	10.10%	.49 Z	.52 Z	JUL 14		94	1.75 C	1.81 C	9.97%	30.09%	9.97%
9.51%	83.03%	9.51%	.22 Z	.23 Z	JUL 14		95	2.42 X	2.56 B	9.18%	16.14%	9.18%
9.13%	92.16%	9.13%	.08 Z	.09 Z	JUL 14		96	3.07 N	3.42 B	0.04%	0.05%	0.04%
9.29%	96.43%	9.29%	.03 Z	.04 Z	JUL 14		97	3.88 N	5.59 T	18.05%	17.22%	18.05%

Source: TD Ameritrade.

FIGURE 3.6 QQQ Smirk

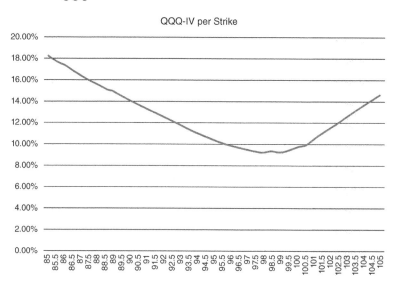

QQQ-IV per Strike

Once we have translated our thinking of the distribution curve to the implied volatility by strike method, there are a number of pieces of information that are immediately available to us. First and foremost, the shape of the curve can tell us a number of things. As we spoke about before, in equities (nonfront month) and equity indices, the shape of the curve often looks like a smirk, where the right side of the upturn is much less pronounced than the left side. We described this in detail before using the QQQ options as an example. But not all underlyings' distributions have this shape. And not all smirks are created equal, either. So, we will first examine the common skew shapes and identify what type of underlyings typically fall into each category. We next look at when and why the steepness of our skew changes. Finally, we will look at exceptions to the rule, why they occur, and how we can interpret them and take advantage of them in our trading. But before we venture into that, let us ponder why a skew exists at all. Were Black and Scholes flat-out wrong about Brownian motion? Does the skew invalidate their work and their pricing model? Or can we explain the skew in concert with the pricing models that exist? Let's begin with a bit of history.

Up until the stock market crash of 1987, virtually no one priced options with a volatility skew that was anything like what we see today. In fact, the skew in equities and equity indices was that of a small smile, where implied volatility moved up slightly the further you moved away from the strike price closest to the underlying's price (see Figure 3.7). That occurred in both directions.

FIGURE 3.7 Smile

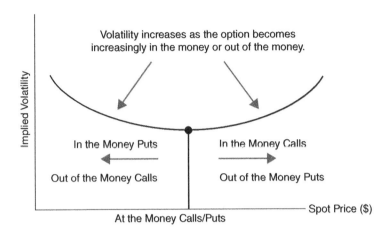

Source: www.investopedia.com.

But after the crash, people recognized that the velocity of down moves was higher than the velocity of up moves, and the "smirk" or, more technically, the "reverse skew" became the norm. Another phenomenon that led to people being willing to pay more for downside protection was just how untradable the markets were during the crash. Markets widened due to the uncertainty of the situation, leading to the conclusion you needed to own "hurricane insurance before you saw the storm coming at you." Thus, from 1987 onward, equity traders were willing to pay up for downside protection, which helped cause the smirk we see today. One other thing that came out of the crash (and the mini-crash that followed in 1989) was the saying that the stock market drifts up and crashes down. This saying is another nod to the theory that the skew exists due to the velocity of movement differential in the stock market between up moves and down moves.

But there is something else that also contributes to the skew, and that is natural order flow. Thinking about how equity options markets are typically utilized, we must place ourselves in the role of a typical money manager. Of course, sophisticated individual investors, in which category I hope you do (or will) fall into, might also think similarly. Money managers will at times sell out of the money calls against their individual equity positions to enhance their yield. These *covered calls*, as they are known, historically have outperformed the market by a substantial differential. This strategy is also frequently utilized on equity index options, such as the SPX, RUT, and NDX, to enhance yield on an entire diversified portfolio in one trade. The Chicago Board Options Exchange quotes a measure of the performance of the SPX buy/write under the symbol BXM (see Figure 3.8).

FIGURE 3.8 BXM versus SPX Chart

Source: TD Ameritrade.

Since buy/writes, as covered calls are frequently called since you buy the stock and write an out of the money call against it, give up potential upside for the right to capture that extra yield, in times of extraordinary upward movement in the stock market the BXM will lag overall market returns. Though these times might discourage widespread use of the strategy, if used systematically over time, it has proven to be a worthy trade. The persistent use of covered calls might cause volatility of upside, out of the money calls to fall as compared with other options in the option chain. This might partly account for some of our upside skew. On the flip side, money managers will frequently purchase out of the money puts to protect their portfolio's downside. These puts will benefit from the down move thereby offsetting some of the losses in their underlying portfolio. This incessant buying of "insurance puts" can cause the implied volatility of those out of the money puts to rise as compared to the at the money options, giving us the type of downside skew we often see. Of course, the purchase of those out of the money puts is a low probability trade, and I am frequently a seller of them to the funds. But the point is that this normal flow of options contributes to the volatility skew we typically see in the equity and equity index options.

Though it makes intuitive sense that the natural order flow would contribute to the skew, is there empirical evidence that supports this hypothesis? I personally believe it is visible at various times throughout the market cycle. After trading for many years, you will begin to discern patterns in the skew that become predictable. One of the most visible patterns has to do with the slope (or steepness) of the downside skew. What I mean by the steepness of the downside skew is the amount of implied volatility increase we see as we move further out of the money on our puts. Though there are many ways to measure this, one common way traders measure the skew is by how much the implied volatility rises for each 10 delta change in the options. I generally subtract the 40 delta option's implied volatility from the 20 delta option's implied volatility and divide the answer by two. This gives me a wider range of implied volatilities from which to discern the slope of the skew. Let's look at an example in Figure 3.9.

Looking at the 41 puts, they have a delta of 42 and an implied volatility of 36.92 percent. The 38 puts have a delta of 22 and an implied volatility of 38.93 percent. So, the delta difference is 20 and the implied volatility difference is 2.01 percent. Dividing 2.01 percent by 2.0 (20 delta divided by 10 delta difference for which we make the calculation), we see a skew of just over 1.00, or 1.005 to be more exact. In the course of normal market movement, the slope of the skew tends to change with certain types of events. For example, when a normal, upward trending, moderate VIX (14 to 19 or there about) environment exists, the put skew tends to have a relatively

FIGURE 3.9 GME Option Chain

Exp	Strike	Bid	Ask	Impl Vol	Prob.OTM	Delta
						34.62% (±1.103)
						39.37% (±2.206)
						37.76% (±4.087)
AUG 14	32	.06	.12	46.17%	95.25%	-.03
AUG 14	33	.10	.20	46.24%	92.82%	-.05
AUG 14	34	.16	.26	44.86%	90.47%	-.07
AUG 14	35	.23	.27	41.71%	88.60%	-.09
AUG 14	36	.35	.43	41.86%	84.01%	-.13
AUG 14	37	.49	.57	40.54%	79.52%	-.17
AUG 14	38	.67	.73	38.93%	74.36%	-.22
AUG 14	39	.92	.99	38.15%	67.80%	-.28
AUG 14	40	1.25	1.32	37.56%	60.45%	-.35
AUG 14	41	1.65	1.72	36.92%	52.67%	-.42
AUG 14	42	2.13	2.20	36.30%	44.71%	-.51
AUG 14	43	2.71	2.79	36.17%	36.99%	-.58
AUG 14	44	3.35	3.50	36.36%	30.00%	-.66
AUG 14	45	4.05	4.25	36.21%	23.70%	-.72
AUG 14	46	4.85	5.05	36.45%	18.50%	-.78
AUG 14	47	5.70	5.95	37.54%	14.70%	-.82
AUG 14	48	6.55	7.30	44.46%	14.64%	-.82

Source: TD Ameritrade.

gentle slope. But if the stock or the market overall begins to fall, investors and traders will often begin to buy out of the money puts in more volume to protect against their long stock positions. This increased demand will cause the slope to steepen. Of course, the overall implied volatility will also rise, but the out of the money puts (and therefore the in the money calls, due to put/call parity) will rise faster due to the demand for the "insurance puts." If the market continues to fall quickly and the overall implied volatility reaches historically elevated levels, this pattern will often reverse itself and the slope of the put skew will actually start to flatten a bit. Why is this? When the skew is steep, purchasing out of the money puts requires you to pay a much higher implied volatility than if you were purchasing at the money puts. But there is a limit to what absolute implied volatility a trader is willing to pay. To put this in perspective, let's go back to the example of hurricane insurance. If you have a home on the Ft. Myers beach that costs $750,000 to replace if it were a total loss after a hurricane, how much would you pay for hurricane insurance? You certainly would not pay over $750,000 even if the hurricane were visible on the horizon. And since your house might not be a total loss even if the hurricane does hit, you probably would not pay near $750,000 even as the hurricane were battering the shore. In much the same way, would you ever pay 100 percent implied volatility to defend a stock position? Remember that with a lognormal distribution, a 100 percent implied volatility protects you down to zero on your stock price for the period of time ending one year from now. You are paying "replacement value" for your home at that point. Thus, as implied volatility gets very high, the extra implied volatility pumped into the downside puts starts to reduce and the slope of the put skew begins to flatten. When the pattern reverses, it does so in a similar pattern. As the market reverses and starts to rise (or even just sit for a day or two), the overall implied volatility begins to recede. But the skew will steepen as the out of the money puts retain more volatility in their prices. The pain of the downside move remains fresh in the minds of investors for some time to come, and thus the skew will not return to its prior slope for months to come.

Interestingly, there is also a steepening of the put slope when implied volatility gets particularly low in a stock or equity index. For example, on July 3, 2014, the VIX closed at 10.32, which is a particularly low implied volatility for the SPX and a 52-week low. At the same time, the skew closed at its fourth steepest slope of the past 52 weeks. This is because with implied volatility so low, insurance in the form of out of the money puts are particularly cheap. Back to our hurricane example: If it is January, when the chance of a hurricane seems far off, and the insurance company offers insurance for $50 per year, you buy it for as many years as you can lock the price in, as it is cheap at twice the price.

You may be wondering how I am figuring the historical slope of the skew for the SPX. The Chicago Board Options Exchange (CBOE) publishes a "skew index" under the ticker "SKEW." Though this is not calculated the way I described earlier, by looking at a chart of it, you can get a relative view of the steepness of the skew very easily. You can read about it on the CBOE website at www.cboe.com/micro/skew/introduction.aspx, or you can dig into the method of calculation by reading the white paper here: www.cboe.com/micro/skew/documents/SKEWwhitepaperjan2011.pdf.

As you can see, predicting the steepness of the skew in normal conditions is not a straightforward process. And determining how the skew will change as the environment changes is also not simple. Most proprietary trading firms will predict the movement of the skew by creating a three-dimensional model called a 3-D vol surface tool, or some similar name. These models have become so common place today that the CME group actually publishes their own version for the S&P 500 futures options on a daily basis. This can be found among the various reports on their website at this address: ftp://ftp.cmegroup.com/volsurface/SNP500_Vol_Surface.pdf.

FIGURE 3.10 Volatility Smile

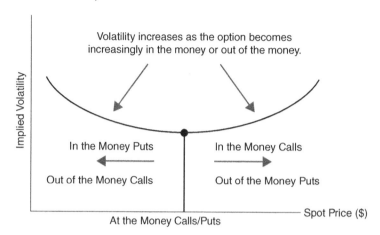

Though the "smirk," or reverse skew, is almost always present in equity index options and frequently present in equity options, with the exception of front month options that are close to expiration and weekly options, there are certain conditions that may arise that will change the shape of the skew. One situation, in particular, warrants its own section as it can give rise to trading opportunities depending on how the skew reacts. This situation is that of a breakout stock in which the price rises to either 52-week highs or, better yet, all-time highs. More on this in a bit.

Though we have now looked at and discussed a bit about two of the three common shapes the skew takes on, we will now review and briefly expand our discussion to other types of underlyings and the type of skew we commonly see in their option chains.

As we described earlier, the volatility smile is one in which the implied volatility rises as the strike price moves in either direction from the underlying price (see Figure 3.10).

This shape occurs when demand for options is higher for both in the money and out of the money options. The volatility smile skew pattern is commonly seen in near-term equity options and options in the forex market and interest rate markets, like bond futures options.

And as we spoke about at some length, the reverse skew, or smirk, is common in equity indices, and nonfront month equity options (see Figure 3.11).

The final skew pattern we commonly see is that of the forward skew, shown in Figure 3.12.

FIGURE 3.11 Smirk

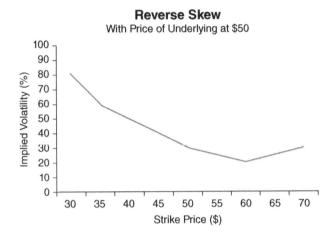

Reverse Skew
With Price of Underlying at $50

Source: www.theoptionsguide.com.

The forward skew pattern is common for options in the commodities market. When supply is tight, businesses would rather pay more to secure supply than to risk supply disruption. This will cause them to pay more for out of the money call options to protect against a price squeeze when demand far exceeds supply.

Though these three patterns represent the norm for the underlyings discussed, there are exceptions to the rule, as there are in almost anything. We will now look at one such potential exception in more detail.

FIGURE 3.12 Forward Skew

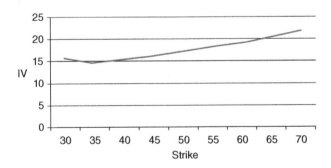

Breakout Stocks

A breakout stock is one that is reaching either a 52-week (one-year) high price, or better yet, an all-time high price. This section is particularly relevant as I write this as the extended rally the market has been enjoying is producing plenty of these. However, when we are in a bear market, we can go for long periods of time without seeing many breakout stocks. What makes a breakout stock different and does it present a trading opportunity? Let us look at these two questions separately.

As we have discussed, implied volatility is a forward-looking predictor of the magnitude of an underlying's movement. As a number (more specifically, a percentage), it says nothing about direction of movement. Directional biases are incorporated in the skew of the distribution curve. Let us now add in a seemingly random thought, but one that is well known and important to always keep in mind: The market hates uncertainty. Usually, we think of uncertainty as entering when the market begins to fall quickly. But this same principle enters our thoughts when a stock breaks above its old highs. We begin to ask, "Just how high can this stock go?" And this uncertainty can cause the implied volatility to rise as the stock goes higher. This is in direct contradiction to what normally occurs as a stock rises, as in general, the implied volatility has a negative correlation with the price of the stock. But as we enter "unknown territory," the uncertainty will sometimes cause the opposite to occur. Furthermore, there will probably be many traders who are shorting the stock against the stock's high price. If the stock breaks through that high price, "many traders" may be forced to (or just desire to) cover. We call this a "short squeeze" as many shorts run to cover their positions at the same time. And, conveniently enough, there is a way to tell just how many open short shares there are for a stock. (Open short shares are the number of shares sold short, but not yet covered.) Thus, we can quantify the "many traders" and not have to guess. The NASDAQ publishes a count of the short interest for each and every listed stock twice per month and keeps 12 months of data on its website. These can be found at www.nasdaq.com/symbol/XXX/short-interest, where XXX is the stock's symbol. For example, to find Apple's short interest, you would go to www.nasdaq.com/symbol/aapl/short-interest. The interpretation of this data takes a little bit of knowhow, however. We will look at this with the aid of an example. As of June 30, 2014, IBM's stock had a short interest of 27,294,767 shares. As of the same date, Apple stock (AAPL) had a short interest of 112,308,789. Does this mean Apple has over four times the risk of a short squeeze that IBM has? In actuality, the story is quite the contrary. We generally predict the risk of a short squeeze not from the absolute number of short shares outstanding but rather from two ratios. The first is the ratio of the number of short shares divided by the number of shares outstanding. This ratio should be somewhat self-explanatory. If a stock has only 1,000 shares outstanding and has a short interest of 750, that is quite a large short interest as 75 percent of its shares are sold short. But if a stock has a short interest of a million shares with 10 billion shares outstanding, there would be little risk of a squeeze. The second ratio, and one that most traders use, is the ratio of the number of short shares divided by the average daily volume of the stock. We call this the "days to cover." The NASDAQ site presents this information already calculated for our use. Using this information, we see that the days to cover for IBM, with a short interest of around 27 million shares, is actually just over 6.5 days, while the days to cover for AAPL, with a short interest of 112 million, is around 2.46. So, despite AAPL having over four times the short interest of IBM, I would perceive IBM's risk of a short squeeze to be more than double that of AAPL. One more point to be careful of is when the volume of a stock changes suddenly. Using our same example, IBM has had a fairly consistent average daily share volume, and I would therefore take the days to cover ratio at its face value. But Apple stock has had wildly fluctuating share volume of late, with a tremendous growth in volume that seems to be falling back a bit during the past few weeks. So, since we cannot be sure of the average volume, we cannot be sure the days to cover is telling us the whole story. Looking at the absolute number of short interest outstanding and its trend might give us more of a clue, as will looking at the first ratio we discussed, that of percentage of shares short. One last note is to be careful of stock splits affecting these numbers when looking at absolute numbers. When a stock splits two for one, the number of short shares will automatically double as each share is replaced with two shares of half the value. We generally anticipate the number of shares traded per day to more than make up for this multiplier. In fact, that is one of the main reasons stocks split. The company splits the shares in order to make their stock more affordable so more investors will purchase them and liquidity will increase.

So at what "days to cover" level do we begin to fear a short squeeze? There is no real answer for that question, as many other issues can contribute to the squeeze. But, in general, I start to get a bit concerned when it crosses above five, more concerned at seven or eight, and the hair stands up on the back of my neck above 10. The high short interest alone does not cause a short squeeze. But if a catalyst causes the stock to reach new highs or take off to the upside, covering a high amount of short interest can certainly cause an acceleration of the upside movement.

One other situation to always be aware of, no matter where the stock price is in its range, is if the shares of the stock are easy to borrow, hard to borrow, or impossible to borrow. As we discussed in our section on broker-ages, when a stock is impossible to borrow, brokerages may have to initiate buy-ins of short positions. This may not only cause high "prints" of the stock price late in the day, but also send holders of short stock to scurry to cover their shares to avoid more buy-ins. Of course, if you try to short stock that your brokerage cannot borrow, you will be unable to execute the trade. But this will not stop you from selling naked calls or call spreads that may soon be in harm's way due to short covering. Furthermore, if you are short stock and the stock's short interest is growing and approaching high levels, you need to be aware that your risk of a buy-in or a short squeeze is growing.

Back to our discussion of the volatility rising with the stock price as it breaks out to new highs, we call this an "inverted volatility path." Now, the key to how this situation might or might not present an options trading opportunity depends on whether the option chain reflects this change in the volatility path. Since we normally expect the implied volatility to fall as the stock price rises, the implied volatility of the out of the money calls will begin to fall as the strike prices exceed the stock price. But if we are seeing the implied volatility rise as the stock breaks out, then this should be reflected in the option chain by each successive out of the money call having a higher implied volatility. If it does, we call this an inverted volatility skew. The fact of the matter is that once we see the overall implied vola-tility of the stock begin to rise with the stock price, the skew will sometimes invert and sometimes it will not. To me, this is one of the few times I believe the market is not showing total efficiency. If the volatility path has inverted, the volatility skew should also invert, in my opinion. In other words, the option chain should reflect what is happening in the marketplace with respect to the implied volatility of the options (see Figures 3.13 through 3.16).

FIGURE 3.13   Stock Price Rising with IV Falling

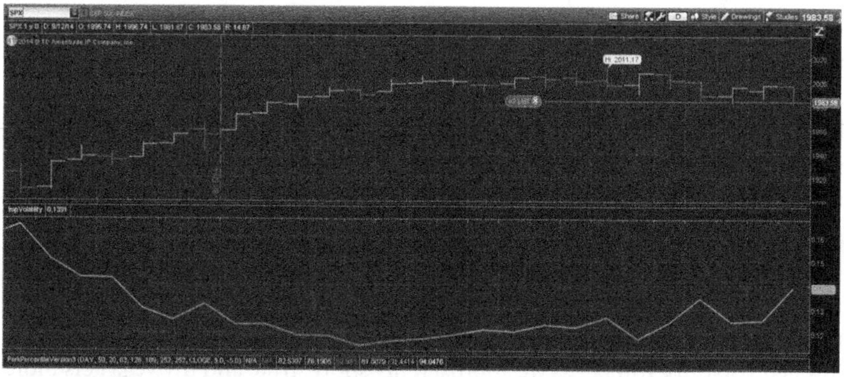

Source: TD Ameritrade.

FIGURE 3.14   Stock Price Rising with IV Rising

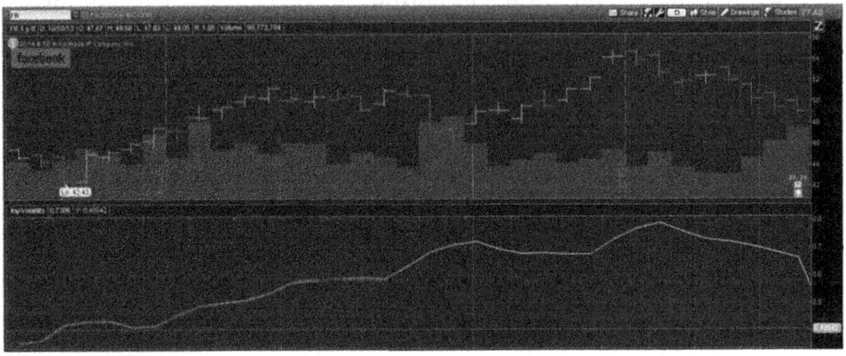

Source: TD Ameritrade.

Depending on whether the volatility skew is reflected in the options, we may or may not sculpt an option trade with good edge in it. Let us look at both scenarios.

If the volatility path has inverted (implied volatility is rising with the stock price) but the volatility skew has not inverted (implied volatility is decreasing in the out of the money calls), we have a mismatch. The overall implied volatility of the options reflects the change in path, but the skew of the options does not. This provides a unique opportunity, in my opinion, to improve the odds of success in your trade. If you expect implied volatility to continue to rise with the stock price and fall if the stock pulls back, but the out of the money calls and puts do not reflect that (and, in fact, reflect the opposite), it is time to take action. Your assumption should now be that the out of the money calls are too cheap and the out of the money puts are too expensive. You can choose to put on a trade on either the upside or the downside, or you can choose to do both. One trade I will often make in this instance is the purchase of a delta neutral risk reversal. For this trade, I will purchase an out of the money call, usually around a 30 delta, and sell an out of the money put with the same or slightly higher price. I will next add up their deltas and sell the appropriate number of shares. I like to choose options that expire around 30 days from the time of the trade. This gives my trade enough time to play out, but not so much that the skew might be unaffected if the rally continues. My hope is that if the stock continues to rally, the volatility skew will eventually invert and I will make money on the volatility expansion as the stock approaches my long strike and my vega grows. Conversely, if the stock starts to pull back, my hope is that the implied volatility will fall as we approach my short strike and my vega gets more

FIGURE 3.15 Option Chain with Normal Skew

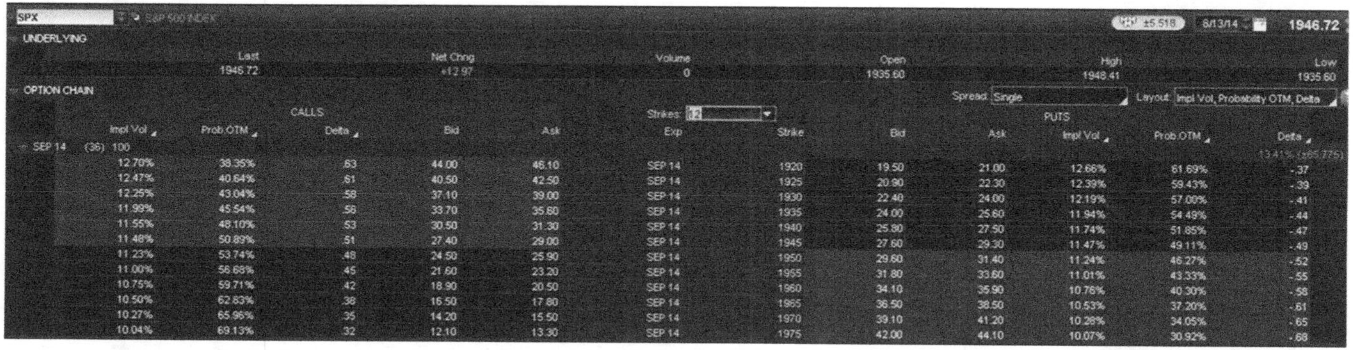

SPX S&P 500 INDEX — ±5.518 — 8/13/14 — 1946.72

UNDERLYING

Last	Net Chng	Volume	Open	High	Low
1946.72	+12.97	0	1935.60	1948.41	1935.60

OPTION CHAIN — Strikes: 12 — Spread: Single — Layout: Impl Vol, Probability OTM, Delta

SEP 14 (36) 100 — 13.41% (±85.775)

CALLS Impl Vol	Prob.OTM	Delta	Bid	Ask	Exp	Strike	PUTS Bid	Ask	Impl Vol	Prob.OTM	Delta
12.70%	38.35%	.63	44.00	46.10	SEP 14	1920	19.50	21.00	12.66%	61.69%	-.37
12.47%	40.64%	.61	40.50	42.50	SEP 14	1925	20.90	22.30	12.39%	59.43%	-.39
12.25%	43.04%	.58	37.10	39.00	SEP 14	1930	22.40	24.00	12.19%	57.00%	-.41
11.99%	45.54%	.56	33.70	35.60	SEP 14	1935	24.00	25.60	11.94%	54.49%	-.44
11.55%	48.10%	.53	30.50	31.30	SEP 14	1940	25.80	27.50	11.74%	51.85%	-.47
11.48%	50.89%	.51	27.40	29.00	SEP 14	1945	27.60	29.30	11.47%	49.11%	-.49
11.23%	53.74%	.48	24.50	25.90	SEP 14	1950	29.60	31.40	11.24%	46.27%	-.52
11.00%	56.68%	.45	21.60	23.20	SEP 14	1955	31.80	33.60	11.01%	43.33%	-.55
10.75%	59.71%	.42	18.90	20.50	SEP 14	1960	34.10	35.90	10.76%	40.30%	-.58
10.50%	62.83%	.38	16.50	17.80	SEP 14	1965	36.50	38.50	10.53%	37.20%	-.61
10.27%	65.96%	.35	14.20	15.50	SEP 14	1970	39.10	41.20	10.28%	34.05%	-.65
10.04%	69.13%	.32	12.10	13.30	SEP 14	1975	42.00	44.10	10.07%	30.92%	-.68

Source: TD Ameritrade.

FIGURE 3.16 Option Chain with Inverted Skew

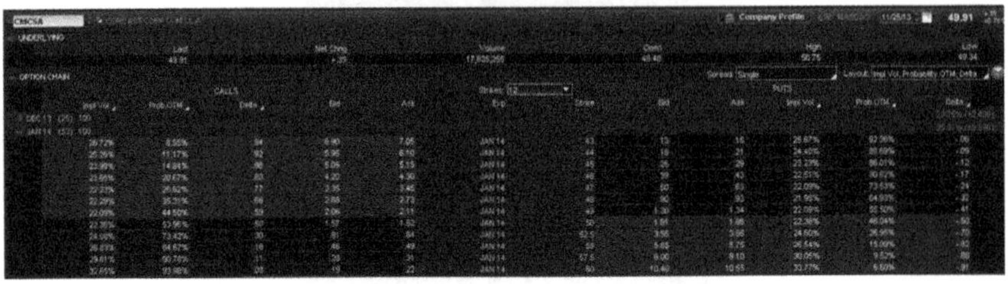

Source: TD Ameritrade.

negative, and I profit again. Of course, the delta hedge I put on is not static, so I either will need to adjust my hedge by trading more stock, or just close out the position before the stock can move beyond my strikes. Though these opportunities do not happen frequently, I find that I am profitable a very high percentage of the times I get to make these trades.

What do we do if the volatility path and the volatility skew have both inverted? We now have a matching aberration to the normal course of volatility. Does that mean there is no play to be made? I do not find this setup to have as high a probability of success as the mismatched situation, but these abnormal skews are infrequent and generally do not last for a very long period of time. Depending on how steep the upside, positive skew has become, I may try to put on a skew play where I sell upside volatility in a hedged manner. I may or may not buy downside puts to reduce my volatility risk, in the event the stock continues to rise. Even a downside put that is hedged with long stock gives you some protection, but it may reduce your profits if the stock pulls back, implied volatility falls, and the skew reverts to normal. Either way, I delta hedge this trade again and solely hope for the implied volatility of the short, out of the money call to fall more than normal due to the implied volatility falling and the skew reversion further reducing the implied volatility of the upside calls. Of course, if the rally continues, you may take some pain on this trade. Therefore, I try to do this trade as far out (the most days to expiration) as the skew inversion allows. This ensures my 30 delta call is far enough away and gives me time to potentially weather a small storm.

Actual versus Historical Distribution Curves

Now that we have broached the topic that the possibility exists for the option chain to inaccurately reflect the actual, historical distribution curve, I would like to discuss this further. Some people consider this topic heresy. Many options traders believe that the option chain properly reflects all known information and is therefore infallible and completely accurate. (Sounds a lot like the "efficient market hypothesis" expanded to include option pricing!) Yet if that were true, there would be no opportunity to make money trading options long-term. The probabilities would lead to that ever talked about "zero sum game" that truly does not exist in trading. Another reason this topic is sometimes considered taboo is that many will continually insist history has no bearing on the future. They use the phrase "Past performance is not necessarily indicative of future performance." While this may be true, the old saying "Those who fail to learn from history are doomed to repeat it" comes to mind. Or perhaps the saying of George Bernard Shaw that states, "If history repeats itself, and the unexpected always happens, how incapable must Man be of learning from experience," might be more descriptive of those naysayers. When we speak of earnings trades later in the book, we will again consider the importance of historical data as an input.

Since we will dare to consider the possibility that the option chain may not accurately reflect the historical distribution of an underlying's movement, let us think about the various ways they may differ. Perhaps the most obvious would be in their standard deviation. This is another way of saying that the option chain might inaccurately predict the future volatility of the stock. This is an obvious area of potential difference and one I think we would all accept as probable, if not merely possible.

The higher the implied volatility, the wider and flatter the distribution curve (see Figure 3.17). It is this movement of the distribution curve due to changes in implied volatility that presents us opportunities in volatility

FIGURE 3.17 Distribution Curve with Varying IV

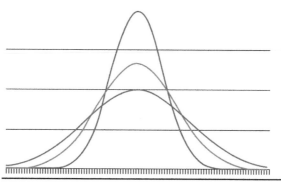

arbitrage trading. We try to sell options in underlyings whose distribution curves are wider and flatter than normal (high implied volatility) and hope for a reversion to the mean in the implied volatility. On the flip side, you might try to buy options when the implied volatility is very low and the distribution curve is high and narrow in hopes that the volatility will widen the curve.

Earlier, we spoke of the distribution curve as lognormal, skewed, and usually leptokurtic. So, those will represent the next three areas in which they might differ from historical movements. We will look at each area individually.

It would be difficult to make a case against the distribution being lognormal, as that would invalidate our option pricing models. However, when earnings come around, or when other large known news events are coming, our option prices will often brace for a jump in the stock price in one direction or the other. This "event risk" actually represents what is known as a discontinuous price jump. All of our common (Black-Scholes style and binomial style) models rely on continuous pricing. These events represent a break from the lognormal distribution of the stock's price for a short period of time. We often handle these events in a different way or with a different model, like a jump diffusion model. (See the section on trading earnings.) But, overall, our distributions can be characterized as lognormal in nature, in my opinion.

The skew is perhaps the biggest area where we see differences between the distribution curve carved out by the option chain's pricing and the historical movement of the underlying. To illustrate this, let us look at the SPX's distribution curve for the past five-year period in Figure 3.18.

The bell-shaped curve is the distribution curve of the 30-day options based on the option chain from July 15, 2014. This means it is using the then current implied volatility, skew, and kurtosis. The bars represent the 30-day movement of the SPX for the past five years overlaid on the option chain's distribution curve. If you were to draw a curve on top of the bars, you would

FIGURE 3.18   SPX Five-Year Eztrade Graph

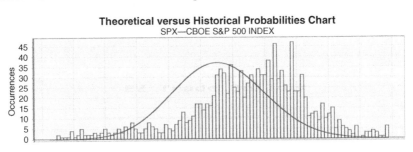

Source: Eztrade.com.

see that the skew is much farther to the right (upside) than the option chain is predicting. This differential would mean if we sold strangles, when our short strikes got breached, they would be breached to the upside (short calls) far more frequently than the downside (short puts). We will test this theory in the next section. As you can see, the actual skew is not well represented by the option chain. If we believe that the actual historical movement pattern has any predictive value, or at least more predictive value than the option chain gives us, this information can be extremely valuable in our trading. We can, in fact, take the actual distribution curve and create new, more accurate probabilities for our trading than those presented by the option chain. If we are delta neutral traders, this would affect our delta, or our hedge ratio, as well. But if we are less sophisticated traders (but intelligent, nonetheless), a simple view of the distribution curves overlaid like the one we are showing can give us a glimpse into what we can expect and guide us into a better trade selection. For example, using the SPX distribution curve, if we were to sell strangles every month we may want to sell our calls a bit farther away from the stock price than our option chain tells us. In other words, if we normally sell the seven delta calls and seven delta puts, we may want to move the call side up to the four or five delta while maintaining our puts at the seven delta point. Another choice might be to sell three puts to every two calls, or even to skip the call side entirely and sell only puts or put spreads. All of the foregoing choices lessen our upside risk somewhat at the behest of the actual, historical distribution curve.

Figure 3.19 shows the distribution curve of Green Mountain Coffee Roasters (GMCR).

As you can see, though the option chain (theoretical curve) has a no-ticeable upside skew to it, the actual historical stock movement is not only

FIGURE 3.19 GMCR Eztrade Graph

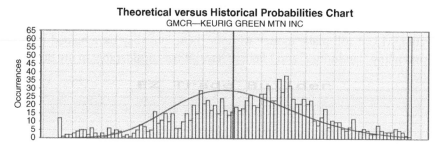

Source: Eztrade.com.

skewed even more to the upside than predicted but also characterized by many outsized moves that are not predicted by the options' prices. Though a majority of these outsized moves are to the upside, we can see that there are also many more to the downside than we might expect. There are a number of stocks that have these characteristics. Before I had this wonderful software to help me in finding the stocks, I instinctively, and financially, knew many of them. How? It seems every time I sold premium in certain stocks, they incurred vicious moves and turned into losers quickly. Now, I tend to stay away from selling premium in stocks that have a high frequency of "black swan"–type moves. In fact, when the implied volatility gets cheap in these types of stocks, I may purchase straddles in them as a protective measure against the short premium I carry elsewhere in my trading portfolio and hope for a repeat of these moves.

One important point to note is that in the illustrations of the overlaid distribution curves, the curve (the one described by the option chain) is built off the current implied volatility at each strike in the chain. If the overall implied volatility of the underlying were to rise, more of the bars would fall within the option chain's distribution curve and the probability of profit for short premium trades would rise. This would be readily apparent by viewing the distribution curve both before and after the implied volatility changes. However, the differences in the skew between the theoretical and historical distributions would still exist and be viewable in the graph. So, to further describe the two (SPX and GMCR) curves we viewed, I will add a bit more context to them. At the time of the snapshot, the SPX implied volatility was trading in its second percentile of its 52-week range. That is, its implied volatility was very cheap as compared to its normal levels. GMCR, on the other hand, was trading in its 57th percentile of its 52-week range and was therefore a bit over its normal level. Remember, when trading cheap, the distribution curve is higher and narrower than normal, and when trading expensively, the curve is flatter and wider.

I use these curves in my everyday trading in both an offensive and a defensive mode, depending on how they compare. Are they necessary to my trading? I can still make money without them, but they have helped me to avoid many "landmines" and I believe have added considerably to my bottom line.

CHAPTER 4

Trade Probabilities: What to Look For

Like every other type of investment you make, each option trade should be made with an eye to the risk versus return ratio. In other words, for each unit of risk that you incur in a trade, you should expect a commensurate return. What does that mean in practice and how can we assess what a reasonable risk versus return ratio might look like? While there are no hard and fast rules, it is important to examine the difference in nature of long premium trades versus short premium trades in the context of risk versus return.

First let's examine long premium trades and what their risk versus return ratio looks like. Earlier we stated that each time you purchase an option you pay more than that option is currently worth. In other words, you pay for both intrinsic value and extrinsic (time premium) value. And furthermore, since the extrinsic value you pay for decays a bit each day, other things must occur with your trade for you to break even, much less turn a profit, on your trade. For example, either the stock must move in your direction or the implied volatility of the option must increase for the value of your option not to decrease by the value of the theta (time decay) each day. Because of this, all other things being equal, long premium trades are considered to have a probability of profit that is less than 50 percent.

Let us look at an example to further drive this point home. On August 1, 2014, with the SPX trading around $1,925, the August $1,960 calls were trading for around $5. The calls had a theta of $0.40 per day and a delta of 20, with two weeks left until expiration. What this means is that on that trading day, all other things being equal, the option will decay in price by $0.40 to $4.60. Leaving volatility out of it and just focusing on market movement means that the SPX must move up $2 on that day just to maintain the $5 price for the calls. Why $2? If the stock moves up by $2.00, the option, which has a delta of 20, will see its price go up by $2.00 ∗ .20 (the delta), or $.40 just based on price movement alone. This exactly offsets the theta (decay) for the day, leaving the option at the same $5 price. On the next trading day, the theta will grow since we are getting closer to expiration, and the delta will fall (for the same reason). So, the SPX will need to go up by even a greater amount for the price of the option to stay the same. And so on and so forth until the option expires.

In contrast, when you make an option trade in which you sell premium you receive more for the option than it is currently worth intrinsically. That is, you receive not only the intrinsic value of the option but also additional monies for the extrinsic (time premium) value of the option. So now, the stock price needs to move against you or the implied volatility needs to rise, or else you will make money on this trade. Therefore, by their very nature, short premium trades have a probability of profiting that is greater than 50 percent.

Having looked at the nature of long premium and short premium trades, you may be asking yourself why you would ever buy an option. Shouldn't you always sell premium, thereby giving yourself a greater than 50 percent chance of making money? Well, there is another consideration we must address before making that decision. Long premium trades have an unlimited profit potential while having a limited loss profile. You can lose only the amount of money you spent purchasing the option or the option spread. If you purchase naked calls, theoretically the stock price could go to infinity, thereby giving you unlimited profit potential for the options. And when you purchase naked puts, the stock could go bankrupt, giving the puts not unlimited but huge profit potential. So the less than 50 percent probability of profit we receive when purchasing options is offset by the limited risk and unlimited profit potential of the trade. Short option trades, on the other hand, incur unlimited loss potential while enjoying limited profit potential. And this nature is offset by the greater than 50 percent probability of profit we enjoy with the trade.

This is why the risk versus return question is such a difficult one when dealing with options. So, in general, which style of trading proves to be more profitable, long premium trades or short premium trades? From my experience, I know very few long premium traders who are consistently profitable. The vast majority of consistently profitable traders I know run a short premium portfolio. This does not mean that every trade they make is a short premium trade. Rather, it means that their portfolio generally has a positive theta (collecting time decay). And though not 100 percent accurate, this generally means they are short premium overall. So the increased probability of profit will generally win out over the risk profile (unlimited versus limited) of the two styles of trading.

Of course, due to the limited potential upside of short premium trades, we can liken short premium traders to baseball players who hit for average. Long premium traders, with their trades' large potential upside, are more like home run hitters who strike out a lot. But when they get ahold of one it sure can be exciting.

Just as I keep trying to teach my children not to believe everything they read, I believe it is important to show you through empirical evidence that the foregoing statement about short premium winning over long premium is true. Though this is not the forum for lengthy research pieces, I felt it was necessary to at least examine the S&P 500 index (via the SPX) over the past five years to see how short premium trades performed versus long premium trades.

The first thing I did was count up the number of days the 30-day implied volatility exceeded the 20-day historical volatility. Though this is not a foolproof measure by any means, if there was a consistent pattern, it would certainly lend credence to one side of the argument or the other. And, of course, if implied volatility exceeded historical (also called realized) volatility, then short premium strategies should have generally been successful. On the flip side, if historical volatility exceeded implied volatility, long premium strategies had a higher probability of being successful. As it turns out, implied volatility exceeded historical volatility a whopping 95.64 percent of the time for the past five years. So, when you are selling premium, you are collecting more premium than the SPX's movement warrants a vast majority of the time. There are two potential fallacies in this argument, both of which will be unable to tip the scale due to how heavily weighted the numbers we just discussed were. But to be thorough, I want to address them both.

First, there is the fallacy that historical volatility always properly represents the realized volatility of the stock. Historical volatility is the standard deviation of an asset's returns over a past period of time. If the stock closes at the same price every day for 20 days, its historical volatility is zero. I find that to be intuitively obvious. What I find to be less obvious is that if the stock rises (or falls) 5 percent each and every day for 20 days, its historical volatility is also zero. The bottom line is that a stock that is trending steeply will have a historical volatility that is lower than one might expect. In this instance, the implied volatility may be far higher than the historical volatility, yet a short premium position may prove to be a loser. Fortunately, over the past five-year period of our study, this has not been the case nearly often enough to tip the scales in favor of long premium trades.

The second issue is that of magnitude. Our 95.64 percent implied volatility over historical volatility reading says nothing about the magnitude of the differences. If we make $1 96 times but lose $100 four times, we are still out $304! Of course, since we manage our trades and do not let our losers grow large (as we will learn in our section "The Kelly Criterion" in Chapter 7), from a practical standpoint, this objection goes away. But for sake of argument, I performed the following five-year studies:

- I sold an SPX strangle every month.
- Each side had a probability of expiring out of the money of 90 percent (approximately 10 delta options) and then 95 percent (approximately 5 delta options).
- I sold the strangles with 45 days until expiration of the options.
- I let the strangles expire into cash.
- No position management was performed at all.
- Profit and loss were summed and statistics collected.

Though this study should have far worse results than what I would experience in the real world, I wanted to take a "worst-case scenario" and see how a short premium strategy would perform. In my normal trading, drawdowns (losses) are managed at an appropriate percentage of maximum potential profit, as are profits. This management technique, which we examine in more detail during the Kelly Criterion section, gives us a far higher probability of success in our trading. But for this study, I wanted to see the worst-case effects of short premium strategies unaided by management techniques.

Before examining the results, I feel it is important to view this time period from a macro perspective to give color to the study. The past five-year period has taken the SPX from $875.32 to a high of $1,985.59. During this period, we experienced two rather hard downdrafts of approximately 20 percent of the price of the SPX before the fall. We also had a couple falls of 10 percent and several falls of between 5 and 10 percent. But overall, this was an extremely bullish five years, and as such, we would expect most of our losses in our studies to be on the call side of the strangle. This is particularly true since the volatility skew leaves the short calls much closer to the index's price at the time of the sale than are the puts. In fact, the SPX skew leaves the calls less than half the distance away from the SPX price than are the puts. Further exacerbating the risk in the study is that this period is also characterized by its relatively low implied volatility, meaning that all the options are closer to the money than they otherwise would be. And to explain that in probabilistic terms: when the implied volatility is low, the distribution curve gets higher and narrower. This leaves the strikes at any given probability of getting touched or surpassed closer to the money than if the implied volatility were high and the distribution curve were flatter and wider (more dispersed).

My point is that there is more risk to selling a short strangle in this environment than in most other environments and that risk is greatest in the upside, out of the money calls. This makes this a particularly illustrative study with respect to long versus short premium. Since we are trying to show whether long premium or short premium trades make money over time, I have taken the directional bias out of the study as best I can. Though the skew adds some directional bent to the test, this is something outside our control and is present in the marketplace. Of course, we could mathematically remove the skew, but I do not believe that would provide us with tradable information.

The Results

Before looking at the results, let us examine what we should expect from the study. We will begin by examining the 95 percent probability of expiring out of the money options. When we sell a strangle that has 95 percent probability of expiring out of the money calls and 95 percent probability of expiring out of the money puts, we expect to have one or the other of our short strikes exceeded 90 percent of the time. One way to think of it is to think of a normal distribution curve. If each strike is predicted to be exceeded 5 percent of the time, that leaves 90 percent of the time where the strikes are not exceeded, as illustrated by the area between the two arrows in Figure 4.1.

FIGURE 4.1   Normal Distribution Showing 90 Percent

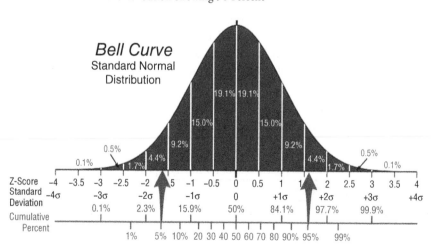

Source: www.mathisfun.com.

But, because the break-even points on each side are farther away from the stock price by the total amount of credits received for the strangle, we actually expect to make money a bit more frequently. In our SPX study, this amounted to, on average, about 1 percent expected improvement to our results. Illustrating how this works, let us assume we sold the 1640/1930 strangle for $5 and that each strike had a 95 percent probability of expiring out of the money. That would mean we expect the SPX to close at or between $1,640 and $1,930 on the expiration date of the options approximately 90 percent of the time. But we will make money if the SPX closes between $1,635 and $1,935. That is due to the $5 in credits we received from the sale of the strangle. By going back to our option chain (or by simply calculating the probabilities, as in the next section) and finding the probabilities of the break-even points, our five-year period averaged around a 1 percent total improvement to our odds of making money. Thus, I expected to make money around 91 percent of the time. If either of these probabilities are off by a large amount in our study, our conclusion must be that the options markets are inefficient and that the pricing of the SPX options are incorrect and provide us with an arbitrage opportunity beyond what we expected. If the strikes are exceeded too frequently, our short premium strategy might prove to be a loser. If the strikes are exceeded less frequently than expected, we might expect to make more money than otherwise hoped for. However, if they are close to expectations, we then need to look at the profit and loss of our historical strangle study. This profit and loss will speak not to the frequency of the events but to the magnitude of the times the strikes are exceeded.

For the five-year period, as it turns out, our numbers were as shown in Table 4.1.

Summarizing the results, we found that the strikes were exceeded around 11.67 percent of the time, instead of the 10 percent we expected. So, the strikes were exceeded slightly more than expected, but not by much. And we expected to make money 91 percent of the time, but actually made money

TABLE 4.1   Five Results of SPX 90 Percent Strangle Study

Year SPX Short Strangle Study					
95 Percent Out of the Money Options					
Exceeded Strike			Made Money		
Probability	Actual	Difference	Probability	Actual	Difference
90%	88.33%	−1.67%	91%	91.67%	0.67%
Total Five-Year Profit: $11,921 per strangle					

TABLE 4.2 Five Results of SPX 80 Percent Strangle Study

	Year SPX Short Strangle Study				
	90 Percent Out of the Money Options				
Exceeded Strike			Made Money		
Probability	Actual	Difference	Probability	Actual	Difference
80%	78.33%	−1.67%	81.50%	81.67%	0.17%
Total Five-Year Profit: $12,413 per strangle					

91.67 percent of the time. So, we made money slightly more than expected. As for the profitability of the short 95 percent out of the money strangle options, each strangle made $11,921 (before commissions) for the five-year period. Had you purchased the strangle (instead of selling it), this would obviously have been the magnitude of your loss.

As for the 90 percent probability out of the money options, our expectations were for our strikes to be exceeded 20 percent of the time (within our strikes 80 percent of the time), and we expected to make money around 81.5 percent of the time. This was again calculated using our break-even points' probabilities. Our results were similar to that of the 95 percent probability of expiring out of the money options (see Table 4.2).

The SPX closed within the expected range 78.33 percent of the time, just shy of the expected, but close enough to consider the option chain accurate. The short strangle would have made money 81.67 percent of the time, almost exactly as we expected. And, perhaps most importantly, the strategy would have made $12,413 before commissions, which is just slightly more than the amount our 95 percent probability out of the money strikes would have yielded. Thus, both short strangle studies would have made a nice yield, illustrating the power of short premium over time. Our study not only showed that the magnitude of our losses does not "overpower" the probabilities of our wins, thus doing away with our second potential fallacy, but also supported the validity of the probabilities predicted by our options chain. With the end results being nearly the same, are there any other differences between the studies we need to consider? There are actually two.

First, and this is particularly true if we do not manage our trades (as in this study), we need to consider our maximum drawdowns. Since this was just a theoretical study, we need to add some common sense and realism into it by considering what it might be like if we actually traded this way. Though many will try to tell you psychology plays no role in trading, I can

TABLE 4.3 Drawdowns on SPX Strangle Study

	90% Strangle	80% Strangle
Nbr put breaches	1	2
Nbr call breaches	6	11
Largest put drawdown	$2,985	$8,145
Largest call drawdown	$1,962	$3,725

tell you from experience that large losses take a toll. It is difficult to stay true to a chosen trading strategy, even one you have thoroughly tested and whose effectiveness you are convinced of, when losses start to build. And if you veer from the tested strategy due to the "pain," you completely invalidate all your prior work in developing the strategy. Again, I deal with this issue by carefully choosing my exit points, both winning and losing, prior to executing the trade. But in this study, we have chosen to assume no management takes place, and therefore we need to think of those painful moments and what they might mean to us. Furthermore, we must be sure we can financially absorb a large loss, particularly if it occurs early in our trading of the strategy.

With that in mind, let us look at the maximum drawdowns of both our strategies and compare them in Table 4.3.

Looking at the graphic, we see that we had far more frequent losses to the upside. That is, our short call strike got breached far more often than our put strike. In the 95 percent probability out of the money study, the put side was breached only once, while our call side was breached six times. Yet in keeping with our velocity of movement to the downside being a greater argument, our maximum loss occurred the one time the put side was breached. This loss occurred in August 2011 and would have yielded a drawdown of $2,985 for each strangle. Considering our average annual gain for this five-year study was $2,384, this single loss would have given back over a full year of gains. This illustrates why many traders are so fearful of their downside risk. Even though downside events are far less frequent than upside "drives," when the downside events happen, they can get ugly quickly. Knowing where you want to take losses, and abiding by your strategy every time, certainly gives you an advantage over most other traders.

In our unmanaged short strangle study where we sold the 90 percent probability out of the money calls and puts, we lost to the put side twice and lost 11 times to the call side. This is a very similar ratio to our 95 percent probability study. And, just as in the prior study, our greatest losing month was one of the downside put breaches. Not surprisingly, this occurred in the same expiration cycle also. Thus, in August 2011, our put side strike was surpassed and cost us a total of $8,145. This amount, lost in a single month, is actually 65.6 percent of our eventual total winnings for the five-year study and therefore wipes away over three years of eventual kept profits. That constitutes an unacceptably large loss and, once again, is the reason I manage my trades according to a well-thought-out plan.

Comparing the two strategies, we see that though they both yielded a similar profit, the drawdown in the 90 percent probability out of the money strike strategy caused far greater drawdowns and thus imparted quite a bit more mental anguish for very little extra gain. Furthermore, and this is the second point I wish to make about this study, the 95 percent probability out of the money strikes utilized less capital, no matter in what type of account you are trading. (Of course, you cannot sell a strangle in a cash account or a partial margin account, like an IRA.) This reduced margin requirement leads to a higher return on capital. Furthermore, even if you do manage your positions, the farther out strikes could lead to less necessary management, leading to fewer commissions.

Having dispensed with the two possible fallacies of our implied volatility versus historical volatility argument, I believe I have shown that short premium is the winning strategy over time and that long premium is, in general, a less than 50/50 proposition and one that generally leads to losses if done systematically. But in my opinion, we have proven only a generality. Since we do not always find ourselves trading generalities, we will now return to our discussion of distribution curves and dig a bit deeper into the topic.

How to Calculate Option Probabilities

We have repeatedly spoken about option probabilities. And though I do not think it's important for you to memorize the formula, it is important for you to understand the inputs and the relationships that go into calculating the probabilities. If you remember our earlier discussion about the inputs into all option pricing models, you will see a considerable overlap between those inputs and those of the probability formula. In fact, all the inputs to the Black-Scholes model are accounted for in the probability formula with the exception of the basis. (Once again, the basis is the cost of carry minus the dividends.) It is also critical for you to note that the probability calculation, just like the option pricing models, assumes a normal distribution. That is, it assumes that movement of the underlying is normally distributed and therefore random. And at the risk of repetition, all option pricing models, all probability calculations, and thus all of options trading are nothing more than a probability exercise.

$$P_{\text{put}} = 1 - N\left(\frac{\ln\left(\dfrac{S}{X}\right)}{v\sqrt{T}}\right)$$

$$P_{\text{call}} = N\left(\frac{\ln\left(\dfrac{S}{X}\right)}{v\sqrt{T}}\right)$$

where

$N()$ is the normal distribution function
S is the stock price
X is the strike price
v is the implied volatility (percentage)
T is the time to expiration

Looking at things from a short option viewpoint, other relationships you should take note of include the following:

- The further out of the money the option is, the greater the probability of success
- The higher the volatility, the lower the probability of success, all other things being equal
- The more time to expiration, the lower the probability of success, all other things being equal.

Focusing in on the latter two points, we need to realize that as time passes and implied volatility changes, our probabilities change. In other words, when we calculate the probability of profit of a given trade we are really calculating an instantaneous probability for that particular point in time. We can use this probability in choosing our trading strategy, but after placing our trade we have no control over how these probabilities will change. What we do know is that the passing of time, all other things being equal, helps our probabilities. And more importantly, we know that if we can predict the future movement of implied volatility we can make use of this to improve our odds. And this, though easier said than done, is at the heart of successful options trading.

Expounding further on this, many people think that if they sell volatility high and buy it back lower they will make money. And though this may be true, the point I will continually try to hammer home in this book is that this strategy often makes money because of the effect changing volatility has on your probability of profit. In fact, in both the Black-Scholes model and the probability calculation, the volatility component is wrapped within the normal distribution function. So though the volatility plays an important role in our trading, the overriding, controlling component is the distribution curve itself. So probability theory reigns supreme with respect to our options trading.

CHAPTER 5

Choosing Your Trades

Now that we have covered the theoretical background and probability formulas, you may be wondering, "What good is all this and can it help me to make money?" I'm glad you asked, as it's time to put this theoretical background to use. Once again, there is no guarantee that a given trade will be profitable. But if we can create a methodology that takes advantage of what we know about the probabilities of an options trade, we can make money in the long run. Taking advantage of the probabilities is the key to our success.

Choosing Your Underlying

Before you can search for trades, it is important that you create a list of underlyings that you like to trade. This list should consist of liquid products that have sufficient volume and open interest to ensure an efficient marketplace. If the bid/ask spread is too wide, you may be giving up any edge you fought so hard to achieve. The list should be long enough to give you ample underlyings to trade, yet short enough to filter out any "noise" and provide you with only viable trading candidates. Furthermore, I like to get to know each one of the underlyings I trade. Therefore, I recommend you start with a shorter list of core trading candidates and add new underlyings as you are able. Though I know and have traded over

1,200 underlyings in the past few years, my main watch list of stocks currently consists of 157 underlyings. I can tell you a great deal about each and every name on my list. These names are made up of stocks, indices, exchange-traded funds (ETFs), and futures that have futures options that are liquid and tradable. It is from this list that I choose the underlyings I will trade.

The first step in lining up a trade is to choose an underlying that you feel will give you a probability edge. We now look at a number of processes that will aid us in this quest.

From a simplistic standpoint, if our goal is to buy low and sell high, or to sell high and then buy low, we need to discern which inputs of option pricing have the greatest effect and are of the greatest importance. Looking back at the inputs into the Black-Scholes model, we can quickly dismiss interest rate and dividend (both building blocks of our basis calculation), as they are fairly static in nature. Days to expiration, though important when we choose a strategy, have little effect on our choice of underlyings, as time passes equally for all. Furthermore, the same can be said for strike price, as that is also part of the strategy we choose and not part of our choice of underlyings. That leaves us with two inputs that will mainly drive the success or failure of any given trade. These two inputs are stock price and implied volatility.

Let's first look at stock price and its effect on our choice of underlyings. If you have an understanding of the option Greeks that are derived from the option pricing model, you will know that the option's delta predicts the change in an option price for each $1 move in its underlying. Ultimately, it is in fact the movement of the underlying that has the greatest impact on whether a trade is profitable. So why do we spend so much time and energy talking about an option's implied volatility? To answer this, let's spend a few moments to think about the implications of making trades solely around our predictions for the underlying's future movement.

The question that must be answered is whether you can consistently predict the direction and magnitude of a stock's movement within a particular time frame. An option has a limited life span. Though we will discuss this in more detail later, it is important we consider this fact now. If you believe XYZ stock will rise in the future, that belief alone is not sufficient to warrant purchasing a call option with 30 days left until expiration. You must in fact believe XYZ will rise greater than a certain amount within the next 30 days in order for that information to be useful in your options trading. Does that mean we should ignore our beliefs about what a stock will do in the future? Not completely. But I am suggesting that it is very difficult to consistently predict a stock's direction and magnitude of move within a given time frame. And though I know I will incur the wrath of my friends who are technical analysts, I do not believe the amount of time, money, and energy spent trying to determine this is worthwhile if you are an options trader. That is not to say that technical analysis has no merit or has no basis in our options trading decisions. Personally, I use technical analysis in an attempt to determine short-term supply and demand imbalances. Beyond that, before each trade I do look at the stock's chart. But I do not find enough information there to consistently make me a profitable trader. I say this for two reasons. First, after almost 27 years as an options trader, I have seen very few technical analysts who consistently make money. And of those few who do, I would suggest they make money more due to their strategic choices than to their directional choices. There is one other point I would like to emphatically make. Remember that all option pricing models and probability of profit formulas assume a stock's movement is random or somewhat random. I cannot reconcile random stock movement with technical analysis. And I say this being fully aware that over 90 percent of all traders utilize technical analysis in their decision-making process.

If I am going to dismiss predicting the future movement of an underlying as a means of putting the odds in my favor with my trading, that leaves me with only one input left to examine. That input is the implied volatility of the option, and as I am sure you are aware, due to the great deal of press volatility indices like VIX, RVX, VXX, and UVXY have been receiving of late, we are not alone in our focus.

There is a term you might often hear used in finance and that term is "mean reversion." Some analysts will say a stock's price is mean reverting. In other words, what goes up must come down. But when we speak of a stock's price there is little evidence to support this claim. For example, even if we speak of a stock's price movement being random, we are quick to also assert the stock's price distribution has a positive drift. That means that a typical stock price will drift upward over time. Now, I fully recognize that not all stock prices move upward over time. In fact, if we think about stocks like Lucent or WorldCom, we recognize that some stocks might not only fail to drift upward but also in fact go to zero. That is, these companies might go bankrupt, clearly violating our upward drift theory. The point I am making is that stock prices are typically not as mean reverting as many people think. In fact, I find that thinking about stock prices as being mean reverting in the short term often gets in the way of creating a consistently profitable options trading methodology. Trend followers will agree with this statement, while contrarian traders might find fault in it.

Why talk about mean reversion at all if I do not believe stock prices are mean reverting? Well, in fact, I believe implied volatility is one of the most mean reverting functions we see in finance. Let's take a closer look at this statement.

Pull up a stock chart that spans one, two, three, or five years, for any 10 underlyings that pop into your head. As you move from chart to chart, you will most likely find many charts that do not have a clearly defined top end and bottom end within which the stock's price oscillates. On the other hand, if you pull up an implied volatility chart for the same underlyings with the same time frames, you will most likely see that the implied volatility tends to oscillate within a range. Looking more closely at these charts you should be able to discern a much tighter range within which the stock's implied volatility normally resides. It is an expectation that a stock's implied volatility will return to this tight range over time that we can rely on when choosing an underlying to trade. This is exactly what we mean when we talk about implied volatility being a mean reverting function.

How can we use this in our trading? If we look back in time and determine a "normal," a high, and a low expectation for a stock's implied volatility, we can determine where in this range the current implied volatility resides. There are actually two ways that traders do this. The first is to determine where the current implied volatility is as compared to its range for the time frame in which we are looking. So the calculation would look like this:

$$IV\ Range\ (or\ IV\ Rank) = (IV\ Current - IV\ Low)/(IV\ High - IV\ Low)$$

So, for example, if we are using a one-year time frame and the highest the implied volatility has been is 40, the lowest it has been is 20, and the current implied volatility is 25, the stocks IV percentile would be as follows:

$$(25 - 20)/(40 - 20) = 5/20 = .25, or\ 25th\ percentile$$

Some traders will mistakenly call this metric "IV Percentile." Mathematically, that is incorrect and I will call this "IV Range." Although this calculation makes intuitive sense, it does not always reflect where in its normal range the current implied volatility currently resides (and is, in fact, a ratio and not a percentile). To illustrate this, let's assume that the underlying illustrated earlier normally trades in the 20 to 25 IV range. In fact, let's assume that in the past one year, or 252 trading days, the implied volatility for the underlying exceeded 25 on only one day. On this day the implied volatility stood at 40 due to some unusual event. If today the implied volatility of this underlying stands at 25, the foregoing calculation shows it to be in its 25th percentile. Yet it surely is trading at a fairly rich implied volatility for the underlying as on all but one day the implied volatility was less than or equal to its current reading. And this defines the second means of calculating the implied volatility percentile. Again assuming we are using a one-year period, we can take the current implied volatility and determine how many days the implied volatility has exceeded or been beneath the current reading. Using this calculation, our implied volatility percentile for the foregoing stock would be 99 percent or 100 percent as the 25 percent IV was exceeded only once in the past year out of 252 reading days. While these two calculations do not always show such a dramatic difference, it is important to take note of the strengths and weaknesses of each, as some software packages you will encounter may use one or the other of the calculations.

I, personally, use the second method of calculation as I find it to be more accurate and predictive of the future movement of the implied volatility. So how do we use this number in our trading? It would seem logical that if the underlying was trading at greater than its 50th percentile, we might be interested in selling premium. And if the underlying was trading at less than its 50th percentile, we might be interested in buying premium. After all, if we believe that implied volatility is mean reverting, doesn't that mean we believe the implied volatility will trend back toward its 50th percentile? In practicality, it is not that simple for three reasons.

First, as we have discussed, our option trades have a limited life span. So though I believe in mean reversion with respect to implied volatility, I do not assume an option will complete its mean reversion prior to my option's expiration.

Secondly, when the market gets quiet and realized volatility slows, most underlyings will fall to below their 50th percentile. It is often the case that during those times, selling option premium gives us the best edge (the widest margin) between implied volatility and realized volatility. And unlike periods of high implied volatility in the general market, these quiet periods tend to last for long periods of time. In fact, they often last for over one year and have been known to last for as long as two years. If we traded underlyings only when their implied volatility percentile was greater than the 50th percentile, we would have very little to do during these quiet periods and would be missing out on money-making opportunities.

Lastly, underlyings that are trading high in their IV percentile are often trading that way for a reason. Perhaps the stock has earnings coming up or some other type of announcement. Or maybe the stock's volatility has increased for another reason, such as the stock breaking out to new all-time highs or falling below its 52-week low, or simply because the industry the stock's business falls within has come upon hard times. Whatever the reason, recognition of the "event" and its timing will help you to make more informed trading decisions.

Rather than keying all my trades off that 50th implied volatility percentile, I will often compare an underlying's implied volatility percentile to that of the overall market. I will generally use either the SPX or the SPY as the representation

of the overall market. In general, I want an individual equity's IV percentile to be
at least 15 percent higher than that of the overall market. I require that because
an individual equity is subject to what I call "binary moves," whereas the SPX, as
a diversified portfolio of stocks, is not nearly as affected by such events. I also require that the IV percentile of the individual stock be over 35 percent. In this way,
if the stock does mean revert in a short time frame, I do not get hurt too much
by the volatility move. And this allows me to still build a short premium portfolio
during the long, low volatility environments we experience.

This implied volatility percentile, or implied volatility rank if that is all
you have to work with, is the first thing I look at when trying to find an
underlying I wish to trade. It allows me to compare underlyings' implied
volatilities on a relative basis, one against the other, and choose the underlying whose implied volatility is particularly high or particularly low for itself.

You may be wondering how I isolate these stocks on a practical basis. My
broker provides a trading platform for me, free of charge, which allows me to
program custom "scripts." These scripts are actually small programs written in
a user-friendly proprietary language that I can use to sort all of the underlyings
I like to trade by virtually any parameter I choose. Of course, one of the first
scripts I wrote was for IV percentile. When I begin looking for new trades I
simply sort this column, first from largest to smallest, in order to find stocks on
my watch list whose implied volatility is high in its one-year range. Having an
underlying trading high in its range does not guarantee I will find a trade that I
like, but from my experience this is the best place to start looking. So I begin my
search with the underlying with the highest IV rank and continue through my
watch list until I get to the name whose IV rank is 15 percent higher than that
of the SPX. All of those underlyings are potential premium selling candidates.
I will now sort the IV percentile column from low to high. I look through all
candidates whose IV percentile is less than 10 percent and research them as
potential premium buying trades. Admittedly, "less than 10 percent" is a bit
of an arbitrary number. If the overall implied volatility in the marketplace is
relatively high, I may look for purchase candidates up to the 15th or even the
20th percentile. But in a normal environment, I am looking for a single-digit
percentile. And remember that since the edge is, in general, in a short premium
portfolio, I use long premium trades as partial offsets to my short premium positions. We will talk more about this when we discuss portfolio management later.

Continuing our discussion of how to choose an underlying, let's assume
we found XYZ stock to be high enough in its IV percentile to warrant further
research. What do we do next? The first question that should come to mind
is "Why is XYZ stock trading with such a (relatively) high implied volatility?"
So we do a little research. The first thing I check is when earnings are due

out. We will spend time later discussing earnings in detail. For now, suffice it to say that as earnings approach a stock's implied volatility, percentile will appear high as it builds in extra IV for the potential binary move to come. If I find XYZ will be reporting earnings within the next two weeks, I will move on to the next underlying in my list. During earnings season this can get a bit tedious and frustrating, as most stocks that are high in their implied volatility percentile are high due to upcoming earnings. It is extremely helpful if your broker's trading platform in some way flags those stocks whose earnings dates are approaching, as mine does. But if earnings are not approaching and XYZ's implied volatility is high for other reasons, we need to continue our search. At this point, I will pull up XYZ's chart. You should be aware that every trader likes to look at charts in his own unique way. If you pull up a chart in my platform, you will not see any technical analysis–oriented information. There are no moving average lines, no momentum indicators, and so forth. It is not that I believe that you should not have them. However, I make no use of them in my particular trading style. It has been suggested to me by friends who do make use of them on their charts that it is my lack of understanding of their usefulness that produces their absence. That is a debate for another day. I have been trading successfully for many years without those indicators, have learned many new things (thus the adage "You can't teach an old dog new tricks" does not apply), but have never found use for those indicators in my trading. So, what does appear on my chart page?

My chart page contains three separate charts. The first one is a simple chart of the stock's price for the past year. I will frequently change this time frame when doing deeper research on a stock, but one year is my default. As I stated before, I generally trade options on underlyings with which I am familiar and therefore do not always find the need to lengthen the time frame. My broker is kind enough to put past earnings and dividend dates directly on the chart. This aids in determining how the stock performed as a result of past earnings announcements and explains, without further research, some of the gaps on the stock chart. So, what am I looking for on the stock chart after I determine the options are trading high in their IV percentile? To be honest, I am like a shopper who in response to the salesman's inquiry states, "I am just browsing." That is, I am not looking for anything particular (as I am not a technical analyst) but I'm hoping the chart will "speak to me." For example, maybe the stock price started fluctuating wildly five days ago. Or maybe the stock price is breaking out to the upside or breaking down below its 52-week low. I am looking for breadcrumbs that might lead me to a theory as to why the implied volatility is trading so high. Oftentimes I will find clues on the chart that will lead me to perform more research. Other times I might be lucky enough to find answers (e.g., with breakout stocks).

The second chart is a chart of the implied volatility percentile for four different time frames overlaid on each other. Those time frames are three months, six months, nine months, and one year. (This chart is courtesy of Park Research LLC.) Though we already know that the one-year implied volatility percentile is high in its range, as that is the reason we got this far in our research to begin with, the additional time frames add color to the picture. For example, if 11 months ago some news came out on this particular stock that caused a great deal of price fluctuation and the implied volatility rose for 45 days, a 9-month picture would exclude that event. I may consider the past nine months as a more normal picture for the stock, or I may not, but at least I have that choice when I look at multiple time frames.

The final chart on my page contains both the absolute implied volatility and the 20-day historical volatility on the same chart using the same scale. Some people ask me why I look at the implied volatility percentile before I look at an option's absolute implied volatility. I will frequently answer with a question of my own. Which would you rather do: sell premium in KO at a 25 percent implied volatility or sell premium in FSLR at a 32 percent implied volatility? Clearly, my point is that each company's stock marches to its own drummer. For KO, a 25 percent implied volatility is very high. Yet for FSLR, a 32 percent implied volatility is cheap. Implied volatility percentile allows us to compare which underlyings are trading cheaper or more expensive than normal as compared to their own history. Then why look at absolute implied volatility at all? Thinking back to our discussion of risk versus return, if a stock has a low absolute implied volatility, the sale of its options may not bring in enough premium to warrant the risk you are taking. Though not the first thing I look at, this is one of the reasons why absolute implied volatility is on my chart.

We now turn our attention to the term historical volatility, or realized volatility as it is sometimes called. Unlike implied volatility, which is a measure of future stock movement as predicted by (or built into) an option's price, historical volatility has nothing to do with options. In fact, it is not a predictor of future stock movement at all, but rather it is a reporter of past stock movement. The industry norm, if you will, is the 20-day (or 21-day) historical volatility of a stock's movement. Though I find historical volatility to be a useful indicator, at times its value can be deceptive. To understand this we need to review how historical volatility is calculated once again. Historical volatility is the standard deviation of an asset's returns over a past period of time. If the stock closes at the same price every day for 20 days, its historical volatility is zero. If the stock rises (or falls) 10 percent each and every day for 20 days, its historical volatility is also zero. So a stock that is trending steeply will have an historical volatility that is lower than one might expect. Thus, I am always careful to review the stock chart to ensure I understand the stock's past behavior. If the stock is trending steeply, I discount the value of the historical volatility calculation.

Now let's assume that the historical volatility calculation seems to fairly show the past behavior of the stock. What good is it to our trading process? Many traders will say it has no value. They will say, "You have seen the disclaimer that past performance may not be indicative of future performance, have you not? In the same manner, looking at past stock performance has little bearing on future stock performance and therefore the historical volatility tells us nothing." Though I understand their point, I disagree. Certainly, past performance has some predictive value, or why would we prefer to sell KO implied volatility at 25 before we would sell FSLR implied volatility at 32? For this reason, many traders simply look for a large differential between an option's implied volatility and its underlying's historical volatility when lining up trades. Though I find this information to be useful, you need to remember that historical volatility is calculated using only 20 days of data and can therefore change quickly. What I find even more meaningful is the trend in the historical volatility. What I mean by that is, how does the 5-day historical volatility compare to the 10-day historical volatility and the 20-day historical volatility? Why is that important and what does it tell us? From my experience, I find that stocks have inertia. That is, when a stock's price starts fluctuating at a greater than normal rate, it continues to fluctuate for some period of time. It may last for a few days or a few weeks, but it is generally more than a one-day event. I utilize the historical volatility trend to alert me when a stock's fluctuations are picking up speed or are slowing down. When the fluctuations are picking up speed, the 5-day historical volatility will generally be higher than the 10-day historical volatility, which will be higher than the 20-day historical volatility. This is because, with only 5 days of data, the 5-day historical volatility is more sensitive to recent events than is the 20-day historical volatility. On the flip side, when the fluctuations are slowing, the 5-day historical volatility will be lower than the 10-day historical volatility, which will be lower than the 20-day historical volatility. Though I don't require a falling historical volatility trend in order for me to sell premium in a stock, a rising historical volatility trend may exclude a premium sale until the stock's price fluctuation normalizes. Of course, a falling historical volatility trend will lend credence to the idea that a premium sale is warranted. And this is where I will compare the absolute historical volatility level to the implied volatility level. If the historical volatility is falling, but is still above the implied volatility, there is little room for error. If I sell premium and the historical volatility does not continue to fall, my trade may have a rough road ahead. But if the historical volatility is falling and its level is already below the current implied volatility, I can sell premium with more confidence in my trade, since as long as the historical volatility does not reverse and rise, my trade has a better probability of success.

How do I see these trends? Once again, by writing custom scripts in my trading platform, I can see these trends as they occur. There is one other way that I use these historical volatility trends in my trading. In fact, I find this second way to have even more value at times than what we have discussed. As I stated earlier, I currently have 157 underlyings in my watch list. Each day I sort these underlyings to see how many have a rising historical volatility trend and how many have a falling historical volatility trend. Typically in a quiet market (low VIX), I will see a long list of stocks with a falling historical volatility trend and a very short list of stocks with a rising historical volatility trend. As one who believes that the market generally takes on one of only a handful of "personalities," the length of these lists often tells me its current personality. Why is that important? I will often sculpt my portfolio based on my reading of the market's current personality. For example, if the market is in a quiet, upward trending pattern, my portfolio will typically contain a good number of naked short puts in stocks I am willing to own at prices well below where they are then trading. So a long list of stocks whose historical volatilities are slowing gives me confidence to sell more puts below the market. A long list of stocks with a rising historical volatility trend is a warning sign. Most of the time the length of these lists is fairly static. When this daily exercise is most valuable is when the length of the lists begins to reverse. When a short list of rising HVs starts to lengthen, I will start looking for trades that protect my short premium portfolio. I also cut back considerably on my premium selling for the time being. And perhaps the best use of this exercise, and one that happens very infrequently, is when the market slows after a period of frenetic movement. Let me give you an example. Back in the beginning of August 2011, the market started to fall quickly and implied volatility exploded. From then until early October 2011 the VIX kept bouncing between a little above 30 and a little below 50. In fact, it did so four separate times. I know many traders who kept selling premium throughout this entire two-month period. Most had a rough go of it. Interestingly, during that entire period, even when the VIX was in one of its several falling phases, my HV rising list was much longer then my HV falling list. But, on or around October 7, the length of these lists started reversing. This was my signal to push many more chips onto the table and to sell more premium. Though I did not sell the top tick in implied volatility, I also did not suffer from the volatility whipsaw that many others suffered. There are times when this technique will give false signals, but they are far fewer than in any other method I know.

Many traders will debate whether historical volatility leads implied volatility or whether implied volatility leads historical volatility. Personally, I often see historical volatility lead on the way up and implied volatility lead on the way down. But before I change the nature of my portfolio, I like to see historical volatility trends clearly moving in one direction or the other. After all, the historical volatility calculation requires 5, 10, or 20 days of data, whereas the implied volatility is a snapshot in time and can whip back and forth much quicker.

Since this chapter is about choosing an underlying, I would be remiss in not talking about underlyings I systematically exclude from my trading. As we spoke about previously, option pricing models assume a stock's price movement is somewhat normally distributed. Furthermore, they assume continuous pricing. From a practical matter, what this means is that they are not equipped to handle binary moves. Though we will discuss how to deal with earnings binary moves in a later section, there are other events that can cause discontinuous gaps in a stock's price. And, in fact, there are entire industries that are subject to these gaps on a more frequent basis and in a more explosive manner. Biotechnology is one such industry, and I make a practice of never selling premium in biotech stocks. Biotech stocks frequently have products in FDA testing. The results of these tests will often cause stock prices to gap dramatically in one direction or the other. Another industry that has frequent gaps, though less frequent than biotech stocks, is oil and gas E&P stocks. E&P stands for exploration and production. These companies deal in a high-risk, high-reward type of business within the oil and gas industry. When one of these companies succeeds in finding large wells, they frequently become takeover targets at large premiums to their current price. Though I will occasionally sell premium in the larger E&P stocks, for the most part this industry is also on my excluded list.

There are other types of news events that may keep me from selling premium in a particular stock or particular industry. For example, from early December until late January retail stocks experience a great deal of price movement due to holiday sales reports. These reports are not earnings reports and are often forgotten about and not fully built into the implied volatility of the stocks, in my opinion. Therefore, I typically do not sell premium in retail stocks during those two months. Likewise, natural gas will frequently see its volatility rise during the winter months as the weather raises or lowers expectations of natural gas usage. There are also industry conferences that come up from time to time where companies will typically make major announcements. It is worthwhile, in my opinion, to be aware of these upcoming events and to "trade around them." Individual stock news can come at any time and in any shape, so to speak. For example, it may not be a good idea to sell Apple premium prior to the conference where they are set to roll out new products, unless you believe recent implied volatility increases overcompensate for the event. To be clear, I am not saying you should never trade events. But I am saying you should be aware the events are occurring and convinced the implied volatility either incorporates or overcompensates (or undercompensates) for it. As my first mentor in the trading world used to often tell me, being profitable is about avoiding the landmines.

On the flip side, I am almost always short index premium. The only time I am not is when all heck is breaking loose and the historical volatilities exceed the implied volatilities. But a low implied volatility percentile does not stop me from laying out some strangles if there is a large differential between the current implied volatility and its 5-, 10-, and 20-day historical volatility. This is because, though an index's implied volatility could mean revert at any time, not only does its implied volatility stay low for (up to) years at a time, but also its largest "edge" between historical and implied volatilities tends to be when the markets are very quiet. When I sell the low implied volatility index strangles, I am aware that I have a bit more risk of mean reversion hurting me than normal, so I trade a bit smaller. But when implied volatility is low, I am lowering my overall profit goals in my short premium trading anyway. Instead of 3 or 4 percent per month, I may be looking for 1.5 or 2 percent per month. So, my reduction in volume of options sold during periods of low implied volatility matches my expectations and my risk versus return assessment.

Making an Assumption

Every trade is driven by an assumption of some kind. It might be a directional assumption or implied volatility related. Though most of my trades are driven by volatility assumptions (after all, that is the "edge" options most readily provide), most traders will be driven by directional assumptions when making trades. This is true of technical analysts, fundamental analysts, contrarian traders, and your average investor. And this kind of directional trading can be done with virtually any instrument, options included. The advantage of directional options trading is the leverage you receive. The disadvantage, unless you are trading deep in the money options, is that to obtain unlimited upside for your trade you must purchase options (as opposed to selling them). As we have discussed, when you purchase an option you are paying more than the option is currently intrinsically worth. So your underlying must move a certain amount in your favor just for you to break even on the trade. If you are trading stocks or futures this is not true. So purchasing options for a purely directional trade is akin to running the first 20 meters of a 100-meter dash in sand.

When you execute a directional trade by selling options, you have a limited profit potential with the possibility of unlimited losses. Of course you gain the advantage of selling extrinsic value, and thus the underlying can actually move against you a bit and you still make money. As such, you put the odds in your favor as a premium seller. But as you can see, this discussion has quickly moved away from using options as a directional vehicle to using options as a strategic vehicle. And that is as it should be. I will leave others to spend hundreds of millions of dollars trying to find a way to continually predict market direction more accurately than "Brownian motion with an upward drift" would predict. I would not be 100 percent honest if I told you I never had a guess which way a stock, or the market, was headed and that I never acted on this impulse. But the bulk of my decision-making process, my trade assumption if you will, is not based on a directional assumption but on a volatility assumption. This is the beauty of options trading. You can be as bad at choosing a stock's direction as I am and still be highly profitable. Volatility assumptions are much easier to make, leave more room for error, and have a tendency for mean reversion that can guide you on your way. None of these things can be said of directional assumptions.

Though I led with the conclusion of the section, I will make a few brief comments on each of the means of making directional assumptions I touched on earlier. Let's begin with technical analysis. I've heard it said, and my experience reinforces the idea, that over 90 percent of all traders use technical analysis in one form or another. I suppose in some small way I am one of those 90 percent. However, I do not consider myself a technical analyst, and in fact, though I've spent years trying to hone my technical analysis skills, I find it truly lends little value to my trading. But I do want to stress that this does not mean it will lend little value to your trading. Each trader is different. There is a well-known trading psychologist by the name of Dr. Van Tharp who begins each one of his newsletters with the statement, "I always say that people do not trade the markets; they trade their beliefs about the markets." I agree with Dr. Tharp 100 percent. You may be thinking, "If every person reading this book is trading his or her own beliefs, and they differ considerably, how can we all be profitable? Isn't it the market that pays us?" This is to my point. It is your strategy and not your assumptions that can make you a consistently profitable trader. If you believe that statement, doesn't it make more sense to spend your time and money choosing and refining a strategy that can consistently grow your account, instead of spending your time and money trying to predict the direction of a stock or of the market in general? For me, the answer is a resounding yes. So why do I use technical analysis at all even in the minimalist form? After many years of trading, I believe there are patterns I recognize that aid me in making an assumption. They bring me to the table to place a trade. The value of that pattern recognition is not that I am correct in what will happen to the underlying in the near future, but that it brought me to put on a trade. The trade, though it began with an assumption that may or may not be correct, will always be supported by a volatility assumption, a proper choice of strategy, and a mathematically supported, positive expectancy exit strategy. And this is the crux of trading success, in my opinion.

When pressed to expound on how I use technical analysis in my trading, I describe it in terms of supply versus demand. This can easily be translated into a support and resistance discussion. Let us say, for example, that during the past year, every time XYZ stock has hit the $37.90 level, buyers have stepped in and propelled the stock higher. And every time the stock rose to $43.85, sellers hit the stock price back down. This has established a long-term pattern of support and resistance in my mind. How do I use this information? One way might be to set a stock alert for 30 cents above its support and 30 cents below its resistance. When the stock gets down to $38.20, I will assess the environment to see if I believe anything has changed with XYZ or the market in general. If not, I might look to sell a put below the support, knowing that IV percentile is likely to be high as the stock falls. If support is broken by 20 cents, I might buy my put back and take my loss since my assumption that support will hold has failed. That gives me only a small loss since I "bought" close to support. But if I am correct, I might wait for the stock to get back to the middle of my support/resistance range to start scaling out of the trade. One might argue this is a true technical analysis victory. But I believe it is a strategic victory, where I used my assumptions, my "beliefs about the market," to my best advantage. I set up a situation where I would cut my losses short and gave my winners a chance to grow wings. This makes sense to me in terms of the Kelly Criterion, which we will speak about in detail in Chapter 7. So again, strategy is what makes me money.

Fundamental analysis holds great merit in my opinion. Being a mathematically inclined person, I rely on and believe in numbers. If a company is growing at a long-term growth rate of 17 percent and its stock is trading at a 12 P/E, I find that pretty attractive. Based on those numbers, you might scoop up some stock or you might sell some puts below the market in hopes of either capturing that premium or buying stock lower than it is trading. Those are rational actions to take based on the information given. But to assume the stock price will move up in the next 30 to 50 days (the time frame of my typical option trade) is overreaching the limits of what fundamental analysis can do for you. The current price of the stock, in an efficient market, theoretically takes into account all known information. To assume that the marketplace is mispricing a company so dramatically that you think the stock will move considerably in the next 30 to 50 days is a fool's errand, in my opinion. So, though I believe in the validity of fundamental analysis, I believe it has little application in the short time frame world in which my options trading resides. In other words, it is a timing issue and not a problem with the analysis itself.

The third means of arriving at a directional assumption that I spoke about earlier is what we term contrarian trading. Contrarian traders generally take the other side of extended moves in a stock or in the overall market itself. They try to take advantage of markets that are overdone on either side. When a stock catches fire, so to speak, and runs up very far, very fast, a contrarian trader will often step in and get short that stock, hoping for a turnaround in its price. As I said, the same is true on the downside. When they feel the "baby has been thrown out with the bathwater" and the stock has taken more abuse than is warranted, they will be there to get long the stock. I have watched many contrarian traders in my career and find them to have a decent track record when measured by the percentage of time they are correct. Unfortunately, when measured by their profitability, they seem to have less success. Intuitively those statements don't seem to go together. But thinking about the nature of those stocks, we can make some sense of it. As I will state several times in this book, I believe stocks have inertia. A stock that has run up very far, very fast is what we term "in play." It has acquired significant velocity, and the farther up it runs, the more speed it seems to pick up. We used to term getting in front of these moves "picking up nickels in front of a steamroller." In other words, when you are wrong, you are dead wrong. My experience with this technique has been very far from pleasant. I would be right three times and make decent profits, and then the loss would come. Due to the velocity of the stock at the time the contrarian steps in, when one is wrong, the losses can be brutal. In fact, many of my biggest losses were during my time experimenting with contrarian trading.

Interestingly, my best directional picks have come from my more personal experiences (nontrading experiences). A few years ago, I realized I was watching a lot of programs on the Discovery Channel. So, I bought some stock and sold some puts below the market. This gave me half the position I wanted immediately and premium coming in until I got put the rest of the stock, which happened seven months later. I rode the stock to a "double" and a little bit more. (That means the price of the stock more than doubled.) Though I still trade this way in my IRA, once again the time frame of the predicted moves does not lend themselves to our everyday options trading.

The bottom line here is that unless you can predict stock movement in a time frame that matches your trades' timing, spending a lot of time and money trying is wasted effort. And even if you believe you can learn to predict direction and magnitude of short-term moves, I still believe option strategy is easier to learn and provides a better outcome.

CHAPTER 6

Choosing a Strategy

By now, we have chosen an underlying that is liquid and that we believe will give us an edge with respect to some kind of volatility assumption. I want to be clear that you do not have to think the same way I do to be successful. Many friends of mine who are accomplished and profitable traders look for other "setups" than those that I look for. In fact, there are few successful traders I know who think perfectly alike with any other trader. In many ways, that is what makes options trading so intriguing and fun for me. If you understand and respect the probability and math behind option pricing and trading, there is ample room for creativity as well. There were many times on the floor of the CBOE that I traded with other professional market makers (my peers) and we were both making money on the trade. They might have been closing a prior trade or mitigating risk, while I might have been taking on their risk for what I considered to be a price that gave me edge.

That being said, the biggest "variable" to be exploited is the implied volatility of the option. So it should come as no surprise that the comparative level of the implied volatility be used to choose not only an underlying but also a strategy. Some strategies will take advantage of an implied volatility we believe will rise, some take advantage of implied volatility we think will fall, and others are reasonably "volatility neutral." Our assumption on the future movement of the stock and/or the implied volatility will dictate which trading strategies are best suited to take advantage of your perceived edge.

Before we launch into the strategies themselves, it should be noted that the type of account you trade within would affect the strategies you are allowed to use. For example, if you trade in an IRA, or any other "cash" or "partial margin" account, you are not allowed to be short stock or short naked calls. You can, however, sell call spreads (though not ratio spreads where you are short more calls than you are long) and trade covered calls. You may also sell naked puts, as this has less risk than merely buying stock. But overall, this limits your strategies as well as the type of return on capital you can hope to achieve. Some brokerages will limit you further, and if they do I would seriously consider changing brokers. The foregoing restrictions are the only ones required by law. Any others would be broker-imposed, which generally occur out of laziness and/or a lack of understanding of the product and its risks.

These restrictions eliminate short straddles, short strangles, and short naked calls (including as part of a ratio spread) from your consideration. Your upside trades must be defined risk trades, but the downside can have "undefined" risk. I put "undefined" in quotes as a stock can go only to zero and therefore the downside risk might be large, but is not technically undefined nor is it unlimited.

Though we can parse our discussion of the different trading strategies in several different manners, I prefer to first place them into the defined or undefined risk category, for the foregoing reasons. This categorization is also important for newer traders and traders with small account sizes. Defined risk trades typically have a much smaller margin requirement, or buying power reduction, than do undefined risk trades, making them more suitable for small accounts. Also, the maximum loss for a defined risk trade is typically relatively small, or can be made to be so, thereby limiting the damage a newer trader can do to his account while learning or while still inexperienced.

Within each category, we will then break down each strategy by the implied volatility environment for which the strategy is best suited. We will break them down into three subcategories: low volatility, high volatility, and inconclusive (or average) volatility. Though I am not going to get into an in-depth explanation of the Greeks, I will briefly review vega and theta, as an understanding of them is essential to our discussion. However, if you are not familiar with the Greeks, I would suggest you spend a few minutes on the Internet researching the topic. It is basic enough that you can get a (free) understanding of their meanings on any one of at least 1,000 sites. It is the intelligent use of the Greeks, to give you an edge in your trading, that we will discuss in this book. So, let's launch into a discussion of some of the more common trades.

Likewise, if you are unfamiliar with the strategies I am discussing, you should consult similar sites on the Internet. I assume you are familiar with each strategy and will discuss only when to use them and not what the strategy actually is.

Defined Risk Trades

As I stated, defined risk trades are great for beginners and for smaller accounts. But I have to be honest. Though the principles of trading hold for defined and undefined risk trades alike, the bulk of my profits come from my undefined risk trades. I use defined risk trades like I would use training wheels on a bike. They do get me where I want to go, but at a much slower pace. They let me learn without incurring any bad injuries. I can get familiar with a new underlying, a new strategy, a high-risk situation, or a new trading platform without risking much of my bankroll. But when you are ready to ride without the training wheels, you become better off. I believe every trader should set their sights on getting to the undefined risk side of the equation when they are financially able and when their skill set supports it—but not before, and this is why I cover defined risk trades first.

Credit Spreads

Not all credit spreads are created equal. This is actually true of all of our spreads. You might be trading a $30 stock. This stock may have $1-wide strikes, or if you are trading weekly options, they might even have $.50-wide strikes. In one credit spread, you might sell the $28/$29 put spread for $0.35. In another credit spread, you may sell the $31/$36 call spread for $1.25. Though both have defined risk, they have vastly different risk profiles, buying power reductions, and Greeks. It is the latter that plays a part in the strategic use of options, and yet all three are important considerations before placing a trade. Let's use these two trades as an example and discuss them in terms of their risk profiles, buying power reductions, and Greeks in the cash account or partial margin account.

First we examine the 28/29 put spread, which we sold for $0.35. As in any short spread, or short naked option, the most we can make on the trade is the credit received. So in this case we can make $.35. How much can we lose? In a worst-case scenario, the most we can lose is the credit received subtracted from the width of the strikes. In our example, the most we could lose would be (29 – 28) – $0.35, or $0.65. If we were risking $.65 to make $.35, why would we make the trade? As always, probabilities give us the answer to this question. If we expect to win on this trade greater than 65 percent of the time, and thus lose on the trade less than 35 percent of the time, then this trade would have a positive expectancy of profit. Does that mean we would take this trade every time it is offered? And how would we know what our expectation for profitability would be?

The answer to the first question depends on the return on capital of the trade as well as the return on capital of other available trades. In general, we would like to maximize the returns we receive per dollar invested. Therefore, our $0.35 credit spread should be one we would choose if we felt the probabilities of profit were in our favor. Since the most we could lose on the spread is $65, that is the margin our broker would expect us to put up against the trade. So if we make the maximum $35 profit on our trade, our return on capital would be $35 divided by $65, or 54 percent. If our spread had 30 days to expiration, this would make our annualized return on capital a whopping 646 percent! Why would we not fill our entire portfolio with similar spreads? The answer lies back in Chapter 5. The sure edge in options trading comes through the effective use of an option's implied volatility. When implied volatility is high in its percentile, and the underlying's movement is slowing and less than its option's implied volatility, then we get a perceived edge when we sell premium. The effectiveness of the trade, if our volatility assumption plays out, is mostly measured by the vega of the trade. A tight spread (one or two strikes wide), in general, has a relatively small vega, especially when compared to an outright sale of an option. In fact, a one strike spread similar to the one described earlier will generally have around one-fourth of the vega of the short option alone. Without much of a volatility edge, our defined risk trade begins to approach a "zero-sum game," though not completely as there is one other "edge" that still exists. That edge is the implied volatility trading for higher than the historical (or realized) volatility. And though that is not an edge you can always count on in the short duration of our typical trade, it gives us an edge most of the time.

Though most academicians and investment advisers will speak of return on capital as the holy grail of benchmarks, in the end it is really about risk versus return. If I am comfortable with the risk I am taking on a day-to-day basis, then my bottom line profitability is my only true concern. I would rather make $100,000 with a bit more (though comfortable and manageable) risk than $50,000 with less risk. But if the risk needed to make the $100,000 does not seem commensurate with the return, I would happily settle for $50,000 if that seems risk-return balanced.

With this in mind, let's turn our attention to the second spread outlined earlier. In this spread we are selling the $31/$36 call spread for $1.25. This means we are risking $3.75 to make $1.25. We are taking on more risk to make a lower return on capital but a higher overall return. Our return on capital, if we achieve maximum profit, would be 33 percent or 396 percent on an annualized basis if this were a 30-day trade. But even though we are charged $375 of margin for each spread we sell, what is our true risk in the trade? You could argue that if extreme events occurred, your true risk is $375 per trade. However, those extreme events are extraordinarily rare. In fact, brokerages and clearing houses do not quantify a trade's risk in this manner and I do not believe a trader should either. As we will discuss in the section on trade exits, before I even place a trade I know where I will exit if things go my way and where I will exit if the trade goes against me. It is that chosen loss level that quantifies my perceived risk in a trade. Though I cannot use that level in my return on capital calculation, I do use it in my risk versus return analysis. Let's look at an example. We will assume that prior to selling the 31/36 call spread for $1.25, we decided to purchase the spread back when its price hits either $0.25 or $3.00, whichever comes first. This means that I will either make a $1.00 profit or incur a $1.75 loss. While it is true that an overnight gap move in the stock might prevent me from purchasing the spread back for $3, it is unlikely that I would have to pay much more than $3. Therefore, I look at the risk in this trade as being $1.75 (my chosen loss level), not the $3.75 that I am charged in margin. And harkening back to our vega discussion, this five strike–wide call spread has a much higher vega (or volatility) component than does our one strike–wide spread. Thus, we can use our volatility assumptions to gain greater edge in the trade. And, again, if we consider our risk to be our exit point and not the maximum potential loss, these wider spreads have a greater potential of being profitable as a longer-term strategy. Furthermore, if you are trading in a cash account (like an IRA), these wider call spreads are a better conduit for mimicking a naked option strategy. This is also true for a smaller account size.

One other trait of a credit spread is that it is a directional trade. Even if the stock moves a great deal, it must move against you directionally to make the trade a losing one.

Furthermore, our choice of a trade will also depend on how it fits into and affects our overall portfolio. We will discuss this in much greater detail in our section on portfolio management.

Debit Spreads

One of the few trades that we will discuss in this part of the book that does not collect theta is the debit spread. The reason for this is that the advantage I find in trading options is that of being able to use the probabilities to give me an edge. The debit spread does not generally accomplish this. But it also does not give up the edge as most long premium trades do. When sculpted in a certain fashion, the debit spread will have close to a 50/50 probability of making money. But, though it does not put the odds in your favor, the debit spread can accomplish a task with a neutral expected value for the trade. It is purely a directional trade, but one that has a limited risk and a limited return, unlike a stock transaction. It also has limited margin requirements and as such allows you to make a levered directional bet that allows you to sleep nights. It can also add deltas to your portfolio to reduce overall directional risk, though its effect is limited due to its defined risk nature.

If you purchase an out of the money debit spread, you are paying for theta each night and your probability of success is less than 50 percent. Though it is cheaper than buying a debit spread the way I propose, if you buy them consistently, I believe you will lose money. No one ever told you that you would lose money purchasing options? Then let me be the first!

So, how do you make debit spreads a 50/50 proposition? You do so by purchasing the one strike in the money option and selling the one strike out of the money option for around half the width of the strikes. Let's assume XYZ is trading for $30. If you were to buy the 29 call and sell the 31 call for $1, you would have approximately a 50 percent probability of making money. You would clearly make money if the stock went higher and lose money if the stock went lower. The spread is relatively unaffected by volatility changes. But these will not always line up perfectly symmetrically due to effects of "basis." Dividends and interest rates may make it unsymmetrical. Also, the volatility skew may affect it slightly as well.

If making it one strike in the money versus one strike out of the money makes the trade a better proposition, why not buy a debit spread where both strikes are in the money? Doesn't that increase your probabilities even more? The answer is yes; it makes the probabilities better. However, a long in the money debit spread is synthetically the same thing as a short out of the money credit spread. The credit spread collects money instead of requiring a significant cash outlay to purchase the debit spread; it is easier to execute and does not have nearly as much of an assignment risk. Let's look at each of these issues individually, not because the minutia is important to the debit spread, but because if you do not understand them, you are lacking some important knowledge when it comes to options trading.

Hearkening back to our earlier discussion of synthetics, let us look at an example. If XYZ is trading for $63, and we purchase the $55/$60 call spread for $3.50, this is the same as if we sell the 55/60 put spread for $1.50. Both trades risk $3.50 to make $1.50. And the payouts are at identical points.

Instead of laying out $350 per spread, why not collect $150 for the sale of the put spread? Furthermore, my guess is the call spread will be far more difficult to get executed in the marketplace, as the prices of the options involved are much larger. As the prices get larger, the spread between the bid price and the offer (or ask) price will generally widen. This makes it less obvious as to the fair price of the spread, unless, of course, you are well versed in the concept of synthetics! Finally, when dealing with in the money calls, if the stock has a dividend and the short calls in your spread are far enough in the money, you could have a potential exercise and/or assignment situation. If you forget to exercise your calls the night before the dividend and get assigned, this could get costly, depending on the size of the dividend. Furthermore, there is a fee associated with both the exercise and the assignment, making it a costly venture unless you are trading a lot of contracts. This is because the fee is per "line" and not per contract. In other words, if you exercise one $55 call, the fee is the same as if you exercise 100 $55 calls.

Thus, in general, debit spreads should be purchased with the long strike one strike in the money and the short strike one strike out of the money.

Butterfly

Though there are traders who claim to make a living trading butterflies, I find my ability to make money consistently is limited with this strategy. Let's examine the nature of butterflies and why it is so difficult to make good returns.

A long butterfly consists of a long spread and a short spread where the short strike from each are the same. Thus, using a 28/29/30 put butterfly as an example, we would be long one 28 put, short two 29 puts, and long one 30 put. Our maximum profit occurs when the stock expires right at 29, as we make $1 on our 30 put and the rest expire worthless. A one strike butterfly, such as this one, would typically trade cheaply, but how cheaply depends on a couple of variables. First, let's look at the effect of volatility on the butterfly. Because this trade yields decent returns only if the stock expires at a particular strike (your short strike), rather than using vega for this, let's think about the effect of volatility on our stock's probabilistic distribution curve to illustrate the point (see Figure 6.1).

FIGURE 6.1 Effect of Volatility on the Butterfly

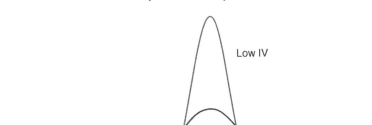

As you see, as the implied volatility rises, the probability of the stock expiring at any one particular price decreases. Since that is the only way to make money on a butterfly (expiring at, or near, your short strike), the higher the volatility, the cheaper the butterfly will trade for and vice versa. Reverting back to vega, since this is a narrow spread (with the long spread being the 29/30 put spread and the short spread being the 28/29 put spread), there is not a lot of vega to the butterfly. Thus, though the higher volatility will lead to a cheaper butterfly, we are probably talking only a penny or two cheaper.

One of the traits of a butterfly is that even if it is profitable, we say the butterfly does not "spread its wings" until a few days before expiration. Referring back to the earlier picture, we can swap out the words "higher volatility" with "more days to expiration," and "lower volatility" with "fewer days to expiration." If we do so, the Greek that we are thinking about now is theta. Theta, or time decay, accelerates in a geometric manner as we get closer to expiration. If you think about our distribution curve as centered on the short strike of the butterfly, as expiration nears the curve gets narrower and steeper. Our long strikes fall off the curve and therefore stop decaying much as their extrinsic value is approaching zero. But our short strike's decay is increasing dramatically. It is this decay that causes the butterfly to "open its wings" late in the expiration cycle and the price of the butterfly expands quickly. But if the price of the stock moves $.50 in either direction, decay for the butterfly decreases quickly and the wings open more slowly (or not at all). With a continued move, they can begin to close again. This description illustrates the fickle nature of the butterfly.

To summarize, the purchase of a butterfly is an inexpensive, low probability trade. To make a decent return even if things are going your way, you will have to hold the butterfly until very near expiration.

Iron Condor

An iron condor comprises two credit spreads, one call and one put. Typically, both spreads are out of the money, though that is not a requirement. What is necessary is that the put spread contain lower strikes than the call spread and that there are no overlapping or shared strikes. Going back to our $30 stock example, a short iron condor might consist of the short 28/29 put spread and the short 31/32 call spread. Just as in the credit spread example, the closer the strikes are to each other, the less effect volatility has on the spread, as the vega difference between the strikes is minimal. Of course, due to the use of two credit spreads, the vega is around twice that of a simple credit spread, and this trade is nondirectional, unlike the credit spread. But you can make the strikes fairly (or very) far apart to increase the vega of the spread and subject it to more of a volatility component. You can also add a directional component by not placing the strikes symmetrically around the stock price. When the small, protective options are low in value (wider strikes), the iron condor begins to look more like a strangle (which we will discuss in the undefined risk section). That means the wider iron condor is much more sensitive to implied volatility levels and will yield much better probabilities and profits when sold in relatively high implied volatility environments. The narrow iron condors, though they perform better when sold in high implied volatility environments, will perform only marginally better than when implied volatility is normal.

I want to stress again that without the assumption of mean reversion of implied volatility, there is a much smaller edge to short premium options trading. Since implied volatility tends to exceed historical, or realized, volatility around 90 percent of the time, that alone gives edge to short premium strategies. However, the limited profitability with unlimited (or larger but not unlimited, in the case of defined risk trades) loss prospects tends to negate much of this edge unless you manage your trades well. But when you put on trades that have a very small or nonexistent volatility component, this implied versus historical volatility is the only edge you have. As you widen the strikes in your iron condor, you add risk. But if you are taking advantage of the implied volatility's mean reversion properties, I believe the expected return of your trading will improve considerably due to the improved risk versus return scenario. It takes on higher risk, but you get paid well to do so, if done properly.

Calendar Spreads

Calendar spreads come in all shapes and sizes. Furthermore, there are many ways to think about what a calendar spread accomplishes, and what it does not. It is perhaps the most misunderstood of all strategies, in my opinion. First, we will describe the nature of the spread, and then talk about a major misconception of how to use the spread, and finally talk about proper usage.

When you purchase a calendar spread, either call or put, you are buying the farther out option (with respect to expiration cycle) and selling the nearer term option. For example, if you purchased an XYZ September 50 call and sold the July 50 call, we would have bought the call calendar. You can buy the second expiration cycle and sell the front month, or you can buy an option one year out and sell any month from the near term to the 11 month out option, which most likely is not listed, but you get the idea. The expiration cycles you choose define the way you use the strategy and which strikes you might choose to trade. We will look at a few variations in a minute. A plain vanilla calendar will have you using the same strike with both options. You can also vary the strikes. If the farther out expiration cycle option is also farther out of the money, you are trading what we call a diagonal spread. An example would be if XYZ was trading for $40 and you purchase the June 45 call and sell the May 40 call. This spread is called a diagonal spread and is actually a combination of a long calendar and a short vertical (credit) spread. Another variation would be if the farther out month call were at a lower strike. For example, if XYZ is trading for $42, you might purchase the June 40 call and sell the May 45 call. We call this a directional diagonal spread. In this case, the trade is a combination of a long calendar and a long vertical (debit) spread.

We will start by looking at the purposes and characteristics of which expiration cycles you choose and then move on to the strike selection criteria. Since you are short a shorter-term option and long the farther out–term option, a calendar spread collects theta. That is the nature of theta. The closer to expiration you are, the greater the extrinsic value of the option decays. So, in a vanilla calendar, as long as the closer-term option has some extrinsic value, you collect theta. The exception is if the calendar is so far out of the money or so far in the money that the front month has little extrinsic value to decay, the farther out option could feasibly have more decay and the theta would then reverse. But not only is that a rarity, I am not sure why you might want to make that trade. So, one of the main reasons for buying a calendar spread is to take advantage of the theta in the spread while limiting your risk. Thus, in general, I will usually have the short side of my calendar in the front month. Just as I like to trade my short premium trades in the 30–60 days to expiration time frame (depending on the probability of profit of the trade), I like the short premium side of my calendar to be in the same time frame. I do not want it too far down the theta curve, as then the calendar spread will cost too much since most of my short premium side will have decayed away. And I do not want it farther out in time as then I will not collect much theta and the underlying has more time to move out of the sweet spot.

As for the long premium side of the calendar, there are several considerations that come into play. First, just as a long calendar collects theta, it is also long vega. The farther out in time the long option is, the greater the vega of the spread. Of course, the farther away in time the long strike is from the short strike, the more the spread will cost you and the greater the risk versus return of the spread. (There is one exception to that statement and that is when we use a calendar as a stock replacement strategy.) But in general, a long second month expiration option and short the front month option is the most common. But you may be thinking, "If the implied volatility of the stock is exceptionally low, why would I not buy a farther out option so I can take advantage of the extra vega the spread will give to me?" The answer to this leads us into two discussions. First, though many people believe the long vega in a calendar will help protect the short vega they may have accumulated in their portfolio from selling strangles, iron condors, credit spreads, or naked puts, this is a fallacy and something you need to avoid when managing your portfolio. Looking at the profit and loss graph of a calendar spread (see Figure 6.2), we see that the trade makes money as long as it stays close to home.

FIGURE 6.2 Calendar Profit and Loss

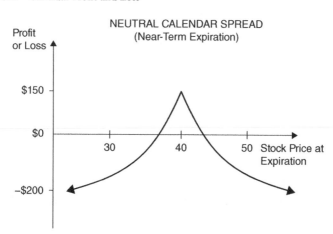

Source: www.theoptionsguide.com.

That is, it behaves like a typical short premium, nondirectional spread (think iron condor). And what generally causes implied volatility to rise? Typically, a sharp move to the downside and occasionally an explosive move to the upside cause an increase in implied volatility. But it is rare to see implied volatility rise considerably when the stock has little movement. And little movement is what a calendar banks on to make money, as can be seen in the graph. So, why do we consider a calendar to be a long vega trade? And why do we look to put the trade on when implied volatility is low in its percentile range? Though a long calendar does little to mitigate and offset a portfolio's short vega risk, it is generally cheaper to purchase a calendar when implied volatility is low. That makes sense since we are purchasing vega overall. Why do I say "generally"? That leads us to the second point in our discussion—term structure. Term structure refers to the relationship between prices, or in our case implied volatility levels, of derivatives with various expiration dates. When each successive expiration cycle's option has a higher implied volatility than the closer in option, we call this a "contango." When the closer expiration cycle has a higher implied volatility, we call this "backwardation." Though "contango" and "backwardation" are really terms that come from the futures world, they are descriptive and applicable to options term structure, and I will use them here. When implied volatility is low, our implied volatility term structure is usually in a contango; the lower the implied volatility, the steeper the contango. (This is true as long as an "event," like earnings, is not looming, in which case the size of the expected event move may invert the term structure "artificially.") Assuming all is normal, implied volatility is low, and the contango is relatively steep, some of the benefit we get from having low implied volatility is lost to us because the option we are buying has a higher implied volatility than the option we are selling. The steeper the contango, the more this is true. To make things worse, when the market starts to move and implied volatility picks up, the term structure begins to flatten or even reverse into backwardation. This means the option we are short will gain more implied volatility than will the option we are long. This again offsets some of the gains we hoped to capture with an implied volatility increase. The bottom line is that though most traders will tell you a calendar spread takes advantage of low implied volatility, the volatility effect is less than many believe. It still exists, but I find my time better spent elsewhere. Does that mean I never trade calendars? No, but it means I trade them for other purposes than to take in long volatility. I may trade them for their theta, but more often it is for a combination of the long theta and it is somewhat of a timing play. My hope is that the front month (short) option expires worthless, leaving me a long option for a cheaper price than I could buy it for in the marketplace. And my directional assumption will then lead me to the proper strike selection, which is the next topic we tackle.

Earlier, we spoke of a vanilla calendar, a diagonal, and a directional diagonal as the three most common calendar spreads. We will briefly discuss the characteristics of each trade.

Since we already dissected a calendar pretty thoroughly, I will begin with a summary. Generally, a calendar is purchased one strike out of the money or at the money. Again, the hope is that the stock sits and the front month decays away, giving you ownership of the back month option at a cheaper price than you could otherwise purchase it. If you buy an at the money calendar, you are hoping the stock stays just below strike and sits so that you are not in danger of being assigned on your short option at expiration. The trade is virtually nondirectional. If you purchase one strike out of the money, your hopes and dreams are similar but you give the stock a bit of room to drift in the direction of your options. Again, you want the stock as close to your short strike as possible without going over. This would give your farther out option its greatest value as the front month expires worthless.

A diagonal is perhaps the most common type of calendar spread I saw on the floor of the CBOE. This is probably due to normal order flow. I would frequently see orders come in from customers who were short calls against their portfolios and were rolling them out to the next month. Due to the "upward drift" in stock prices, this led them to often sell diagonals. As the buyer of the diagonal, I pay less money than I would for a vanilla calendar and therefore incur less risk. This is because the farther out option is more out of the money than in a vanilla calendar. As long as I take my trade off before the front month expires in the money or I am assigned on my short call, my risk is known and defined. But you do need to be alert to the prior events because if you end up short stock, your trade takes on a whole new risk profile and may not be one you are hoping to have in your portfolio. Along with the decreased risk of the diagonal, I also have less chance for a large payout. As always, the "risk versus return" ratio guides my trading—position size, propensity for making the trade, and so forth. With the lower risk and lower payout, I would have to increase my trade size to make it worthwhile.

A directional diagonal is the least common of the three calendars, and yet it is the one I trade the most frequently, though I do not trade calendars often in general. With a directional diagonal, I am buying a calendar as well as a debit spread. I buy the debit spread with my long strike one strike in the money and my short strike one strike out of the money. This gives me a distinct directional bent to the trade. My debit spread has around a 50 percent probability of profit by itself, and my calendar, due to the positive theta, gives me a bit better than a 50 percent probability. But because I am paying for both the time premium of the calendar and the debit spread, the overall trade has more risk but with a bigger payout if I am right.

As I said before, the calendar spread is the most misunderstood of the common option strategies. Some options educators call calendars an "income producing" trade. This is true in that they collect theta, thus giving the trade a better than 50 percent probability of profit with limited risk. But for my money, I prefer out of the money credit spreads unless I want a timing component to my trade.

Undefined Risk Trades

As I stated previously, all options trades are risk transference transactions. If you want me to take on your risk, you will have to pay me a price that I deem appropriate. This entire book is really about pricing that risk transference and subsequently managing the risk you have taken. But rather than a strict mathematical approach, I have taken a more commonsense, strategic approach. There are hundreds of books that explain the Black-Scholes model, the binomial model, the use of Monte Carlo simulations for price modeling, and the thousands of variations thereof. But few lay out how to use these models to put the probabilities in your favor.

With that in mind, we now look at a few common undefined risk trades. To state that risk is undefined is not always accurate, as a short naked put has a clear definition of what you can lose. The stock can only go to zero. But in almost all situations, that would lead to a very large loss that may or may not be catastrophic. So, these trades would be better termed "higher-risk strategies." Be that as it may, the term "undefined risk trades" is an industry standard term, so we will stick with it here. For a trade to fall into this category, we would be looking at a short premium trade. If we buy premium, we can lose only what we pay for it, assuming we manage the trade appropriately. Therefore, a long premium trade is always a defined risk trade. Furthermore, a long premium trade, according to the option models, will always have a less than 50 percent chance of making money. Since I want the probabilities in my favor, I will almost always run a "short premium portfolio." And since as a premium seller of naked options I am taking on an "undefined" or a very large amount of risk, I will be looking for more edge on these trades. The greater the risk I take on, the more edge I want in the trade. Of course, I control this risk through proper position sizing and effective portfolio management. But due to the increased edge I am able to obtain on these trades, they are truly my "bread and butter." I would estimate that 88 percent of my annual trading profits come from short premium, undefined risk trades. I made the statement earlier that once you are able to "take off the training wheels," you need to graduate to these types of trades. Now you know why!

The Straddle

A straddle is a trade where you buy (or sell) a call and a put of the same strike in the same expiration cycle. If you sold the same quantities of the March $46 calls and the March $46 puts in XYZ stock, you would have sold XYZ straddles. A short straddle carries risk in both directions. Any large move in the underlying will lead to losses, and those losses grow the farther the stock moves beyond the straddle's break-even point. A straddle is generally traded at the closest strike price to the stock price (the at the money strike) and therefore is nondirectional. Since the option that has the largest vega, or close to the largest vega, is the at the money option, and since you are selling two options at that level (one call and one put per straddle), this strategy has one of the largest volatility components of any trading strategy we will discuss. What this means in practical terms is that you can often obtain the greatest edge by choosing stocks as we discussed in Chapter 5. By taking advantage of the mean reverting properties of implied volatility, and by looking for slowing historical volatilities to predict that a high implied volatility stock will mean revert within the time frame of our trade, we hope to "beat" the probabilities predicted by the price of the straddle. If we can beat the predicted probabilities, we can consistently make money.

However, though the straddle can give us the largest profit and the greatest trading edge, it also carries the greatest risk. It is not for the faint of heart. But there is another closely related strategy that also carries large profit potential with more buffer to be wrong.

The Strangle

With a short strangle, you are short an out of the money put and an out of the money call of the same expiration cycle. Though they do not truly have to both be out of the money, they are almost always traded that way. The call just needs to be of a higher strike than the put.

A strangle can be traded without directional bias by selling the options with identical deltas, or as close as possible. Of course, due to the typical volatility skew, these options may not be equidistant from the stock price. But if you believe the options are priced efficiently, delta (or probability of profit) is the best predictor of directional risk and therefore the best way to determine your strangle has little directional bias. Of course, you can introduce directional bias into the trade by choosing strikes with unequal deltas. This is a choice you can make based on your own, individual assumption of future stock movement.

Because the strikes of the strangle are farther from the money (the stock price) than those of a typical straddle, the strangle has a lower vega than a straddle. That means the trade has a lower sensitivity to changes in volatility than does a straddle. But it still has a strong vega component to the trade, probably stronger than almost any other typical strategy other than a straddle. Furthermore, when compared to a short straddle, a strangle has breakevens that are farther away from the current stock price and therefore gives you a higher probability of profit than does a short straddle. Even though the potential profit is lower, I will almost always short strangles rather than straddles for this reason. And if I choose to buy premium, I will buy straddles and not strangles to give myself a better chance to profit. Due to the difference in profit potential, I will generally sell more strangles than if I were selling straddles.

In general, since I am a probability-based trader who believes I gain edge by taking advantage of mispriced implied volatility, the short strangle is my most common trade. It has a large enough volatility component and no directional bias, and I can sculpt the trade to have breakevens far enough from the current stock price that I can sleep nights.

Short Naked Puts

My favorite directional trade is the naked short put. Like any other undefined risk trade, there is a large amount of risk in the trade. But what most people do not understand is that there is less risk in selling a naked put than there is in purchasing stock. We will discuss this in more detail in a bit.

Once again, as in all options trading, I can pick my probability of profit to fit my situation and my assumption. Naked puts actually have several advantages over a short strangle.

1. Stocks have a positive drift (upward movement). This is true regardless of whether you believe in randomness of the market. Take a look at any key equity market index over a long period of time and this will

become apparent. In fact, over the past 50 years, the market has averaged a 6.2 percent compounded annual return. So, with that as background, doesn't it make more sense to place a long delta trade than a trade that has upside risk?

2. Though this may sound like a negative, in general, the velocity of movement to the downside is greater than the velocity to the upside. As such, the implied volatility of the out of the money puts reflects this by trading with a volatility skew. In other words, you get more premium selling out of the money puts than out of the money calls that are the same distance from the current stock price. Since the stock market falls hard only on rare occasions, most of the time the skew presents an opportunity to collect some healthy premium by taking on the downside risk. If you are wrong and the stock falls hard, the result is you own the stock at a price that is higher than what the stock is trading for.

This brings us back to my statement that there is less risk in selling a naked put than in buying a stock. For some reason, this is one of the most difficult concepts to get across to prospective options traders. Yet it is also one of the most basic. Let us look at an example. XYZ stock is trading for $34. We will examine the difference between buying stock at that price or selling the $32 put that expires in 30 days for $1.

First, we look at purchasing the stock outright. Our cost for 100 shares is $3,400. In 30 days, we look at the profit and loss of our stock at various stock prices:

Stock Price	Profit (Loss)
$0	−$3,400
$28	−$600
$30	−$400
$32	−$200
$34	$0
$36	$200
$38	$400

Now, we look at selling the naked $32 put for $1. This would take in $100 credit from the sale of the puts. In 30 days, we look at the profit and loss of our option trade at various stock prices:

Stock Price	Profit (Loss)
$0	−$3,100
$28	−$300
$30	−$100
$32	$100
$34	$100
$36	$100
$38	$100

Comparing the two strategies, you will see that at no point does the naked short put lose more money than the stock purchase! In the event the stock price falls significantly, the loss on the short put is always $300 less, in our example, than the loss on the stock purchase. Of course, the trade-off is that if the stock rallies, the most the put seller can make is the credit he or she receives from the sale of the put, while the stock buyer has unlimited upside. But the put seller makes money if the stock stays above $31 and the stock buyer needs the stock above $34 to make money. There is a vast difference in probabilities of making money! The put seller will make money far more frequently.

Bottom line, when we speak of risk, the stock purchase has more than does the short naked put. Go teach that to the masses, and we would vastly improve the liquidity of our options markets (not to mention increase the sales of options books!).

Ratio Spreads and Back Spreads

Ratio spreads and back spreads are two sides of the same coin. With a ratio spread, you are long one strike (call or put) and short more than one farther out of the money strike (same, call or put, as before). An example of a call ratio spread would be if XYZ were trading for $32 and you purchased one $34 call and sold two (or more) $36 calls. A back spread is exactly the opposite side of that trade. It is the mirror image and, in our example, would be if we sold the $34 call one time and bought two or more of the $36 calls. An example of a put back spread would be if we sold the $31 put and bought two (or more) of the $30 puts. What do these spreads try to accomplish and under what circumstances do we get the best edge in the trade?

Let us begin by looking at the ratio spread. Using our previous example, and assuming a one by two ratio spread where we are long one $34 call and short two $36 calls, our best expiration scenario is for the stock to close at our short strike. In this case, that would be at $36 and we would make $2 plus or minus the price of the original spread. In general, I would prefer to put on a ratio spread for a credit. However, sometimes to accomplish that, I need either to up my ratio (one to 2.5 or one to three) or to get closer to the stock price than I want with my short strike. This puts greater risk into the position, and so I will on rare occasions put the trade on for a small debit. But be aware that the debit versus credit decision is critical. The main reason is that the probability of profit of the trade changes dramatically on this fact. And since I am a probability-based trader first and foremost, as I believe it is the only way to consistently make money over long periods of time, this is often the decision that drives my "trade or no-trade decision." Why is debit versus credit such a major driver of the probabilities? Staying with our example, if we put the call ratio spread on for a credit, we cannot lose to the downside. If the stock moves down, or stays below our long strike, we still get to keep the credit we receive from the trade. The only place we begin to lose money is above $38 plus the credit received. Since these calls are far out of the money, our probabilities are probably north of 70 percent and more likely north of 80 (or even 90) percent. Another reason to trade these spreads for a credit has to do with trade management. When you put on a ratio spread, your hope is the stock will move through your long strike but not exceed your short strike. Your risk is when the stock runs through your short strike by a considerable amount. If, after initiating the trade, the stock runs in the opposite direction (down after you buy a call ratio, or up after purchasing a put ratio), and if you put the trade on for a credit, this may provide you with an opportunity to "butterfly the trade off" for a credit. What this means is that if you bought the $34 calls and sold two of the $36 calls for a $.10 credit, if you get the opportunity to buy one of the $38 calls for less than $.10, you have a no-lose situation. You will have created a long butterfly and been paid to do so. Since a butterfly cannot be worth less than zero, you have guaranteed yourself a profit (if you continue to manage the trade properly, meaning there are no early exercise issues). And in our case, you can actually make $2 on each butterfly, since you own a $2-wide butterfly. But if you paid to put on the original trade, the best you can do when the stock moves against you is create a long butterfly that you have paid for. This increases your loss on the trade if the stock never exceeds your long strike rather than creating a no-lose situation. Furthermore, if you pay for the ratio spread, the stock price zone where your trade makes money is far smaller and therefore so is your probability of profit. If we pay $.10 for our spread, we now make money only when the stock expires between $34.10 and $37.95. This is in contrast to our credit spread where we made money with our stock trading anywhere from zero to $38.10.

To be fair, we may be talking a small monetary swing between putting on the trade for a $.10 credit versus a $.10 debit. But I like to win, and the credit side wins far more often. For many traders, the drive to win is a limiting factor in their ability to trade profitably. When a trade turns against them, they refuse to take losses and this can lead to huge problems. I have rarely seen a disciplined trader go bankrupt. It is the inability to take a loss and poor trade size management that are usually the culprits that cause a trader to blow out. I prefer to be stubborn on my win versus loss decision prior to trade entry. This will more often than not keep me out of trouble. Will it maximize my profitability? I cannot state that definitively, as there are too many issues involved. But it limits the amount of time I spend on my trading, gives me a higher winning percentage, and satisfies my "need to win" without adding risk to my trading.

Now we turn our attention to the Greeks of a ratio spread. Though these vary considerably based on time to expiration, when determining how far out of the money our long and our short strikes are, how large our ratio is, and so on, in general, we can make the following three statements:

1. A ratio spread is generally short vega and short gamma. This is particularly true the farther you are away from expiration. This means you get the best probabilities of success by putting on a ratio spread when implied volatility is at a higher percentile. Of course, the reverse is also true. If implied volatility is low and you believe the stock is poised for a large move, you might consider a back spread. As a short premium trader, I rarely put on back spreads, unless I need the extra "units" (contracts) for risk management purposes to reduce my buying power in my portfolio management account.

2. Because a ratio spread is short vega and short gamma, it is usually collecting theta. As such, I will generally put these on in the same time frame I would put on any other short premium trade, which is 30 to 50 days to expiration. If the stock stays where it is at, as the trade gets closer to expiration, the farther out options have generally decayed away and the only option of any value left is your long. So, at some point, the Greeks can invert on this trade. I will generally close my trade before this occurs, unless I have a good reason for wanting to pay out theta to hold the position.

3. The delta of the trade will also be determined by the strike with more units, provided there are enough days to expiration and depending on

the price of the underlying. So, in a call ratio spread where you are short more units than you are long, you will generally be short deltas. As expiration nears, the location of the stock as compared to the options' strikes will determine the delta of the strategy.

What Time to Expiration Should My Trades Have?

If you have read anything at all on options theory, you will have most likely read that theta accelerates as you get closer to expiration. Though this is true for an at the money and slightly out of the money option, this statement is not completely accurate for all options.

Option prices are made up of a combination of intrinsic value and extrinsic value. Intrinsic value is the value the option is currently worth if immediately exercised. The rest of the price of the option is contained in its extrinsic value. It is the extrinsic value that holds all the time value and is affected by implied volatility. And it is the at the money options that carry the most extrinsic value. The farther out of the money the option gets, the less extrinsic value it carries, on a comparative basis. On an absolute basis, an option has more extrinsic value the higher the implied volatility, the longer the time to expiration, and the closer to at the money it is. We can intellectually reconcile this concept by thinking about the distribution curve of the underlying's price, as shown in Figure 6.3.

With a higher implied volatility or more days to expiration, the distribution curve widens and flattens. This means the probability of a farther away underlying price getting reached increases. Traders are therefore willing to pay more for options at these farther out strikes as it seems more likely they could

FIGURE 6.3 Distribution Curve

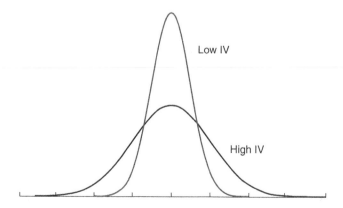

Low IV

High IV

profit from such a transaction. This increase in price is solely attributed to an option's extrinsic value. If the option is at the money or out of the money, its entire value is extrinsic value. This means that if the option never gets in the money, its entire value must decay away by the time the option expires.

With this foundation in place, let's look at the theta curve and how it differs between options. First, if we examine an at the money option, as we stated before, the theta accelerates until the option expires. This is the lesson most frequently taught. But as a premium seller, I am more often selling out of the money options to keep my probability of profit high, yet I still want to take advantage of collecting theta as an option decays. I tend to trade strategies with a similar probability of profit all the time. For example, virtually every month, I sell strangles in the SPX. I choose both the calls and puts such that each option has approximately a 95 percent probability of expiring out of the money according to my options model. Since delta can be used as an approximator of the probability an option will expire in the money, these SPX options have around a five delta. When I believe the overall market is in a quiet, upward trending pattern, I also sell out of the money puts in a variety of equities. Depending on my assessment of the individual equities I choose and just how willing I am to purchase the stock should it fall below my put strike, I might sell puts that have a probability of expiring worthless in the 75 to 85 percent range. These options will therefore have a delta of around 15 to 25, depending on my chosen probability. Therefore, it is imperative I understand how an out of the money option decays over time, depending on the option's delta.

Let's begin logically. The farther out of the money an option is (the smaller the delta) the smaller is its extrinsic value. That means there is less value to decay between trade date and the expiration of the option. The question then becomes "does the option decay exponentially until the time of expiration, like an at the money option (albeit at a slower absolute rate), or does the decay curve take on another shape?" Adding in some empirical evidence (from my years of trading experience), I have observed that my SPX out of the money options will decay at a good pace until the option shrinks to under $1 in value. The decay then seems to slow and eventually comes to a crawl when the option falls below $.25. In essence, the decay curve has an inflection point in it where the decay goes from accelerating to decelerating. Where this inflection point occurs depends on the probability of profit of the option, or the delta of the option.

Let's look at this in a bit more detail. Figure 6.4 shows the decay curve of SPX options having deltas of 5, 10, 15, 20, and 25.

As you can see, the smaller the delta of the option, the sooner the inflection point occurs. Thus, if you are selling far out of the money options, you get more theta (on a relative basis and an absolute basis) by selling a longer dated

FIGURE 6.4 Decay Curve with Various Deltas

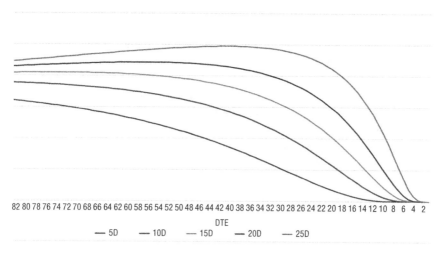

82 80 78 76 74 72 70 68 66 64 62 60 58 56 54 52 50 48 46 44 42 40 38 36 34 32 30 28 26 24 22 20 18 16 14 12 10 8 6 4 2

DTE

— 5D   — 10D   — 15D   — 20D   — 25D

option. In our example where I looked at from 100 days to expiration in to the day before expiration, neither the 5 nor the 10 delta option ever saw a rising theta. That means both a 5 and 10 delta option achieve their maximum theta longer than 100 days before expiration. Our 15 delta option reached maximum theta 88 days before expiration. Our 20 delta option achieved maximum theta 55 days prior to expiration, and our 25 delta option saw maximum theta 39 days before expiration. Since there are other variables at play here, the exact number of days prior to expiration may vary, but the pattern we see will not.

Why is this important? Once again, most traders are reasonably consistent and mechanical in the way they trade. If you are always selling 25 delta naked puts in your portfolio, you would not want to be selling them with 100 days to expiration if you are looking to maximize your theta. Of course, there might be other strategic reasons to alter this. We are admittedly isolating theta to understand its nature better.

Trading Earnings Announcements

Another assumption that goes into all of our common option pricing models, such as the Black-Scholes model or the binomial model, states that the price of the underlying must be continuous. In short, the option pricing model assumes there are no "binary moves" or "gap moves" in the stock. We all know that on occasions, a stock will gap up or down, often during nonmarket hours. These moves are usually caused by news that comes out that could have, or is perceived to have, substantive effects on the stock's price going forward. Many of these gaps come out of nowhere and are not anticipated. There is not much we can do about those. Presumably, they are part of the reason the implied volatility of our options is generally higher than the historical, or realized, volatility of the underlying. But what if we could anticipate the binary moves? How should we handle those events if the option models do not take them into account? Should we just take the option prices the market gives us and assume they are fair?

There are many ways we can go forward, including assuming the market forces are accurately predicting price movement, including the binary move. Another way would be to use a different option pricing model entirely. You may have heard of "exotic options." Exotic options come in various shapes, sizes, and rules. Due to the uniqueness of each type of exotic option, there has been a great deal of financial engineering done to come up with appropriate, usually closed-form models to effectively price the exotic. One such model has gained in popularity among earnings traders. It is a form of a "jump diffusion model." These models can become very complex for the novice trader, and even for the experienced trader. What you need to know is that the model is only as good as your assumptions are for both the jump (binary move) and the diffusion (resolved implied volatility that predicts normal movement for the underlying, exclusive of the binary move). Rather than get lost in the mathematical weeds, I find there is a far simpler way to trade earnings. And earnings are the type of predictable gap, or binary, event of which I speak. An earnings announcement will generally color the movement of a stock for some period of time after the event, since the earnings announcement and subsequent conference call will give an investor fresh information with which to value the stock. But it is truly the earnings event itself that makes our trade profitable or not profitable. Thus, it is the "jump" part of the move we can try to capture, as it generally dwarfs the "diffusion" phase. I will now look at a far simpler, and in my opinion more effective, means of pricing earnings events. This method utilizes past earnings moves as a predictor of future probabilities. And, before I go further, I will reiterate that there are those who will quote the statement that is found in so many financial publications: "Past performance is not a predictor of future results." They will maintain that history teaches us nothing about future events. I find this hard to swallow. If that were so, why do these same people price Green Mountain Coffee Roasters (GMCR) earnings events differently than they price Exxon Mobil? And why does each individual equity trade with an implied volatility that averages a bit above its own, individual, historical volatility?

Many people consider Warren Buffett to be one of the great investors of the modern era. He has a few simple rules he follows when valuing potential targets. Having sat through many of his annual meetings, his message comes out loud and clear that the most important consideration when assessing a company is its management. (As a side note, Berkshire Hathaway's annual meetings are attended by so many investors for a reason. I have learned more about business at each meeting than I learned in the two years of my MBA program. And my MBA program was actually quite good.) Management provides the "marching orders" for its company. This will often include the personality of its earnings guidance and announcements. Hearkening back a few years to a Steve Jobs–run Apple Inc., we have the perfect example of this. Jobs seemed to generally announce guidance for earnings lower than he expected them to actually be. He created a buffer so that in the event the company didn't meet his expectations, the stock would not incur a negative shock. Thus, he insured the street's expectations were lower than his expectations. What this led to was a confluence of positive earnings "surprises" for the stock. In fact, from April 2004, when the stock started to gain traction, until just before Jobs's resignation in August of 2011, the stock moved up on earnings announcements an astounding 22 out of 30 times. Was that a coincidence? I do not think so and neither do many in financial circles, as it was a much talked about strategy while it was occurring. Does every company "sandbag" their earnings guidance? Or are some managers overly aggressive about their estimates? I believe that for the most part, managers make a fairly honest assessment of earnings going forward. But some are better at it than others. Yet some do have patterns of bias. For any given company, can we discern which category its management falls within? As for bias, sometimes I believe it becomes apparent when we look at any pattern that might exist in past earnings announcements. But with respect to the accuracy of management's predictions, I believe we can always find useful information by looking at past earnings events. One caveat to this is that you need to be aware of any management shakeups, either at the top (president or CEO) or within the finance department (CFO or controller). If management personnel that could affect the earnings estimates going forward has recently changed, the history of earnings moves loses much, if not all, credibility. The "personality" of management has changed and so might their ability, or patterns, in discerning earnings going forward.

I want to be clear that I will generally play earnings as an overnight event. In other words, I will put on the trade late in the day prior to the earnings announcement and take the trade off the very next day, often on or near the open. This helps me to isolate my trades to the "jump" portion of the event and ignore the "diffusion" process. This simplification helps me to focus in on and hone my trades to match my earnings expectations in terms of magnitude of the expected move. There are modifications to that pattern, and I will point them out as we get deeper into the trades.

Though, in general, I am a short premium trader, this is not always true for earnings plays. The reason stems from why I am a short premium trader. As I have stated several times, in the long run, an option's implied volatility is usually at a higher percentage than is the stock's historical volatility. This gives us an edge to our short premium plays. Further, much of the edge comes from the theta, or decay, of the options over time. When you hold an option for a short period of time, hours to a couple of days, the option does not have much time to decay. Thus, the profitability of the trade comes almost entirely from the movement of the underlying compared to what the implied volatility predicts, and from implied volatility changes themselves. Since an earnings event is an overnight occurrence, if we hold the trade for a short time, we do not have to be concerned with theta at all. What of the implied volatility changes? Some traders will claim you have to play earnings from the short premium side to take advantage of the implied volatility crush that almost certainly will take place the morning after earnings. Though I cannot deny a volatility crush usually takes place, we need to examine the nature of implied volatility and the path it takes both prior to and after earnings.

First, I want to reiterate a few points about implied volatility. As one of the six inputs into an option's price, it is, along with the stock price, among the most important. Changes in an option's price based on changes in implied volatility are measured by the vega of the option. Vega for a particular option decreases as time to expiration decreases. So, as an option approaches expiration, the vega of the option approaches zero and becomes a much less important factor in the option's price. Another way of stating this is that the extrinsic value of the option approaches zero, and the option price is almost entirely made up of intrinsic value, as the option approaches expiration. That means that as expiration approaches, the stock price is the overriding factor in an option's price, which makes perfect sense.

Even so, some find an implied volatility that is trading over 100 percent or even 150 percent irresistible and they sell it. Let's trace the path the implied volatility takes to get to such a level. According to studies, prior to a known (potentially binary) event, an option will apparently slow down its rate of decay. In other words, theta slows depending on how large the earnings move is predicted to be. And we see this slowing of theta as an increase in the option's implied volatility. How much, and how far before earnings this occurs, is dependent on the size of the expected move almost entirely. Why? What is really occurring is the expected binary move is getting built into the price of the options. So, when it appears the implied volatility is rising, it is actually a fallacy. Once again, our option pricing models are not built for binary, or gap style, moves in the underlying. As such, there is no true mechanism built into the model to account for the gap. We see it as either a slowing of theta or as an increase in implied volatility, depending on your perspective. This increase in implied volatility is deceptive. It appears as a result of an imperfect model for the upcoming event. Once the event has taken place, the extra implied volatility built into the options for the binary move will come out almost immediately. We see this as a volatility crush, yet it truly is nothing of the sort. It is just a return to business as usual for implied volatility after a period of distortion. As such, you can predict where the implied volatility should return to within hours after the opening of trading on the day after earnings. Of course, that prediction assumes an earnings move that is not out of control. And by that, I mean not outside the range the prior couple of years earnings had produced. The implied volatility should return to its pre-earnings level after adjusting for any abnormal market or stock movement. Again, by abnormal stock movement, I mean an earnings move far greater than normal for that underlying.

Tying together this point with the point about vega nearing zero close to earnings, I choose to make most of my earnings plays with as short dated options as possible. This generally will mean weekly options if they are available. What this does is almost entirely takes the implied volatility out of the decision. Rather, I look at the price of the at the money straddle as the predictor of the earnings move.

From a practical standpoint, I will now show you how I line up earnings plays. As I said before, the entire premise of my strategy hinges on the current corporate management having been in place for a while, for it is their performance we are measuring as well as the company's. If there is new management in place, I move on to other trades as the repeatability of their earnings performance is seriously called into question. And since there are almost 1,200 stocks I follow, there is always something else to do that gives me good probabilities.

During earnings season, I keep a close watch on the "earnings calendar." I use several sites for this, as on occasion I will find mistakes in one site or the other. My broker provides a calendar and I find this useful, as it flags which stocks have upcoming earnings in the current expiration cycle right on my watch list of stocks. Next, I will compare the date my broker provides to a free site called "Earnings Whispers," at www.earningswhisper.com. What I like about this site is that it flags earnings dates that are "confirmed" versus those that are educated guesses. Some sites do not distinguish between the two and can, at times, get you into trouble. If I still have questions about an earnings date, I go right to the source. If you perform a search on the company's investor relations' page, you will find out if a date has been officially announced. If it has been, you can take that to the bank. If not, there is still some risk in relying on the date published on the earnings tracking sites. Doing the search is time-consuming, so I only do it when I have a conflict between earnings dates on the various sites. There is not a set location on a company's investor relations' page where announcements are made. Therefore, as each site is different, you often spend a few minutes hunting for the information. I have a third source I use frequently, but be warned that it is a pay site. It is found at www.optionslam.com. Assuming there is no large price increase in the works, I find this site to be inexpensive for the vast amount of data it provides you. Though I could reproduce all the information given on the website myself, it would take an extraordinary amount of time and energy that could be better spent elsewhere.

On a daily basis, I will leaf through the earnings calendar looking for stocks I follow that have reasonably large earnings moves. I generally look at stocks that have earnings both the current week and the following week.

I find little edge in stocks that do not move much with earnings. These "quiet earnings stocks" generally are not good premium purchases, as they rarely pay out much. They are not good premium sales either because, though the trade may be profitable much of the time, their occasional misses can be costly. This, in my mind, makes the risk versus return comparison unappetizing. (By unappetizing, I mean balanced.) I can certainly make money on either side of the trade, but I cannot find much edge in the expected payout of the trade over time. But with the higher volatility stocks (with respect to earnings), there is a greater propensity for edge in the trade. This can be on either side of the premium trade. As I said, though I am a short premium trader in general, I am ambivalent about which side of the trade I play for earnings. When I choose to buy premium, I always use short dated options. When I short premium, I usually also use short dated options, but will occasionally find more edge in farther out options (generally two months out). We will look at this scenario more in a bit.

We will now "line up" two trades by walking through the thought process. These are actual scenarios and actual trades I made. The trades themselves are of far less importance than the mechanical process I go through. To put you in the proper "frame of mind," remember that though we normally look for good probabilities for our trades by assessing implied volatility, with earnings trades we are searching for a new way of assessing our odds. This method is solely based on current "implied move" expectations versus how the stock has moved on earnings in the past.

The first trade we will look at was my earnings trade in Green Mountain Coffee Roasters (GMCR) from February 5, 2014. Green Mountain not only is a relatively high implied volatility stock but also has historically had wild earnings moves. These volatile moves put the stock on my radar screen on January 27, the Monday of the week before earnings. Why on the 27th? Prior to the open of the markets every Monday, I check out all the earnings for the next two trading weeks and create a short watch list of earnings that interest me. They may be stocks in which I have current positions that I am looking to close or defend. Or, as in this case, I could be looking for what I consider to be mispriced options prior to earnings. By "mispriced," I mean that I believe historical earnings moves tell me a different tale than what the current option prices are saying. Back to Green Mountain, the first thing I did was to look at the at the money straddle for the weekly options expiring immediately, or as soon as possible after the earnings announcement. These were the options expiring on February 7. The straddle could be purchased for around $9.25, which represented around an 11.9 percent expected stock move. This is calculated by dividing the straddle price of the weekly options into the stock price. Since these options actually had 12 days to expiration at this point in time, this number really represents the expected move over the next 12 days (10 trading days plus a weekend). Knowing that short-term options decay very quickly as they approach expiration, you might expect this straddle to shrivel over the next week and therefore provide a much better purchase for an earnings play the night before earnings. As it turns out, I will usually wait until the night before earnings, but not for that reason. To illustrate my earlier point about decay slowing or ceasing a couple of weeks before earnings, the at the money straddle was trading the afternoon before earnings for around $9.10! So, even though the option pricing model was predicting that the straddle would decay around $0.55 each day with 12 days until expiration and accelerate up to $1.45 the night before earnings alone (2 days to expiration), the straddle actually decayed only $.15 total for the entire 10 days! With that in mind, wouldn't the straddle be a great buy on January 27? The answer is a definite "maybe." The answer will depend on the reason you are making the trade. If I am looking to make a nondirectional earnings trade (e.g., a straddle or a nonskewed strangle), I prefer to make my trade the day prior to earnings so that I can center my strikes around the stock price just before earnings are announced. In the case of Green Mountain, had I made my trade with 12 days to go, I would have been trading the $78 strike. But on the day of earnings, the closest strike would have been the $81 strike.

So, if I had purchased the $78 straddle, by the time earnings came around, my straddle would have had a 26 delta. Though it may seem like I would have gotten a "head start" by buying early, my trade that was intended to be non-directional would have become nothing of the sort by earnings time. I would have had a long delta trade that might have rendered a downside earnings move unprofitable due to the pre-earnings movement.

Getting back to lining up my trade, by February 5, the day of earnings, the at the money straddle was trading for around 11 percent implied movement. Looking back at how GMCR moved on earnings, in the past, I found the following:

- Six of the past nine earnings moves have been over 20 percent.
- The three-year average earnings move is 22.1 percent.
- The largest earnings move was 47.75 percent on May 2, 2012.

With this as background, purchasing the straddle for $9.10 seems like a cheap play. In fact, on average, it appears I will double my money overnight. And if we get an extreme move like we had in May 2012, I could more than quadruple my money.

Now let us look at what I am risking by purchasing the straddle for $9. In the highly unlikely event the stock opened unchanged after earnings, the straddle would probably open around $3.50, as it has a high IV even during the best of times. So, I am risking around $5.50 at most. If I get a three-year average move (22.1 percent), I would make around $9. So, looking at it in this way, I risk 1 to make 1.62. If you consider this a 50/50 bet (as we are using an average move), I would take this bet all day long. If we look at the fact that six of the last nine moves were greater than 20 percent, we now have a situation where we risk 1 to make 1.62 *and* we win two-thirds of the time! Lastly, we have looked at the worst case (as a $5.50 loss). But best case was in May 2012, and that was a risk 1 to make almost 5.4 trade, as it turned out!

Thus, using simple historical probabilities and projecting them forward, GMCR straddles appeared to be "a screaming buy." And that is the point of this discussion. Since option pricing models do not work well with binary moves, and since predicting the probability of profiting from a trade relies on those option models, we needed to look for a different way to assess our probabilities. After all, I have worked hard for my money and I will not squander it by guessing on trades. I need to feel I have a risk versus return that is palatable and a probability of success that makes the expected value of my trades positive. So, bottom line, I actually bought the straddle for $9. I assumed my risk to be $5.50 (or $550) per straddle and sized my trade (number of straddles purchased) accordingly. As it turned out, earnings were good and I sold stock against my straddle at $110. This meant I paid $9 for the straddle and effectively sold it out for $29! This was a $20 (or $2,000) profit per straddle. A few people called my trade lucky. But in my opinion, I had the probabilities in my favor, just like any other trade I make. Having the odds on my side does not guarantee a winning trade, of course. But if I am correct in my assessment and I continue to trade a high number of occurrences with the same consistent methodology, the "expected value" of my trading will be positive. In other words, I will make money!

The next trade we will look at is the Herbalife (HLF) earnings trade I made on April 28, 2014. Herbalife is a stock that is frequently in the news. Rival, well-known hedge fund managers continually attempt to "talk their positions." Bill Ackman of Pershing Square Capital Management has frequently come out and called the stock an illegal pyramid scheme. Generally, this will cause a sharp down move in the stock. Rival managers Daniel Loeb and Carl Icahn have quickly come to the company's defense, and the stock has quickly reversed course and rallied hard on the news. As such, most investors think of Herbalife as a high-volatility stock that might move considerably on earnings. But the fact of the matter is that HLF's past earnings moves show nothing of the sort. In the past 10 earnings cycles (which, again, constitutes the past 2.5 years) HLF's average earnings move was 5.42 percent. Quite a bit of this was due to a single outlier on April 30, 2012, when the stock fell almost 20 percent. If we remove that data point, the average move was 4 percent. The past five earnings moves, which cover the entire post-Ackman announcement of his views on the company and his shorting of 20 million shares, have averaged a scant 1.85 percent. So, when the weekly straddle was trading for and predicting an approximate 7.4 percent move from earnings, I began looking for a short premium trade. Knowing that the stock has had even one large earnings move led me to look for a bit more coverage than the 7.4 percent the straddle afforded me. And this is generally the case when I choose to short premium for an earnings play. Though I will frequently buy the straddle when I buy premium, I will rarely sell straddles when I short premium. So, I looked for a good risk return play by selling strangles. Due to Herbalife's overall high implied volatility, the stock's distribution curve was wide and flat. This meant I could move farther from the current stock price and still collect some decent premium. In fact, I was able to move around $5 to each side of the afternoon stock price, which was near $59, and collect $1.65 for my strangle sale. This put the breakevens for my trade over 11 percent away from the current stock price. For the past 10 earnings plays, I would have lost money one time and collected the entire strangle price the other nine times. The loss would have been near $3.50, while my winners would have been total and complete. Assuming that meant a strangle that collected around the $1.65 I collected on this trade, my 10 cycle expected profitability, using past data, would give this trade a profit of ($1.65 * 9) − $3.50, or $11.35. So, knowing my probabilities as best as one can, I entered the short strangle trade an hour before the close. As it turned out, the stock closed the post-earnings trading day up 2.2 percent and I had a near total profit on my trade.

Once again, the important takeaway is not the result of any one trade. It is the expected return of your strategy over time. As I frequently stress, trading is a marathon, not a sprint. Just like in a coin toss, we cannot be sure of our outcome. But over time with enough occurrences, we can predict the "expected return" of any strategy using probability theory. In a normal environment, the option pricing model does that for us. But when those models break down due to assumptions the mathematical model relies on no longer being relevant, we must find other ways to arrive at probabilities for our forecasting. Earnings are a prime example.

Though I have attempted to beat to death the point that historical earnings moves will usually provide that probability model for us to rely on (as long as management has not changed recently), I want to once more outline what historical data I generally look at and how I use it.

1. First, I find the expected earnings move of a stock by using the at the money straddle that has the least time to expiration, but at a minimum encompasses the earnings event. If I am looking at next week's earnings moves, I cannot use options that expire this week. Though this sounds obvious, it is a simple mistake to make. Be careful to use the options that expire the soonest after the earnings announcement as possible for this task.

2. Next, I compare the expected move to the prior 10 earnings moves. Why the past 10? There is nothing magical about that number. In fact, 10 is not normally considered a statistically significant number in probability theory, as 30 is often the smallest number of occurrences that make a pattern significant. But stocks change their "stripes" over time. A $20 stock eight years ago that is now trading for $150 will probably not behave the same as it used to. So, I try to stay somewhat close to the current environment as possible with my first pass at the numbers. But I do not end my research there. When comparing the implied move to the prior 10, I look for the following:

   a. What percentage of the time does the historical move exceed the current implied move?

b. When the historical move exceeds the current implied move, by how much does it exceed? By how much does it underperform, if the movement underperforms the options' expectations?

c. On average, how does the implied move compare to the past 10 actual moves? In other words, what is the average move over the past 10 earnings and how does it compare to the current expectations?

3. Now, I look back at the past 40 earnings (10 years). First, I try to determine if I believe the stock is still the same stock it used to be. Does it have the same management? Is its implied volatility close to the same? Do its earnings' moves seem to be somewhat consistent? If so, I do the same three calculations using 40 earnings. I am now in the world of statistical significance. If I do not feel I can rely on all 40, is there a point I can draw a line in the sand? If so, I grab as much data on which I feel I can rely and perform my calculations on it.

4. I now attempt to calculate an expected return of buying or selling premium in the stock. I take into account the number of occurrences in which I feel I will win. In other words, I determine my estimated probability of profit. Next, I look at my extreme wins and losses both to see if I can live with the largest loss to date, and also, in the event I can, for my position sizing. (These are the same three types of data used in our Kelly Criterion calculations, which we will look at in the next chapter.) I will also take a good look at the average move, both over 10 periods and over the longer period of time in which I believe the data is relevant, to determine an expectation from them.

5. I will now assess whether I have a directional bias. As I stated earlier, some CEOs will have a tendency to either over- or underestimate their company's earnings. By using past data, you might see a trend that lends support to a directional stance. Furthermore, there are stocks in which I might have a directional bias for other reasons. For me, this might be fundamental analysis, tape reading, or supply and demand points of interest. (Some might look at this last point as a form of technical analysis.) Usually, I do not have a directional bias and will solely react to the magnitude of the expected move.

6. I will now attempt to turn all this data into a reasonable trade. Again, if I am choosing to buy premium in a nondirectional manner, I will buy straddles. If I am looking to sell premium in a nondirectional manner, I will sell strangles. If I have a directional bias and a magnitude of move bias (the latter of which I usually have or I would not be playing earnings moves), I might choose a ratio spread if I believe the move will not be as large as the options are predicting. Without that magnitude move,

I may choose a purely directional debit spread. The strategies are limited only by your creativity. Just remember what the distribution curve that is dictated by the option chain is telling you compared to what you believe the historical earnings moves are saying.

What I have outlined is what I consider to be "the norm." There are two more situations, which occur occasionally, that warrant attention. One can give you a bit of extra edge when going long premium, and one can improve your odds when going short premium.

As I stated, I will look at the next two weeks of earnings before the market opens on Monday morning. In fact, I often do this sometime over the weekend. When a stock is lining up to be a long premium earnings trade, I will frequently look back to see when and if the options decay has slowed, and if so, by how much. To be able to do this, it is nice to be with a broker who provides this historical option pricing information. This may give me some clues as to what the straddle might look like the day before earnings. But what I really look out for is what the straddle is trading for the last Friday afternoon before earnings. Why? Options decay 365 days per year. Even though there is no trading on the weekends, there can be important newsworthy events taking place that might have dramatic effects on the markets. From my experience on the floor, if the market is not rocking and rolling, traders will generally try to get ahead of the decay and suck two or all three of the weekend days' theta out of the option prices on the Friday before the weekend. The problem with this is that you are now pricing the options as if the weekend will be a nonevent (marketwise) before the weekend even happens. And occasionally, overzealous traders who are eager to get rid of long premium or to get more positive theta on their sheets by adding more short premium will sell the options of pre-earnings stocks down to what I consider "too cheap" of a level. How do you define too cheap? Well, the Monday of the week before a stock's earnings, when I first look at the upcoming earnings, I always assess my buy and my sell levels for each stock. In other words, when I look at XYZ stock, I may say, "Using past earnings moves, I will buy the straddle at 4.5 percent implied move, and I will look to line up a short premium play if the straddle is trading for 9 percent." Anywhere in between, I might not care. If the Friday afternoon before the week of earnings, XYZ straddle is trading for 3.9 percent implied move (for example), I might violate my rule of waiting until the day before earnings to "center my trade" and buy the straddle then and there. If the straddle expands back to within my "normal range" (i.e., it exceeds 4.5 percent but is below 9 percent), I can choose to hold the options for earnings or I can take my quick profit. If the stock moves considerably between the time I buy the straddle and earnings, I will probably have a nice profit on the straddle I purchased. In this case, I will sell the straddle and reassess, as a separate trade, the then at the money straddle for an earnings play. Though these opportunities do not happen often, when they do, they provide me a low-risk trade and give me a very high probability of making money. So, before you plan Friday evening's happy hour, try to fund a few beverages with this simple task.

I also spoke of occasionally getting more edge on your short premium earnings trades. How? This one gets a bit more complicated so we will explore the concept in a bit more depth. Up until now, we have spoken only about trading the shortest dated options on the board for an earnings play. This makes entire sense for a long premium play because, as we discussed, prior to earnings a stock's options' implied volatility is often artificially "inflated" to account for the upcoming binary move. And since the vega of a weekly option is tiny, the "inflation" can seem astronomical. For example, on April 7, 2014, one month before GMCR was to report earnings, the weekly options that expired four days later were trading for around a 51 percent implied volatility. On the same day, the May (39 days to expiration) at the money options had an implied volatility of around 63 percent and the June options (74 days to expiration) had a 55 percent implied volatility—quite an interesting term structure indeed. So, how did this look the day before earnings? The weekly at the money options had an implied volatility of 162 percent, the May options (9 days to expiration) had an implied volatility of 89 percent, and the June options (44 days to expiration) had an implied volatility of 54 percent (see Figures 6.5 and 6.6).

Clearly, the weekly options had the largest increase, followed by May and then June. Why? Again, the artificial implied volatility increase caused by the expected binary earnings move shows itself in different amounts based on the size of the vega of that expiration cycle. Since the front month's vega is smallest, the implied volatility has to go up more to account for the same amount of increase in the price of the options in order to account for the expected earnings move. But if we look at the implied volatility increases and divide them by their vega, this does not account for all of the discrepancy. That is because there is something else at play. And that something else is due to the inability of our "normal" option pricing models to account for binary moves. The "jump and diffusion process," meaning "earnings and then normalcy," disrupts what we might predict would happen. Another way to view how the implied volatilities handle the process is to take a weighted average of what expected movement tells us. Let us review the basics before going further.

FIGURE 6.5   GMCR Chart of Calendar IVs One Month before Earnings

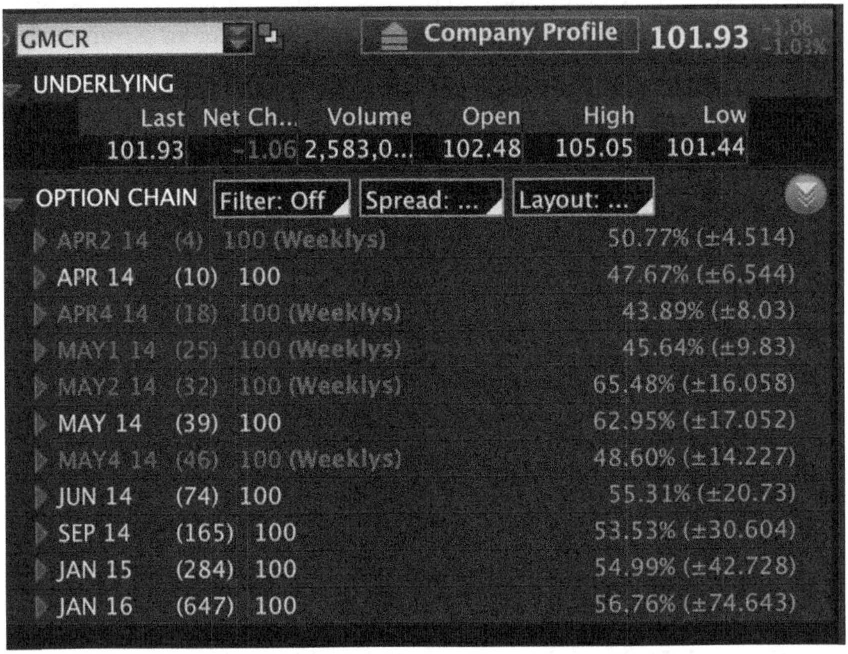

GMCR	⬆ **Company Profile**	**101.93**	-1.06 -1.03%

UNDERLYING

	Last	Net Ch...	Volume	Open	High	Low
	101.93	-1.06	2,583,0...	102.48	105.05	101.44

OPTION CHAIN | Filter: Off | Spread: ... | Layout: ... |

▶ APR2 14	(4)	100 (Weeklys)	50.77% (±4.514)
▶ APR 14	(10)	100	47.67% (±6.544)
▶ APR4 14	(18)	100 (Weeklys)	43.89% (±8.03)
▶ MAY1 14	(25)	100 (Weeklys)	45.64% (±9.83)
▶ MAY2 14	(32)	100 (Weeklys)	65.48% (±16.058)
▶ MAY 14	(39)	100	62.95% (±17.052)
▶ MAY4 14	(46)	100 (Weeklys)	48.60% (±14.227)
▶ JUN 14	(74)	100	55.31% (±20.73)
▶ SEP 14	(165)	100	53.53% (±30.604)
▶ JAN 15	(284)	100	54.99% (±42.728)
▶ JAN 16	(647)	100	56.76% (±74.643)

Source: TD Ameritrade.

Though you may hear this a number of ways, an implied volatility of 19.896 percent implies a 1 percent daily movement in the underlying. You will hear people say the implied volatility that predicts a 1 percent daily movement is 15.7, 16, or 19.1. But these numbers all come from a flawed interpretation of the theory. The standard deviation, instead of reflecting the "daily returns," actually involves the square root of an average of squares. This will make more sense if you think of how a variance is calculated, as the standard deviation is just the square root of the variance. And since the 19.896 percent is so close to 20, we can safely use 20 percent implied volatility as a close predictor of a 1 percent daily move. This simplifies things greatly.

Back to our earnings-driven implied volatility levels—we spoke before about how we could estimate the percentage implied move at which we would sell a weekly option. That means we could imply a one-day implied volatility level for the earnings day. For example, if we think an XYZ weekly straddle with just a few days to go is too rich at an 8 percent implied move, then we can assume we are willing to sell an implied volatility on that day of 8 * 20, or 160 percent (really 8 * 19.896). And if we believe every other day

FIGURE 6.6 GMCR Chart of Calendar IVs Day before Earnings

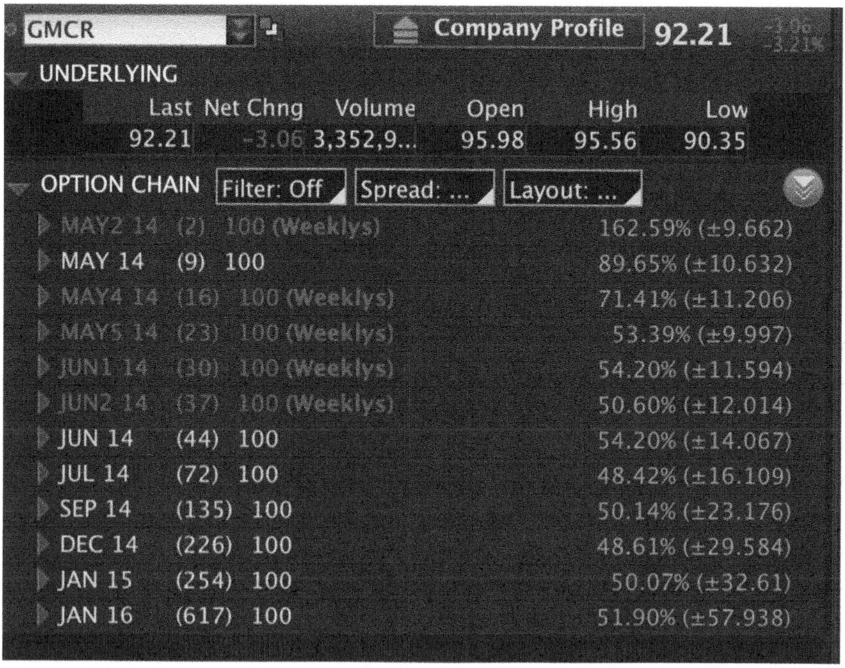

GMCR		⬆ Company Profile	92.21	-1.06 -3.21%

UNDERLYING

	Last	Net Chng	Volume	Open	High	Low
	92.21	-3.06	3,352,9...	95.98	95.56	90.35

OPTION CHAIN | Filter: Off | Spread: ... | Layout: ...

▶ MAY2 14	(2)	100 (Weeklys)	162.59% (±9.662)
▶ MAY 14	(9)	100	89.65% (±10.632)
▶ MAY4 14	(16)	100 (Weeklys)	71.41% (±11.206)
▶ MAY5 14	(23)	100 (Weeklys)	53.39% (±9.997)
▶ JUN1 14	(30)	100 (Weeklys)	54.20% (±11.594)
▶ JUN2 14	(37)	100 (Weeklys)	50.60% (±12.014)
▶ JUN 14	(44)	100	54.20% (±14.067)
▶ JUL 14	(72)	100	48.42% (±16.109)
▶ SEP 14	(135)	100	50.14% (±23.176)
▶ DEC 14	(226)	100	48.61% (±29.584)
▶ JAN 15	(254)	100	50.07% (±32.61)
▶ JAN 16	(617)	100	51.90% (±57.938)

Source: TD Ameritrade.

XYZ should trade to a 34 percent IV, for example, then we should be able to provide a general framework for our term structure. Once again, though we have lined up our trade using the shorter dated option, the implied volatility of these options means little. Only the implied move matters with these weekly or soon to expire monthly options. But as we add more time to expiration to our options, the earnings expected move plays less of a role in the implied volatility of the option. By taking a weighted average of the implied volatilities, let's predict what the term structure should look like.

Using our earlier example, our earnings day implied volatility is 160 percent. This represents the implied move of 8 percent that we are looking to sell. Absent of earnings, assuming we are willing to sell XYZ's implied volatility at 37 percent (since 34 percent is normal), we can predict the following:

Weekly with three DTE:
  One day at 160 percent IV
  Two days at 37 percent IV
  Weighted average = 78.00 percent IV

Front month with 17 DTE:

    One day at 160 percent IV
    Sixteen days at 37 percent IV
    Weighted average = 44.24 percent IV
    Second month with 45 DTE:
    One day at 160 percent IV
    Forty-four days at 37 percent IV
    Weighted average = 39.73 percent IV

As you can see, if there is a significant earnings move expected, prior to earnings, the term structure will invert. This means the normal pattern of each successive month having a slightly higher implied volatility (often called a contango type pattern) will reverse and slope downward (often called a backwardation type pattern). To be more accurate with this assessment, we would probably assume the "normal" implied volatility we might want to sell would differ for each month. We might be willing to sell a 37 percent implied volatility in the front month, but might want to receive 38.2 percent for the second month. If so, we would just incorporate that in our calculations and would now want the second month's implied volatility to be at 40.91 percent before we would sell it.

Second month with 45 DTE:

    One day at 160 percent IV
    Forty-four days at 38.2 percent IV
    Weighted average = 40.91 percent IV

By doing this calculation, when we find a stock in which we are interested in selling premium prior to earnings, we might find that a different expiration cycle's options have more edge in them than the weekly options, based on our assumptions. For example, if in the foregoing situation the weekly options are trading for a 79 percent implied volatility, the front month's options are trading for a 46 percent implied volatility, and the second month's options are trading for a 50 percent implied volatility, I would venture to say the second month is the best sale. I would be careful to check and be sure there is not another event, such as an important trade show where major announcements are usually made, taking place in that second month's expiration cycle. You can do this via the news or via the stock's website. You will often find word of these on the "investor relations" web page under "events or presentations."

One word of caution. With a weekly option, this weighted average is not always quite as accurate. The reason stems from the "inertia" argument again.

(Yes, I was a physics major for a while!) When a stock has a large earnings move, it may continue to have outsized moves for a period of time. Therefore, the assumption that the "other days" in our three days to expiration example earlier are "sells" at a 37 percent implied volatility might not be accurate. So, I assess the edge in my weekly options based on the expected earnings moves, while I compare the implied volatility of the longer dated options using the weighted average technique. When you assess options that are three months out or longer, be careful to account for more than one earnings date or other upcoming binary-style events in your weighted average.

CHAPTER 7

Exiting Trades

The area of trading that receives the least attention (and has the least intelligible educational material available) is "when to exit a trade." One of the reasons for this lack of a strong body of knowledge on the topic is that few traders truly understand the math behind it. Most traders exit by "feel" instead of by mechanics. They stubbornly refuse to take a loss and believe that makes them better traders in the end. As a person who believes strongly in the power of math, I would like to change that. So we will discuss what a proper mechanical strategy looks like and how to design one. We will also look at when it is allowed to deviate from the plan and when it is essential not to deviate. This will take place in the context of a strategy with a positive expectancy. (A positive expectancy means that with a high enough number of occurrences, the probabilities predict we will be profitable.) We will look at the three situations that lead us to exit a trade and dissect what each means to our probability assumptions.

The Variables

What variables must we solve for (or at least understand) to create a positive expectancy trading strategy? Though it sounds like a difficult question, it really has a simple answer. Even traders who work by gut feel have an understanding that the "edge vs. odds" relationship is critical to success. In other words, the greater the odds of success or the bigger the edge in the trade, the bigger the risk you should take on with the trade. But what does this mean in practice? Let's take some examples. If I offer to bet you $1 of my money versus $1 million of yours, would you take the bet? Actually, you do not have enough information to answer! If I told you that you would win 100 percent of the time, would you take the bet then? Of course you would. It is free money! Now let's flip the bet around. If I offered $1 million of my money versus $1 of yours but told you your odds of winning were 2 million to 1, would you bet me once? Twice? A million times? Well, the answer to that one is a bit more difficult as there are multiple things going on at once. But in general, if you took that bet 1 million times, you are probably going to lose. The expected value of the bet is against you. Looking at one more example, if I offered to flip a fair coin 1 million times and pay you $1,001 for each heads and collect $1,000 from you for each tails, would you do it? Is that $1 edge enough? It should be, as you should make around $500,000 from the game. Probabilities dictate that as long as you have a high enough number of occurrences it is a winning strategy. Why? Because you have a 50 percent chance of winning on each flip and your average winner is greater than your average loser. What is important to take away from this discussion is that there are three closely connected inputs to the decision. They are the probability of winning, the average payoff when you win, and the average cost when you lose. These are "three legs of the stool" that make up your strategy, and all three are inexplicably intertwined. When someone asks me, "When should I take my losses?" it is impossible to answer that without the context of when they are taking their profits and how frequently they are profiting and losing. Anyone who tells you differently is missing a big part of the puzzle!

You may be wondering if you will ever be able to understand how to create a winning strategy with all these interconnected pieces complicating the issue. How are they interconnected? How will I know if my strategy has a positive expectancy? Fortunately, there was a scientist by the name of John Kelly working at Bell Labs who, back in 1956, derived a formula to aid in noise reduction for long-distance calls. People quickly realized Kelly's formula (or Kelly's Criterion, as it is often called) had applications for gambling and for position sizing in trading. By boiling his formula down to a more simplified form, it can also help us to design a positive expectancy strategy. Let's examine this little gem and see what we can learn.

The Kelly Criterion

As we discussed, the Kelly Criterion can help us balance the three legs of the stool associated with our trading strategy. The simplified formula, used for position sizing, looks like this:

$$\text{Kelly percent} = W - [(1 - W)/R]$$

where

W = percentage of winners (or if forecasting, probability of profit)
R = average gain of our winning trades/average loss of our losing trades

So, how do we use a formula for position sizing to aid in building our strategy? Let's begin by looking at where our Kelly percent is equal to zero. This would imply the strategy is neither a winner nor a loser, but rather is a breakeven. Then we can "back off" one of the three variables to create a winning formula.

Substituting 0 for Kelly percent, we can simplify our formula as follows:

$$0 = W - [1 - W/R]$$
$$R = (1/W) - 1$$
$$W = 1/(R + 1)$$

These two formulae are the most reduced, boiled-down means of determining what is occurring with our strategies. These determine the break-even relationships between our three variables. Given any two of the variables, you can determine the break-even value from the third. Let's look at a few examples. In these examples, we will assume we have made short premium trades and that the total credit received on each trade will be represented by 100 percent. So, if we sell a strangle for $4 and we let it expire worthless, we make 100 percent. If we buy it back for $1, we have a 75 percent profit ($4 − $1)/$4 = .75 (or 75%).

Example 1:
Let's say we are selling defined risk spreads for 33 cents on the dollar and not managing the losing side. That means our losses can grow to approximately two times credit received, or 200 percent (.67/.33). We will further assume our probability of profit on the trade is 67 percent. Substituting, we get the following:

$$R = (1/W) - 1$$

Since R = Average winner/Average loser

Average winner $/ 2.00 = (1/.67) - 1$

Solving for avg. winner, we get avg. winner = 1. That means, to break even, if we let our losers go to max loss, we also need to let our winners go to max profit. If we take our winners any earlier and let our losses run to max loss, we have a negative expectancy strategy!

Example 2:

We are selling defined risk spreads for 33 cents on the dollar and are taking our profits at 75 percent of max profit. For example, if we sell a $1-wide OTM call spread for 33 cents, we will take our profit at 25 cents ($0.33 ∗ .75 = $0.2475), meaning we buy back the spread for $0.08. Where would we have to take our losses to break even?

$$R = (1/W) - 1$$

$0.75/$Average loser $= 0.50$

Average loser $= 1.50$, or 150 percent

So, we would have to buy back our losing trade for $0.82, giving us a $0.49 loss. If we let the losers run further, we again have a negative expectancy strategy. If we take our losses a bit earlier, we can plan on earning a profit.

Example 3:

We sell strangles at a 90 percent probability of profit and take our profits at 25 percent of max profit. Where would we have to take our losses to break even? We will then compare this to taking our profits at 50 percent and then at 80 percent.

$$R = (1/W) - 1$$

$0.25/$Average loser $= .111$

Average loser $= 2.25$, or 225 percent

If we sold the strangle for $2.00, and took our profits by buying it back when it trades for $1.50 (for a 25 percent, or $.50, profit), we would need to buy it back for a loss when it trades for $6.50 (for a 225 percent, or $4.50, loss). If we let the average loss run further, we lose. If we take our losses earlier, we profit.

If we took our profit at 50 percent of max profit, we would need to take our losses before it hit a 450 percent loss to make money. If we took our profit at 80 percent of max profit, we would need to take our loss before it reached 720 percent of max profit.

Instead of taking my word that the math involved works, let's prove that the relationships work using an example. Using Example 3, where our "W," or probability of profit, is 90 percent, we should win 9 out of every 10 times. If we sold a strangle for $2.00 and took our profit at 50 percent of max profit and our loss at 450 percent (as described earlier), our average winner would be ($2.00 * .50) or $1.00, and our average loss would be $2.00 * 4.50 or $9.00. If we did this trade 100 times, we expect to make $1 ninety times and lose $9 ten times. This makes our expected return:

$$\$1.00 * 90 = \$90$$

$$+$$

$$\frac{-\$9.00 * 10 = \$90}{\$0}$$

You can try this for any combination. If you define any two of the three legs of the stool, you can calculate the break-even level for the third. To simplify things a bit, for any given probability of profit, Table 7.1 gives you the break-even "R" (the ratio between the average winner and the average loser).

Let's look at an example of how to use the information in the chart. If you sell a strangle that has a 75 percent probability of profit, and you plan to take your profit when you have profited 70 percent of the premium received, then you should be taking your losses at less than 210 percent of the premium received. To determine this, look down the Probability of Profit (or "W") column until you find 75 percent. Now, look across that row to determine the break-even "R," which is 0.33 in this example. Since R is the average winner divided by the average loser, and we defined our average winner as 70 percent (0.70), our formula becomes:

$$0.33 = 0.70 / ?$$

This tells us the maximum we should let our losers run is 2.10, or 210 percent of the premium received from selling our strangle. In fact, you should take your losers off with some room before the breakeven.

Now that we have introduced and explained the Kelly formula and its use in defining a mechanical strategy for exiting trades, we need to discuss a few instances where we must diverge from the plan.

TABLE 7.1 Chart of Kelly Break-Even "R"s

Probability of Profit (W)	Break-Even R
5%	19.00
10%	9.00
15%	5.67
20%	4.00
25%	3.00
30%	2.33
35%	1.86
40%	1.50
46%	1.17
50%	1.00
55%	0.82
60%	0.67
65%	0.54
70%	0.43
75%	0.33
80%	0.25
85%	0.18
90%	**0.11**
95%	0.05
100%	0.00

First, there are times when a market gaps overnight and it is impossible to take losses (or profits) at the prescribed level. In these instances, we may have some outsized losses (or profits). The reason I keep emphasizing the losses is that they can deviate considerably from the plan. If you plan on taking profits at 70 percent of maximum, the biggest deviation you can get from a gap is that it exceeds it by the remaining 30 percent profit. But if you plan on taking your losses at 150 percent and a stock you are short gets bought out, you may deviate by over 1,000 percent. In rare instances, this may affect your system's profitability for a while. Does this invalidate the mathematical model? In short, no. It is still the best predictor of success we have with respect to exiting trades. Remember, we are looking at *average* gains and *average* losses when determining our levels. With a high enough number of occurrences and small position sizes, these black swan events should (eventually) get lost in the shuffle.

If my loss level is gapped through, I do not "play with my losses" and give them time to reverse without a *very* strong reason. Rather, I take my loss and move on despite the outsized loss I incur. Remember, probabilities dictate that these occurrences *will* happen. Accept them and move on.

If they gap in your favor, however, I will occasionally "play with my winners." What I mean by that is, for example, if I planned to take my profits at 70 percent of maximum and it gaps through and opens at a 75 percent winner, I may, at times, either:

- Take half of my profi t and hope for a larger (or max profit) on the second half (to off set some of the outsized losses due to gapping stocks).

or

- Set a mental stop-loss where I let the winner run further unless it reverts to my initial profi t level, where I then exit the trade. So, as earlier, my trade opens at the 75 percent profi t level. I wait for it to run to 95 percent or so unless it reverts and revisits the 70 percent level. If it does, I lock in my 70 percent profit, having given up the "extra 5 percent" I could have had.

Not all of our trades will be exited at our chosen levels anyway. As expiration approaches and our distribution curve gets high and narrow, we will often decide the risk to reward ratio favors closing a trade based on timing alone. Thus, some trades will not hit our profit or our loss levels. Once again, this does not invalidate the math used to create your strategic exit plan. It will, however, make your results "inexact."

One last consideration of which you should be aware is that your probabilities are not a certainty. In other words, when you choose your probability of profit upon trade entry, this probability is calculated using a "snapshot" view of the current environment. Of particular note is that the current implied volatility and the current days to expiration are used as inputs. So, after the trade is made, our probabilities will change. And if we have done our job as traders well, we hope this will usually be in our favor either due to decay (shortening of days to expiration) or due to a change in implied volatility, thus changing our distribution curve and our probabilities. Also, we generally anticipate that short premium trades, in general, will give us a 2–4 percent probability of profit "boost" due to implied volatility generally trading for a higher level than historical volatility. But there is one other decision we make that will also affect our probabilities. Assuming we make high probability trades, the quicker we take our trades off (due to profits or losses), the quicker those trades are replaced by new high probability trades. So we can increase our probabilities slightly by taking profits and losses a bit quicker. But that does not always increase our absolute profit level. So, beware of false prophets telling you to take winners quickly to boost your bottom line!

The real point of this discussion is that trade exits are every bit as important as trade entries. Options trading is a probability game. Though you have no control over what the market does, your probabilities of success are "controlled" by statistical theory. And since math never lies, ignoring this math is not a wise choice. Define the three legs of the stool to fit your personality, but make sure they mathematically provide you a positive expectancy.

Morning Routine

If you are a baseball fan, you might have seen David Ortiz or Nomar Garciaparra go through their "prepitch" routines. David Ortiz rests his bat against his leg, spits on his right hand, and claps when preparing for the batter box. Nomar had more batting ticks than anyone I can remember. While their rituals were mostly superstitious in nature, it mentally prepared them for the next pitch. They found their "zone" of concentration. Though I do not have the time or patience for unnecessary rituals, I tend to prepare for each trading day by going through a routine of sorts. While each step may lead me off on various tangents, I would like to briefly outline the tasks I perform each morning. If I do not complete them, I feel wholly unprepared for the trading day.

1. *I make and consume my first cup of coffee.* Maybe that does not sound much like a necessary trading preparation task. But there is a point that this step makes that is very important. At this time in my career, I consider myself a professional educator. In an academic setting, much ado is made over a professor's ability to teach. Though I do not mean to downplay that skill, it is my belief that it is the student's ability to learn that is vastly more important. And for students to be at the top of their game, they need to be prepared to learn. They should be rested, if possible. Their attention should be focused and their desire to learn piqued. Each morning, before I sit down at my computer to trade, I prepare myself to be a good student of the market. I want to be mentally sharp and ready to absorb the information the market will throw at me. For me, my cup of coffee and time to unwind and shake the cobwebs off is part of that preparation. Whatever accomplishes those tasks for you should be the first thing you do each day in preparation to trade.

2. *Take a step back and look at the big picture.* It is often easy to get caught up in the minutia of trading. Once the day begins, we can get absorbed in the excitement and have a harder time putting what we see into perspective. That is why I find it helpful and important to kick back and take a longer view of the market. Maybe we have had a 3 percent pullback in the last few trading sessions after an extended 25 percent market rally. By contrast, it feels like the next market crash is right around the corner. Yet despite the feeling the sky is falling, a 3 percent pullback, in the scheme of things, may be not only a small event but also actually healthy for the market. However you assess the events you have recently experienced, a great time to do so is before the market opens and you are caught up in the faster-paced tempo of the day. Clear your head and listen. Drop your preconceived notions and try to hear what the market is saying, rather than what you think or hope it will say.

3. *Check the overnight markets.* As you know, the markets throughout the world have a good deal of correlation. We are becoming much more of a one-world marketplace as time goes on. As such, while we sleep, events take place around the world that may affect our markets. By two hours or so before the market opens, much of the overseas action has been absorbed and many, if not all, of our morning's earnings releases have come out. It is a good time to begin assessing how today's opening markets may behave. I always look at our equity futures markets (S&P's, Russell 2000, and NASDAQ), foreign equity markets (in particular Germany, Great Britain, and the Asian markets), 30-year government bonds and 10-year notes, commodities (especially gold, silver, oil, and natural gas), and currencies (Euro, Yen, dollar). Though those are not the only ones I watch, they are a good start and will give you a good core view of the markets.

4. *Check the overnight movers, in particular those on my watch list.* My broker provides a free interface between their trading platform and Excel. A few months ago, that link was done via a facility of Excel called "DDE," which stood for "Dynamic Data Exchange." Microsoft recently deprecated that function and replaced it with a function called "Realtime Data" (RTD). These functions allow you to pull live data into an Excel spreadsheet where you can manipulate the data any way you would like. I will often use the functionality for getting real-time quotes on spreads across products, such as risk arbitrage trades or pairs trades. But I have one spreadsheet that just shows me the overnight moves on each and every symbol in my watch list. Furthermore, since this is in Excel, I can sort this data to see the largest gains and largest losses on stocks whose options I like to trade.

It is this spreadsheet that I look at each morning. It lets me know if there is considerable movement in a stock in which I have a position. It also helps me focus my eyes on stocks in which I may want to create a position once the market opens. If you are a stock trader, you may find premarket opportunities to get involved. Once I have looked at the biggest movers, both up and down, I close the sheet. From here on out, I have my eyes on the next piece of my checklist. I do not let the moving markets absorb my attention yet. There will be time for that after the market's open. Until then, I am just surveying what has taken place overnight.

5. *Check out your favorite financial news sources.* Every trader has his or her own favorite places to catch up on the financial news for the day. Some watch it all day, either on TV or on the Internet. Some check in when they can. Others, though these are few, try to isolate themselves from the news entirely as they believe all the news is already built into the markets and the markets are all they need to make intelligent decisions. Though that sounds a little extreme, there is some wisdom in that stance. Remember that not all news is created equal. Many moons ago, when I was a young college student, I had a roommate who was a journalism major. Back in those days, the first rule of journalism was to report only the facts. No opinion was allowed to be imparted. Opinion was left to the editorial pages. A word of caution: Those days are long gone, and it seems that pretty much every news story nowadays has some editorializing occurring. Unfortunately, this seems particularly true in financial media. Pretty much every pundit comes on (including me, at times) and lets you know which way they believe the market is going to go in the future or what is going to happen to a particular stock or trade. Most of this information I find useless. Worse, it can become noise that takes me away from focusing on valuable tasks that could be making or saving me money. So, why not give up news entirely? Because there are nuggets of gold in many stories. There are two very difficult things to learn when dealing with "financial news." Both tasks sound easy enough, yet it literally took me two decades to become accomplished at them. Of course, I never had anyone warn me about the dangers of not accomplishing them! The first task is to never accept conclusions of news reports. I use news to focus my eyes and attention on events taking place in the market that I might have missed. In other words, I want the news to say to me, "Hey! Look over here at this!" I block out what the reporters are telling me is going to happen because of the event. I just want to know there is activity, or management change, or an event, or a stock split, or any of 1,000 other things that can affect a stock. I do not want to know if they believe the news is bullish or bearish. I can draw my own conclusions. Remember, every

trade begins with an assumption. That assumption needs to be my own or I should not take the trade. If I could wipe away every trade I took using someone else's opinion, I would be far wealthier than I am now. And it is entirely my fault for taking the trade and losing money based on someone else's opinions. When Warren Buffett comes on the screen and says, "I like XYZ Company," I put my fingers in my ears and start humming. Many traders will think, "Warren Buffett is one of the greatest investors of our time. If he likes XYZ Company, then so do I!" Yet that is worthless information to me. Why? Warren buys companies. He has a long time horizon. He knows nothing (and cares even less) what the implied volatility of XYZ options are and whether they are liquid or illiquid. I, on the other hand, mostly sell options with short time horizons based on the volatility and liquidity profile of the stock and its options. Though we are both trying to take money out of the market, that is where our similarities end. But maybe during Warren's interview he stated that XYZ was going to be announcing a new product at a trade show the following Wednesday. That is news I can use! That might affect the implied volatility of the options and potentially change the risk profile of any trade I might make or already have on. Those are the distinctions you must learn to make. Hone your listening skills to hear only what is useful to your trading. And, even more importantly, learn to ignore the advice. Focus on the news you can use to formulate tradable ideas based on your own opinions. The second task is a close corollary to the first. Too much news will become noise. This noise not only is useless but also can be harmful to your trading and to your psyche, in general. Some traders I know rabidly absorb financial news. They know every CEO by name, reputation, and shoe size. They can tell you about, and quote from, the past 10 big blockbuster financial books that were written. Though they sound very intelligent and interesting at a cocktail party, none of this information is useful to what I do. While they were reading and absorbing all that information, I was digging into the implied volatility trends, finding skew aberrations, and studying correlations for my risk management and potential pairs trades. I may be boring at cocktail parties, but I am clear-headed, confident, prepared, and in control when I sit down to trade. So, what news sources do I use in my premarket routine? That depends on if I am on the train going downtown, sitting in my office, on a plane, or driving. But I use all forms of media. I will generally get one financial newspaper, usually either the *Financial Times* or the *Wall Street Journal.* I may watch, or listen to, TV reports on Bloomberg Television or whatever is available. I will certainly use the Internet if possible. There, I try to keep up with some of the shows on CBOE TV. I also peruse various websites, such as marketwatch.com, finviz.com, Twitter, and a host of others, depending on what I am looking for. You need to find the ones that "speak to you." But the rules of engagement are the same no matter which sources you use. Let them point out stocks, industries, commodities, currencies, or world or national events that might be good inputs to use in formulating trading ideas. The news sources are only the catalyst for you to research an idea or a stock—nothing more and nothing less.

6. *Review which stocks have upcoming earnings in the next two weeks.* As I addressed earlier, each weekend, I will generally take a look at the next two weeks of earnings releases for potential opportunities. From that research, I will create a checklist of stocks to watch. Each of these will have dates next to them for follow-up. Each morning before the open, I look through every stock on the list for news and to reassess opportunities. If it has earnings that evening or the following morning, I will drill down quite a bit more and try to determine trades that I believe are appropriate. I will, of course, revisit these at around 1:00 p.m. and make any trades I wish to take. I would estimate I make one earnings trade for every 10 stocks from my watch list each cycle. That means if I have 100 stocks on my watch list, I may make 10 earnings trades per quarter. That is not a large number compared to the amount of trades I make. The reason is that earnings plays are a whole different animal than a normal trade. It gives you immediate feedback, both positive and negative. And the profits and losses can at times become outsized and are often difficult to control. Therefore, I require what I would consider to be very strong odds before I take a trade of a binary nature such as these.

7. *"Balance my sheets."* This last task is a bit more mundane, but extremely important. The term "balance my sheets" comes from my days on the floor. You have to remember the nature of the old floor trading environment. We were trading millions of dollars of options, often via hand signals to other traders across the trading pit. After making the trade, we wrote on a trading card the trade, the trade size, who I made the trade with, and what clearinghouse held that trader's account and cleared his or her trades. This left plenty of room for error. So, each morning the second thing I did (after getting my spot in the pit for the trading day, or at least until nature called) was to "balance my sheets." This included making sure every one of my trades cleared exactly as I thought they should. If they did not, I had what was termed an outtrade. This means that the trade I thought I made with Johnny across the pit was not what Johnny thought we did. It could be he thought he was buying 5 contracts and I thought I sold him 50. Or I thought we traded calls and he thought we traded puts. Or Johnny was

trading with Tom, who was standing behind me, and not with me at all. It was a rare day that I did not have outtrades on my sheets. Fortunately, most were due to clerical errors (the keypuncher typed it in wrong) or I wrote 50 but remember trading only 5, as Johnny wrote. Today, with all my trades being made electronically, there is much less room for error. Yet there have been days when the positions I thought I should have on my sheets did not match what my broker thought I had. Once another trading day has begun, it gets much more difficult to fix those errors, especially if they are due to a "fat finger" mistake where you meant to sell five contracts but actually hit that extra zero. So, always take the time each morning to verify your account looks like what you expect. If you started the day yesterday with an account balance of $28,455 and thought you made $300 yesterday, your account should be around $28,755 minus any commissions and fees for which you may not have accounted. Anything far afield of that amount must be reconciled before the day starts. If not, not only might you be incurring unnecessary risk, but also it may affect your ability to concentrate and focus on today's trading.

With these tasks out of the way, you now have the trading day ahead of you. Your mind is clear, your thoughts are focused, your perspective is sharp, and your coffee is consumed. Bring on the day!

To Log Your Trades or Not to Log Your Trades

Often a subject of intense debate is whether it is worth the time and effort to log your trades. After all, you will remember your truly painful trades without the need to write them down. And if you write down the really good trades, this might keep you from effectively embellishing the stories over cocktails at a later date and time. So, why bother with all the small trades or trades that had little effect on your account? As I hope you remember by now, options trading is a probability-based activity. As such, collection of proper statistics can be an educational and important step in validating your mechanical trading strategies. Here are a few reasons you should keep a detailed trading log and a few ways you should use your log to guide you as you move forward.

1. Though the option chain predicts your probability of profit for you, there is no guarantee that your results will match them exactly. If you collect your trading data for an extended period of time and find that your actual percentage of trades that are profitable does not match what

the option chain predicted, you have a flaw in the way you are choosing either your underlyings or your trades. However, it is usually the choice of underlyings that causes the probabilities to veer off the predicted path, from my experience. Going back through those sections of this book that cover "choosing your underlying" or "choosing a strategy" should help you in determining where you are going wrong. If not, you may need a session with a good options coach to point you in the right direction. The good news is that for any decent options coach, this is generally a quick fix.

2. As we discussed in our section on trade exits, the Kelly Criterion defines a "three-legged stool" that helps us create a trading strategy that has a positive expectancy (i.e., it defines a profitable trading methodology). And one of the three legs is our probability of profit. Without this piece, we cannot determine the appropriate levels to close our trades, both on the profit side and on the loss side. Using the probabilities from the option chain is a good place to start. But over time, if we study our logs and the statistics that come out of it, we can get better probabilities to guide us in our exit levels. I may choose to utilize the Kelly Criterion more "categorically" based on strategy, as in all strangles (since I tend to trade them with a similar probability profile of 85 percent probability of profit and demand a 13 percent edge, for example) use a Kelly Criterion where I close my winners at 80 percent of max profit and my losers at 200 percent of max profit, for example. Or I may use the Kelly Criterion on a trade-by-trade basis. If I do that, I might keep a consistent edge to my trading. Thus, if my probability of profit is 85 percent or 65 percent, I might choose to use a 13 percent edge in my Kelly Criterion formula, but vary the probability of profit in the Kelly Criterion formula. Or I may use a different edge for each type of trade. For example, I may want more edge to my undefined risk trades due to their increased risk, and a lower edge to a defined risk trade, since my losses are limited. Either way, with all the trades I make, if each trade has its own exit levels, it would be next to impossible to keep it all straight without writing it down. Traders who are against keeping a log are invariably not using any kind of exit strategy based on probabilities. If they are, and are not logging their trades, they are trading so infrequently that they can track them in their heads. And that is an entirely different problem, as you need a reasonable number of occurrences for the probabilities to work. Back to my point: If you do not log your trades, it is difficult to remember and abide by your Kelly Criterion exit strategies.

3. Though this may seem silly, I find that without logging his trades, it is much more difficult for a new trader to believe the discipline of trading is as easy and as necessary as I find it to be. And when that is the case, it

is much easier for a trader to veer off plan. So, a trade log can hammer home the point that trading is indeed a "discipline." Looking through six or nine months of trades and seeing that your trade probabilities are within a couple percent of what was predicted by the option chain can be an eye-opening exercise for newer traders, and even for experienced traders who try logging their trades for the first time.

4. Though this is a close corollary to number one, a log is the easiest means of finding errors in your methodology. Patterns you may not expect to see will often pop out of a careful examination of your log. For example, one of my current students had kept a log for three months. She was hitting her probabilities about 3.1 percent lower than the option chain predicted. Since she had chosen a 10 percent edge in her Kelly Criterion, she was regularly making money (three for three in terms of profitable months). During a coaching session, we broke down the results as chronicled in her log, which was quite complete. What we found was that her undefined risk trades were outperforming the expected percentages of profit by almost four percentage points, but her defined risk trades underperformed considerably. In total, a 3.1 percent shortfall did not appear to be out of line, but her defined risk trades lagged by almost 6.6 percent (as she had more defined risk trades than undefined). This is a significant shortfall. When we dug deeper, what we found was that whenever she was comfortable with an underlying, she traded an undefined risk strategy, like a short strangle. But whenever she was nervous about the risk associated with an underlying, she traded a defined risk strategy. The risk versus return thought process made sense at many levels since she was reducing the riskiness of the trade when she felt unsettled. But what she was actually doing was trading underlyings that had distribution curves that were not well represented by the option chain. As such, those trades were actually unprofitable and led to a far lower profitability for her account than if she traded only the undefined risk trades. After a quick review of how she needed to choose an underlying and how to verify that an underlying's option chain matches the historical results for the underlying's movement, she took 17 underlyings off her "short premium trading candidates" on her watch list. The next five months were far more profitable. This is just one example of positive results that can be obtained through the use of a trading log.

So, what kind of information is useful in a trading log? The more information you choose to log, the more of your time the log takes up. And since time is money, it makes sense to try to keep this data collection to a minimum. But no one ever said trading did not require some effort. The beautiful part of creating a trading log is that it can be populated after trading hours or after work hours. Though a few numbers might change during the day, you can easily either re-create or interpolate those numbers in the evening or on the weekend. Of course, the closer to the trade time you log the trade, the easier and more accurate it will be. And the more information you collect, the more useful the log will be to your trading. So, this is a place I would not skimp. I would collect all the information you feel you might need. It is far easier to collect it up front than to attempt to go back in time and re-create the numbers.

When keeping your log, remember that the main purpose is to be able to compare expected probabilities to actual probabilities over an extended period of time. As such, you will be logging information from when you made the trade and expectations from the trade, as well as logging your exits and the actual probabilities you incur. Also, since the results of your log are useful in tweaking your Kelly Criterion levels, I find it useful to combine the exits the Kelly Criterion defines for me in my log. I can best illustrate this with an example. Here are a few fields I find are useful for a trade log and how they can be utilized.

1. Trade entry date: I always log the date I made the trade. This will be useful in a couple of ways, which we will outline later.
2. The symbol of the underlying traded: As we spoke about before, when we do our "trade forensics" after at least several months of data are collected, one of the things we look for is symbols that consistently do not perform as their option chain predicts. Thus, we need to be able to sort by symbol in our spreadsheet to easily accumulate this information.
3. The trading strategy employed: Not only do I like to see how my strangles, my iron condors, and my long straddles are doing, but I also like to code whether my trades are undefined or defined risk strategies. I can then see how my probabilities are tracking expected results on several different levels.
4. The price of the underlying at the time of the trade: This allows me to see the magnitude of the move in the underlying from trade entry to trade exit. You may begin logging your trades (or begin trading, for that matter) right at the beginning of some high historical volatility. These numbers will help you to decipher if that is so.
5. The strikes traded: This is helpful when managing your trades, but can become a difficult thing to track if you roll your trades in any manner. If you do roll a trade, there is a multitude of ways to track this. Think through the best way to set up your own log.
6. The number of contracts traded: This is important in tracking your profitability and to look back to insure you are sizing your trades correctly. If your probabilities are tracking well but you are not making money,

sizing is the most common cause. More on this during our section on portfolio management.

7. The probability of profit as defined by your option chain: This is a vital piece of information for the way we use our logs. Remember that this is not the probability of finishing out of the money, but rather the probability of breakeven. With short premium strategies, probability of breakeven will be higher than probability of expiring out of the money.

8. The implied volatility at the time of the trade: This can be tracked in one of several ways. You can either keep the implied volatility of the at the money option for the expiration cycle you are trading or keep the implied volatility of each strike you trade. Though the latter provides far more information, for the beginning trader, I find the data to be excessive. The extra data can be used in discerning skew and other changes in the distribution curve. But determining that information is difficult. So, I find keeping the at the money implied volatility is enough. I find it interesting to see how frequently I am correct on whether the implied volatility mean reverts (drops) from the time I sell premium until I buy it back. I also find it interesting to see how frequently my long premium trades get wings and incur expanding implied volatility. This information can go a long way toward reinforcing your trading mechanics and in giving you confidence in what you are doing.

9. The premium received or spent during the trade: Having the net price of the trade is absolutely necessary if you are going to utilize the spreadsheet to track your trade exits as defined by your Kelly Criterion. It is also necessary if you are tracking your profit and loss information.

10. The Kelly Criterion percentages at which we want to exit: I like to set up my log so that I either input the percentage of max profit at which I want to take my profit and the edge I want from the predicted probability (usually between 10 and 15 percent), or input both the percentage of max profit at which I want to take my profit and my percentage at which I want to take my loss. Either way, I calculate the prices, both profit and loss, at which I want to exit my trade. Whichever price the trade hits first is my exit point. By having this calculated at the time I enter the trade into my log, I know immediately where my exit points are. And by having them in my log, I can refer to them at any time. This keeps me focused and aids me so I do not miss my exit and wreak havoc with the discipline the Kelly Criterion imparts to my trading strategy.

11. Certain pieces of information on the exit: The first piece of data is the date we make the exit trade. From that date, we can calculate and log the number of days we were in our trade. This piece of information can be used

to refine our Kelly Criterion percentage of profit at which we want to exit. Personally, I like to try to sculpt my exits so that the average number of days I am in my trades is around 28. This allows me to continually recycle my positions so that I am putting on trades each expiration cycle with around the same days to expiration. If I am taking profits at 80 percent of max profit and my trades are averaging 38 days, for example, I need either to take profits sooner (maybe at 65 percent of max profits) to move my average time down toward my desired 28 days, or to sell premium a bit closer to expiration for the same purpose. Either way, these dates are useful pieces of information to help you refine your mechanical strategy.

12. The price at which you close your trade: From this data, you can determine your actual probability of profit for comparison with what the option chain predicted. You can also determine your profit or loss for the trade. Thirdly, this data tells us how effectively we are following our Kelly Criterion strategy by determining if we exited at the percentage of max profit we anticipated. As we discussed, there are often reasons to exit our trades earlier than Kelly predicts, and infrequently, there are reasons to let our winners go a bit further than planned. But I never voluntarily let my losers run further than my Kelly Criterion exits, yet gaps in the stock can occasionally cause that to occur. Our log will help us to see patterns we might otherwise miss.

13. A number of other fields: We can calculate profits and losses, number and percentages of winners and losers, and percentage differences from expected. We can break these fields down by categories, like defined risk trades versus undefined risk trades, or by specific trading strategies, like strangles or iron condors. We can find out how we are doing with our long premium trades versus our short premium trades. We can see if we are effective with our earnings trades. We can find underlyings that are performing well or performing poorly. The type of information you can pull from your log is limited only by your imagination.

As you can see, a trade log is a very useful tool for helping refine and track our trading strategies. I use Excel for creating my log, but some of the traders I coach use Google Docs spreadsheets, FileMaker Pro, or other programming languages to track their trades. So, it can be a very basic program or a more complex means of accumulating the data. Start simple and grow your log as you see fit. The goal is to get the best return for your time. But once you begin logging your trades and pulling information out of it, it becomes quite addictive. It is an invaluable tool to aid you in your trading.

CHAPTER 8

Executing Your Trades

One of the topics in options trading that you will read and hear the least about is trade execution. Though each trading platform has its own particular traits when it comes to trade execution, there are a few principles that permeate all platforms and are essential for you to understand if you are to be successful. Trade execution is one area where novice traders often give up the most edge in their trading. For example, if you are trading SPX options and the calls you want to sell have a bid/ask spread that is $1.40 wide, how do you proceed? For example, suppose the calls have a market with a bid of $5.60 and an offer of $7.00; do you sell the calls at $5.60? Do you try to sell the calls at the midprice of $6.30? Or do you choose a different price entirely? Or, as many traders choose, do you avoid the underlying altogether due to the width of the spreads?

Before digging into this, let's reiterate that learning to get the best price out of your trade execution is far more important than getting the best commission structure from your broker. Yet many traders will leave their broker and run to a cheaper broker just to save 25 cents per contract. Now, I am not saying you should not get the best rates you can, as controlling costs is important to the profitability of any business. And you should run your trading activities as a business. But if one broker does a better job filling your orders in between the bid and ask prices, that may be a far more important factor in your profitability.

And though some brokers will tell you all brokers get you the same fills, that has not been my experience. It may take a bit of trial and error to find that broker who does the best job for you, but it is worth the effort in the long run.

Before we begin dissecting the art of getting the best execution, we will look at some of the more common order types. We will also look at some other background material necessary to your understanding of good execution skills, such as where your orders go when you submit them and who might be taking the other side of your trades.

Order Types

Though part of this discussion is quite remedial and I expect most readers will know much of it, I will discuss when (or if) I ever use these order types and why. You do not have to follow my lead, as my goal is not to create clones of myself, but rather to give you enough information for you to find your own unique style. However, I will try to caution you against using certain order types, or at least urge you to use them only in certain situations.

Though market orders are one of the most common types of orders, I almost never use them. With a market order, you are saying, "I will pay whatever your offer is or will sell whatever your bid is." The strength of a market order is you are guaranteed (or virtually guaranteed) an immediate fill. So, if you are desperate to put a trade on or take a trade off, a market order will accomplish that goal. The downside is that you really have little guarantee at what price that fill will be. When dealing with options that are traded on many exchanges, you theoretically will get filled at the displayed prices. Why theoretically and not "in actuality?" Well, most of the time they will be the same. But if the market happens to momentarily change when you send the order, your fill can be quite different and unwanted. Furthermore, in situations like the 2010 flash crash, placing market orders was financial suicide. The flash crash was one of those rare situations where the options market-places declared a "fast market" due to a sudden, sharp increase in volatility. When a fast market is in effect, brokerages (and market makers) are not held to the same constraints as during a normal market. As such, bid/ask spreads can often get very wide and fill prices can become very erratic. To avoid an extremely costly and painful experience, during these periods, you should never place a market order. If you do, you are asking for a good beating, and a beating you shall take. Unfortunately, it is often during these times that you most desire, or need, to get filled. So, what can you do? This question is the perfect segue into our discussion of limit orders.

With a limit order, you are setting a top price that you will pay for an order. Obviously, the advantage is you will know ahead of time what the highest price is you will pay. Let's put this into perspective. When was the last time you walked into a store to buy a pair of jeans and said, "I will buy those jeans at whatever price you want to charge me?" You may have seen them advertised at another store for $79, but that does not mean this store will sell them for that price. Paying whatever the store wants to charge is the equivalent of a market order. You may pay $79 or you may pay $300 if there was a sudden spike in demand for those particular jeans. Of course, in many instances, the options marketplace insures you will not pay more than the best price for an option, but that is not always the case (as we discussed with regard to fast markets). As such, I cannot remember the last time I placed a market order. Even if I want to pay the offer, or I am willing to even pay a bit more than the offer, I will submit a limit order at a price I am willing to pay. So, I might bid $80 for the jeans and hope I end up paying no more than $79. So, why bid $80? I will bid $80 only if the market is a bit volatile and I do not want to miss my fill. Else, I will bid $79 and if I do not get filled, I will cancel/replace my order up, or if I am not anxious, I will wait for the market to "come to me," though that may never happen and I will miss my fill. But I will not risk a market order getting filled at a far higher price than anticipated.

A stop order is an order that becomes effective only when a security trades at or surpasses a particular price. For example, suppose I had a large, diversified portfolio of short premium trades and the market kept running higher and higher and the SPX was approaching $2,000. My volatility risk was not taking any pain, but my deltas kept getting shorter and shorter. Suppose I am not afraid of the delta risk unless the SPX breaks above $2,000, as I believe that level will provide significant resistance. But if the SPX breaks through that resistance, I believe the market will accelerate its upward movement. If I wanted to hedge some of my delta risk in the event $2,000 did not hold, how could I do that? This is where a stop order would be a good solution. I could place a buy stop to purchase a number of S&P futures in the event the S&Ps trade $2,001.75, as I would consider that level a "breakthrough." Once the futures trade at $2,001.75, my broker's execution platform will enter a market order to buy my futures. Though this does not guarantee a particular price at which I will be filled, it does guarantee a filled order. As long as the product I am trading is highly liquid, the price should be close. But in the event of a gapping market, it is possible for the price to be significantly different (meaning higher). In the section on market orders, I stated I almost never submit a market order. This type of order is my exception. Again, once my limit is hit, my order is sent as a market order. I will generally use this type of order when I am away from the market and not able to defend my positions. This provides a means for me to cover some of my risk in the event the market hits a level at which I want to take action.

Suppose you like what you see with a stop order, except that you are not happy with the risk of getting filled far from your price in the event of a gapping market. What can you do then? There is a closely related order type called a stop limit order that "has your back." A stop limit order is triggered in the same way as a stop order. But instead of sending a market order upon execution, a limit order is sent. Using the last example, when I send a stop limit, I may designate the stop price at $2,001.75, as I did before. I will also have to give my broker the top limit I am willing to pay for the futures. I will generally place that limit around 50 cents higher if it is during normal trading hours. It is not common, though it does happen, that the S&P futures will jump over a limit price 50 cents higher without executing the order. So, I am covered for a vast majority of the occurrences where my stop is hit. What you need to weigh when choosing between a stop order and a stop limit order is how important it is that you get filled "at all costs." Since I manage my individual trades per the Kelly Criterion, it is rare I have an "emergency" and feel the need to get filled at any price. My level of urgency, though, will help me in determining how far above my stop price I will set my limit. For example, if I am trading a future as a scalp (meaning I am opening a trade due to the future or stock passing through a level), I will keep my limit very close to my stop price. If I do not get filled, it does not cost me anything. If the market is very volatile, I am busy elsewhere, and feel the need to defend my position while I am not able to watch the market, I will give my limit more room. I may bid a full dollar (or more) above my stop. You will need to find your own style when using stop and stop limit orders. And you will have to get a feel for how much room you need to give the limit order based on the particular product, the volatility in the market, and the level of urgency you are feeling to get filled.

There is one other type of stop order we will cover. It is one I use frequently when I am scalping stock or futures, and it is called a trailing stop. Though this is an options book, there are often times I will scalp "around my position." We will discuss the purpose for these scalps in more detail in the section on portfolio/trade management, but for now, suffice it to say it is a means of mitigating risk in your portfolio. However, before we discuss the trailing stop, there is a different type of order we will discuss first.

An "OCO order," standing for "one cancels the other order," is a means of entering two orders simultaneously, only one of which will be executed. One of the orders is a limit order and the other is a stop order. When one of the orders is executed, the other is automatically canceled. As my goal is not to just teach you about order types, let's look at how I use the OCO order. As we just discussed, I will often scalp around my positions. Let us assume I am short an XYZ strangle with my short calls at the $100 strike. XYZ's all-time high was $94.70, which the stock just broke through and is trading at $95.12. Implied volatility is starting to rise, and I am looking at this stock as a breakout stock. Looking at my short calls, I still have a good amount of loss left to incur before I hit my Kelly Criterion (loss) exit price. I am now short-term bullish on the stock as I feel like there should be some short covering by technical analysts who were shorting against the all-time highs. Yet I feel like the stock will not get through the century mark, meaning I believe the stock will not break above $100. So, I decide to leave my trade alone, but want to cover some of my deltas for the short term. So, I buy some stock at $95.12. I am hoping to ride the stock up a bit to cover some of the pain from the short calls. But if this is not a true breakout and the stock reverses, I do not want to lose too much of the profits I hope to make on my options trade. Thus, after buying the stock, I enter an OCO order to close the stock trade. I might enter a limit order to sell the stock I bought at $99.12 and a stop order to sell the shares at $94.12. The two orders are linked via a "one cancels the other" umbrella. Thus, if the stock keeps running up, I hope to make $4 per share on the scalp. But if this is not a breakout and the stock loses steam and starts to fall, I will incur only a $1 loss per share. When either of the orders is executed, the other is canceled so that I do not get filled on both and end up short the stock, which would add to the risk of the portfolio instead of mitigating risk. The cancel is handled by the broker's computer due to my instructions, upon entry, to cancel one when the other is filled.

I use OCO orders not only when trading stock or futures to protect my positions but also frequently when scalping futures or stock for "offensive purposes." A quick example occurred recently when the S&P futures recently pulled back from its all-time high of $1,985.75 to $1,895. The futures were then starting to rise again and were trading for $1,903.50. I felt like the market was beginning a rising trend again and chose to buy some futures to profit from the move. However, since the bread and butter of my trading is my options trading, I keep these scalps' losses to no more than a day's theta that my overall portfolio is collecting. What does this mean in practice? At the time of this scalp, suppose I was collecting around $1,800 per day in theta. Thus, I wanted to lose no more. The next question I asked myself was, "At what price will I assume my bullish assumption was incorrect for purposes of this scalp? If the S&P futures broke below the $1,895 (recent) low, I will assume I was incorrect. So, I decided my stop price would be $1,894.50, which is $9 lower than the S&Ps were trading at that point in time. Since the S&P futures are worth $50 per point, should I get stopped out, that would mean I would lose $450 for each future I purchased. Though I could then purchase four futures and be risking only the $1,800 that makes up my theta, I chose to purchase only three futures. This gave me room to account for a bit of extra losses I might incur if I did not get filled at my stop price. Also, again, scalping is not my main money-making activity, so I prefer to keep some of the theta I hope to collect. So, now I knew my stop price and the size of my trade. All I needed next was my profit level. I will generally look to receive around three times what I am risking when I scalp. So, I chose to enter my limit order at $1,930.50. With all three parameters decided on, I went ahead and bought my three futures and as luck would have it, I got filled at $1,903. Since I liked my stop price, I now entered my OCO order to sell three futures on a stop order at $1,894.50, and I readjusted my profit price to be three times the $8.50 at risk and entered my limit sale at $1,928.50. As luck would have it again (since the market goes up only around 53 percent of the days), the market took off to the upside. We entered into the teeth of what felt like a nice, strong rally. Risking falling prey to the "Bulls make money, bears make money, pigs get slaughtered" saying, I started to think I was too conservative with my limit order to sell my longs at $1,928.50. What choices could I see to potentially take better advantage of the move?

Well, this leads me back to the trailing stop discussion to which I promised we would return. A trailing stop is a stop order that is triggered based on the distance from the top tick after order entry (in the case of a sell stop) or the bottom tick (in the case of a buy stop). Let me illustrate by continuing the discussion of the three S&P futures I was long. The S&Ps were now trading for $1,921. At this price, I had a $2,700 profit thus far as the futures were up $18 from where I bought them. Rather than see this profit turn into a loss should the market turn around, I reduced my original OCO order to command only one futures contract. I then entered two separate trailing stop orders. With one contract, I wanted to insure I kept at least an $8.50 profit to offset the $8.50 loss should the worst happen with my OCO order. To give it a bit of room in case my fill was not at my stop price, I placed a $9 trailing stop. This means that anytime that the S&Ps dropped $9 from its top tick from here on out (meaning from the top tick of the current price or any higher price subsequent to this point in time), my platform would enter a market order to sell one S&P future. The trade monitor page of your trading platform should keep a running sell stop price for you. So, at point of entry, with the S&Ps at $1,921, my system considered this order to be a sell stop at the price of $1,912 ($1,921 − $9). When the market now ran up $1.50

to $1,922.50, my sell stop price became $1,913.50 (1,922.50 - $9). If the S&Ps fell from $1,922.50, the price of the sell stop would not change. I now had two futures "spoken for." With the third future, I wanted to give it more room to "breathe." What I mean is, if the market pulls back $9 and stops me out on one of my futures and then runs up a lot further, I would have a profit but would have missed out on additional gains. So with the third future, I entered a trailing stop with the trailing future the full $18 of gain I already had on the future. In other words, I was willing to accept a scratch for that future. This left plenty of room to weather temporary pullbacks on the road to what I hoped would be a healthy profit. But if the market turned ugly and hit new lows (below $1,894.50), I would not be out any money. The OCO order would incur an $8.50 loss, the first trailing stop would incur a $9.00 (or there about) profit, and my last trailing stop would be a scratch. I would have given up the $2,700 profit I currently had in order to try for a larger gain. And the only way I would get a scratch is if the current price was the top tick from here on out, until the futures traded below my final stop in my OCO order. If I even got another $1 of up move to $1,922, I was virtually guaranteed at least a $100 profit. As it turned out, the futures got up to $1,941 before pulling back a bit over $9. Thus, my OCO limit sell order got filled at its original price ($1,928.50) for one contract on the way up for a gain of $1,275.00. And my $9.00 trailing stop got filled at a price of $1,931.75, for a gain of $1,437.50. My $18.00 trailing stop came within $0.50 of getting filled before the market reversed and ran higher again. To my surprise, the S&Ps went through the $1,950 mark, a price at which I expected to see resistance, without hesitation. I now had a much larger than expected profit on this last future, and I decided to tighten up my trailing stop a bit. This insured I would not give back too much of my profit. I moved my trailing stop up to be a $10 trailing stop. A few days later, after peaking at $1,961.00, the S&P futures fell over $10.00 and I got stopped out at a price of $1,950.75. This last future added $2,387.50 of profits for a grand total of $5,100.00 of profit, before commissions.

Trade	Order Type	Price	Future P/L	$P/L
+3 /ES	Limit	$1,903.00		
−1 /ES	OCO Limit	$1,928.50	$25.50	$1,275.00
−1 /ES	Trailing Stop $9	$1,931.75	$28.75	$1,437.50
−1 /ES	Trailing Stop $10	$1,950.75	$47.75	$2,387.50
Total				**$5,100.00**

The point of following this trade was not to illustrate the size of the profit. In actuality, the trade size was much larger than what I described and I scaled it down to make the math easier to follow. The point is the creative use of the various ways you can use order types to aid you in your trading. When scalping, I almost always begin the process with an OCO exit order. It is not something everyone does, but it fits my personality perfectly. But if the market runs my way, I will often convert the OCO order to a trailing stop. How far away I place my trailing stop is determined by several things, not the least of which is the current volatility of the marketplace. If the market is extremely volatile, I will place my trailing stop farther away to give it more room to breathe. In that way, a normal intraday swing will not take me out of a good trade. And since I have more risk with the trailing stop far away, I will size my trade down (fewer contracts) to keep the dollars risked in the trade consistent with my theta. You do not need to size the trade to your theta, but I believe that since my bread and butter is my options trading, I never want to dwarf the profits and losses from it with lower probability scalps. Recognition must be given to that probability differential, as that is why I trade options. The probabilities rule my trading!

Though this is not strictly an "order type" per se, I want to discuss closing orders and how I treat them differently than opening orders. I am speaking here of a normal, short premium options trade that constitutes the bread and butter of my trading. As we discussed, I generally close my trades based on the calculated levels from my chosen Kelly Criterion parameters. For any given trade, there are two levels calculated at trade entry: a profitable exit and a losing exit. Almost immediately after I place my trade, I will enter a GTC (good until canceled) order for my profitable exit. For example, if I sell a strangle for $2.00 and I like to take my profit at 75 percent of maximum profit, then I will immediately enter my order to purchase the strangle back for $0.50. I am aware that I may make adjustments to the trade throughout its life, such as rolling the untested side of a strangle closer, that may affect my exit price. If so, I will adjust the closing order accordingly. But having the closing order with my desired exit price on my screen each day helps me to track the progress of the trade. In this way, there is no confusion. So, if I have my closing profitable trades entered, do I also enter my losing trades as an OCO order? The answer, in short, is no! Though I know my level, I generally do not place stop orders in options. This is particularly true in options that have a wide bid/ask spread like the major indices. I am almost always short SPX strangles and often also short RUT strangles. The bid/ask spread is often well over $1 wide for these options. Since I can almost always get a trade price somewhere near the midpoint, it would make no sense for me to place a stop loss order in these options. Furthermore, if volatility picks up, the bid/ask spread of most options will widen. Again, this does not mean I cannot get filled near the midpoint, though there is no guarantee of that. For these reasons, I prefer to never place stop loss orders in options. If I am away from the marketplace when one of my trades is approaching my Kelly Criterion loss level, I may place a stop loss order in the stock or future that hedges the options as a temporary "holding place," or hedge, for my short options. Though this carries its own risk (in the event of a whipsaw move), I trade only stocks and futures that are highly liquid, and therefore I do not give up too much edge with stop orders on the underlyings. When one of these stop orders is hit, I receive a notification on my cell phone of my underlying trade and will get to my trading platform as soon as possible to unwind the underlying trade and take my loss in the option trade. In the same way, if I do not want to place an underlying trade, I can just set a text alert to let me know when a stock level has been breached. That will also send me scurrying to my trading platform at my earliest opportunity.

Very briefly, I will now touch on a few important notes on trading different products. This is not intended to be even close to exhaustive. I am assuming you have done your homework and are relatively well versed on trading a product before you venture into its marketplace. But there are a couple of key elements of each I want to reiterate,

Earlier, I made the comment that you will usually get filled at the market you see, except for in a fast market or if the market "moves" in the split second you are sending your order. There is actually a law in place guaranteeing this for equity securities. In 2007, the Securities and Exchange Commission passed Regulation NMS (Regulation National Market System). This was a three-part regulation, but the important part for you and me is that we are guaranteed a trade at the National Best Bid and Offer (NBBO). This means we get to buy at no worse than the lowest offer price from any exchange or market maker and we get to sell at the highest bid from the same participants. Regulation NMS requires brokers to guarantee their customers the NBBO pricing. One issue to be aware of is we are not guaranteed that our order will be filled at those prices. The NBBO also will be displayed with the size of the bids and offers (see Figure 8.1). So, for example, say I want to sell 50 January AAPL 90 puts and there are traders bidding $2.73 for 36 contracts; I am guaranteed the NBBO bid price for only that number of contracts. I would still send all 50 contracts in my sell order. More often than not, I will get filled on all 50, as there are potentially other buyers at that price who will accept that offer. But I am guaranteed only a partial fill. If after selling the 36 contracts that were bid, the market coming out is $2.72 bid, at my $2.73

FIGURE 8.1   Apple Trade Grid

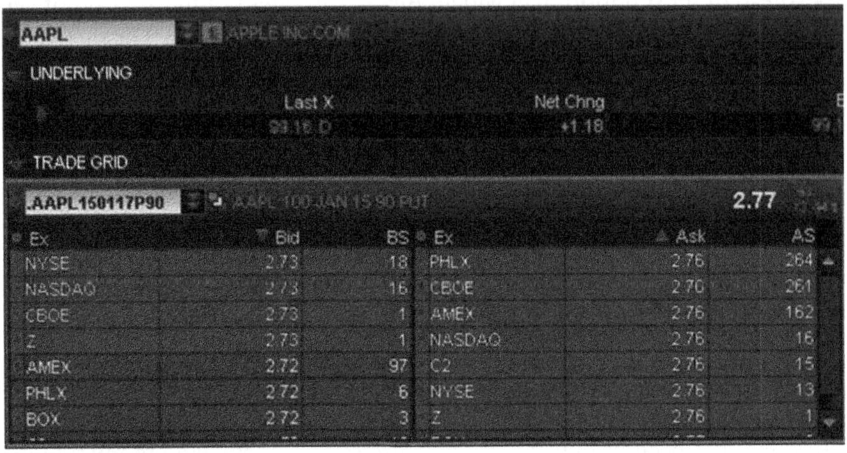

AAPL			APPLE INC COM			
UNDERLYING						
	Last X			Net Chng		E
	93.18 D			+1.18		93
TRADE GRID						

AAPL150117P90		AAPL 100 JAN 15 90 PUT			2.77	
Ex	Bid	BS	Ex		Ask	AS
NYSE	2.73	18	PHLX		2.76	264
NASDAQ	2.73	16	CBOE		2.76	261
CBOE	2.73	1	AMEX		2.76	162
Z	2.73	1	NASDAQ		2.76	18
AMEX	2.72	97	C2		2.76	15
PHLX	2.72	6	NYSE		2.76	13
BOX	2.72	3	Z		2.76	1

Source: TD Ameritrade.

offer (pretty cool that the entire world is looking at my offer), I can choose to wait or I can cancel and replace my order to sell the remaining contracts at $2.72. Your broker should have a means of displaying the data as shown in Figure 8.1. When you first begin trading, your trade size will most likely be small enough that this grid of the best bids and offers and their sizes will be of less importance. But you should still understand what the grid is telling you as there is still useful information in there. As I said before, I will almost always try to trade a market somewhere in between its best bid and its best offer. In our AAPL example in Figure 8.1, the NBBO was $2.73 bid and $2.76 offer.

If I wanted to try to sell my contracts at $2.74, how would I best accomplish that? If you just send a $2.74 offer through your broker without designating where you want to send it, your broker will send it to the marketplace that has the lowest fees for it. This is not normally a problem for you, and I do not believe (despite all the coverage it is receiving) that this is a conspiracy to harm the client for the benefit of the brokerage. I want my broker to make more money if it costs me nothing. In that way, with the brokerage flush and making money, I hope to have more room to share in that profit by getting my fees reduced. I believe a profitable brokerage will be more willing to accommodate that request than one that is barely scraping by. But if I hope to get filled at $2.74, I would prefer to send my order to the exchange that has the most aggressive $2.73 bidders. Someone from that group may be willing to step up the extra penny to get filled. And if they happen to be market makers adding liquidity to the exchange, they will most likely get the best fees, or even paid, for their order flow. Thus, they may be incentivized to make the trade on their own exchange. Without viewing the trade grid, seeing where the best bids are coming from, and routing my order there, I may be depriving myself of a fill.

Though this is all true of individual orders in equity securities, it is not so for spreads. There is no "national best bid and offer" for a spread. In fact, each exchange has its own spread book where it houses spread orders. Therefore, when I send a spread, I will send it to the exchange that seems to have the most volume for the options of the equity security. I will let it rest there for a minute or two so that market makers and other traders can view it. If it is not filled, I will then cancel/replace it to the next most active exchange. I will cycle through the major exchanges, and if they are not filled anywhere, I will then put it back to the most active location to rest. Or I may then look for a way to get filled at my price by legging the spread. Legging the spread means I will trade each option in the spread individually. I will often get filled at better prices this way, though I add risk to my execution in that I may get filled on one side of the trade and have the market move against that leg, thus leading to a worse fill in the end. Note that when trading a spread, it is possible to be attempting to sell a bid and purchase an offer and still not get filled. If both the bid and the offer are at the same exchange, I will likely be filled immediately. But often the highest bid and the lowest offer are found at different exchanges, and I may have to leg the trade to get it executed. Of course, even if I am willing to sell the bid and buy the offer, I will most likely look to get at least a tick better on the first leg to give myself either a better fill or room to chase the other leg if the market moves. I am more likely to leg a spread in a quiet market or if the market is running in one direction than I will be in a whippy, two-sided market. The main point to remember, though, is that when trading a spread, there is no central repository or national best bid and offer for the spread. You may sell it at one exchange for $1.00, when it is $1.10 bid at another exchange, as long as no leg is traded through. So, you need to move your order around and test the waters, or leg the spread if so desired, to have a better chance of getting the best fill price.

As we stated, the NBBO that is guaranteed by Reg NMS is for equity securities. In general, this means the rule holds for stocks and individual stock options. Each of these securities is traded on multiple exchanges at the same time, thus necessitating (at least in the eyes of regulators) a means of protecting investors from getting inferior pricing on their trades at one exchange when better pricing exists elsewhere. Futures, on the other hand, are generally traded on only one exchange. There is no necessity for any rules or regulations to insure pricing fairness. The markets you see are what you get. Your order is routed to the only place the future trades and the disseminated quotes, by definition, reflect the best markets available.

When trading spot forex, there is a completely different marketplace for you to navigate. The first thing you will note is that most brokerages do not charge commissions for spot forex trades. Do they do that as a courtesy to their customers? In actuality, when you trade spot forex, you are trading the markets as set by your brokerage. There is not a single or small number of brokerages making markets. Each brokerage can set their own markets, and they make their money by "market making." That means they hope to make money by buying on the bid and selling on the offer. This is just the opposite of what we do as customers, where we have to pay the offer price and sell the bid price. But, though your broker gets to set their own market, they are not truly independent of others' markets. If your broker is off the market, an arbitrage opportunity presents itself. Traders will open (if they do not already have) accounts at more than one brokerage and will take advantage of the discrepancy to force the markets back in line. Therefore, if you are using any reputable broker, you can count on the markets being in line with everyone else's. But what you need to be careful of is to choose a broker who has tight markets. That is, the bid/offer spread should be as small as possible. Remember that that spread is your broker's fee. And your broker takes on risk when they take the other side of your trade and therefore must be further compensated for that risk premium. But paying the bid/ask spread can also amount to a hefty fee for you. You need to carefully choose your broker based on this spread if you are a frequent spot forex trader. This does not negate the need to vet your broker on all other issues, but this hidden fee can truly be a game changer for whether you are profitable as a spot forex trader. With forex being the largest marketplace in the world, trading over a trillion dollars' worth of currencies and currency futures each day, you have many alternative places to trade. I urge you to do your homework well.

CHAPTER 9

Portfolio Management

We have spoken about how to choose individual trades, how to best execute your trades, and when to exit trades both as winners and losers. Once you have a number of trades on your sheets, what should you do to control your overall portfolio's risk? How do you know what the overall risk really is? This is perhaps the most difficult area of trading. There are many schools of thought on the issue. We will begin our discussion by exploring a more academic viewpoint on the issue and proceed to a more practical approach. I must caution you that for every educator you read or listen to, you will more than likely get a different answer as to the best way to control your risk. And even if all educators had a similar answer, each individual trader has his or her own risk appetite, financial situation, and pain threshold for withstanding losses. Therefore, there is no "one size fits all" solution. What I will deliver to you is a solid framework for how to view your risk, some potential trade ideas to help mitigate your portfolio's risk, and some rules of thumb as to how to size your trades. You may be wondering why sizing your trades appears in a portfolio management discussion. In actuality, proper trade sizing is probably the single most important area of risk management. Let us begin by talking a bit about risk and diversification of risk.

Two Types of Risk

Most people hear the term *risk* and think it refers to how much they can lose. Though that is not entirely wrong, there is much more to the story. And knowing a few more of the details will help you better understand the nature of your portfolio. So, we will revert to a bit of "Financial Management 101" speak.

People, by nature, are risk-averse. Most of us would prefer not to take any risk, all else being equal. There are those few daredevils out there who take on risk just for the sake of the rush it provides. I would highly advise those individuals to stay away from trading. They will get their rush and then the call from their broker letting them know their account is closed due to lack of funds. A rational individual takes on risk only if he feels appropriately compensated to do so. We call this compensation *risk premium*. We discussed this in some detail back in Chapter 5. Every trade is a shifting of risk. By lining up trades where the implied volatility exceeds its norm and its historical volatility, we feel appropriately compensated in most instances. But we need to understand a bit more about risk to manage it appropriately. There are actually two types of risk of which every trader should be aware. The first type of risk is unique risk. This refers to risk specific to a stock or a company. Examples of unique risk are numerous. They include management changes, quality of management, company earnings surprises, lawsuits, bad press, and getting outcompeted, among others. When considering unique risk, think of an event that will affect only one company or a small circle of related companies. This risk can also be expanded to an industry, though industry risk is a bit of a hybrid. The point you need to be aware of is that unique risk can be diversified to limit the amount of risk new trades might add to the portfolio. We will talk about this in more detail in a minute. The second type of risk is systematic risk. This refers to macro level risk, such as that provided by political events or large monetary policy events. Examples might be war breaking out, oil prices spiking, a surprise rate hike, or health issues of a high-ranking official in the federal government or Federal Reserve. These events affect virtually all instruments. This is the type of risk that cannot be diversified away, often comes unexpectedly, and must be premitigated, in most instances. In other words, your portfolio should maintain some type of balance with respect to direction, volatility, industry, and asset class. That is not to say you should be perfectly balanced. It just means you need to be aware of the level of systematic risk your portfolio carries and insure you feel you are getting enough risk premiums for the level of risk you carry. Though you do not diversify systematic risk away, you can mitigate the amount of risk you carry with appropriate types of risk-offsetting trades. Again, we will speak more specifically about these after a bit more foundation-building discussion.

The Goal: Diversification—Minimizing Unique Risk

At this point, we will look in more depth at the theory behind diversification of unique risks. First, as options traders, we are distinctly aware of implied volatility as a risk in every trade we make. And, as we have discussed, implied volatility is really nothing more than the standard deviation of the distribution curve of our underlying's movement. Each individual underlying has its own, distinct standard deviation. In modern financial management courses, we use that standard deviation as a measure of risk in a company. We can look back over at least a 60-month (5-year) period and determine what that standard deviation is. Any statistics book can help you with this, if you are not aware of how to calculate it. Also, you can use a spreadsheet, like Excel, and utilize its built-in standard deviation function to arrive at a solution. And thanks to our friends who bring us stock indices, we can also calculate the standard deviation for a diversified portfolio, such as the S&P 500 (as represented by the SPX). I have chosen to calculate the standard deviation for 12 securities for a 20-year period to aid in our discussion. These 12 securities consist of 11 members of the SPX, and the SPX itself. See Table 9.1 for the data.

TABLE 9.1   20 Year Average Implied Volatilities

1989–2008: Standard Deviation	
Stock	Standard Deviation
AA	30
C	31
DIS	26
GE	21
GM	33
HD	30
INTC	40
PFE	25
PG	22
T	25
XOM	16
SPX	15

Looking at this data, we see a wide range of standard deviations, and therefore risk, among our underlyings. But the one thing that should stand out is that the diversified portfolio of stocks, the SPX, has the lowest measure of risk. If we were to take all 500 securities, calculate their standard deviation, and average them (weighted or not), the average standard deviation would be far higher than the standard deviation of the SPX. In fact, that is the working definition of diversification. Diversification is the phenomenon whereby the average standard deviation of the parts of a portfolio is much greater than the standard deviation of the combined portfolio. Why is this? It is because the unique risks are canceling each other out! One caveat to be aware of is the underlyings in your portfolio need to be diverse in nature. That means they should be relatively uncorrelated or inversely correlated. The unique risks will not cancel if you are trading two closely related securities. For example, a portfolio with only Home Depot (HD) and Lowes (LOW) has far more unique risk than a portfolio with only Home Depot and Google (GOOG). Home Depot and Lowes are in the same business and will likely be moved by similar, nonsystematic risks. That is, they share some of the same "unique" risks. Though that sounds like a misnomer, I hope you get the point. Home Depot and Google, however, are in totally unrelated businesses and will have separate unique risks. (Systematic risks may batter both stocks, however, no matter how unrelated their businesses are.)

The Methods: Correlation and Number of Positions

To determine how much of the unique risk is diversified away, there are two numbers that we can utilize, depending on the nature of our portfolio. The first, and the easier to calculate, is correlation. A formal definition of correlation (from Wikipedia) is, "In statistics, dependence is any statistical relationship between two random variables or two sets of data. Correlation refers to any of a broad class of statistical relationships involving dependence." More specifically, correlation will give us clues as to how the movement of one underlying will be related to, or not related to, the movement of another underlying. The degree to which they are related can be determined by the underlyings' correlation coefficient. Correlation coefficients have a range of -1 to $+1$. If two stocks have a correlation coefficient of $+1$, they move in lockstep. In other words, when Stock A moves up 1 percent, so does Stock B. We say these stocks are perfectly correlated. In reality, no two stocks of different companies are ever perfectly correlated. A correlation coefficient of -1 would tell you that when Stock A moves up 1 percent, Stock B moves down 1 percent. These stocks are said to be perfectly inversely correlated. Two trades that are inversely correlated provide the best means of diversifying your portfolio. However, stocks that have little or no correlation, having a correlation coefficient near zero, are also excellent means of diversification.

Knowing what a correlation coefficient is will not help you if you cannot calculate it. My goal is to give you the tools you need to be a successful trader, and I do not wish to get caught in the mathematical weeds. But a little understanding can go a long way. Correlation is calculated by dividing the covariance between the two securities by the product of the two securities' standard deviations (or volatility). And rather than give you the math of covariance, I just want to explain that it is a measure of how much two random variables change together. In other words, it defines the relationship between the two variables, or in our case, two securities. To calculate the correlation coefficient between any two securities requires good historical data, a decent spreadsheet (like Excel, Numbers, or Google Docs, among others), and a couple of seconds or minutes of your time. (You do not need to calculate covariance and standard deviations.) I created spreadsheets to show you how to calculate the correlation coefficient, and they can be found on this book's companion website. But you should be aware that correlation coefficients can be calculated using various time frames. Correlations can break down, or change, at times. For example, from the summer of 2007 to the summer of 2008, when oil was breaking out to new highs, every time oil surged, the market (SPX) sold off. Thus, the two securities were highly inversely correlated. But after oil peaked in July 2008, correlation changed and the two securities became positively correlated. Does this negate the value of correlations in our trading? Though it might diminish it a bit, correlations can still be valuable information. On a gross level, it still helps us in our effort to diversify our portfolio. By looking at the correlation over various time frames, we can get a feel for how closely two securities move together. And on a macro, nonmathematical level, we should have some sense of relationships between securities, as we saw with the Home Depot/Lowes versus Home Depot/Google discussion. This knowledge alone should aid you in determining whether trades added to a portfolio are helping to diversify it.

I will frequently break down my portfolio by industries to get a macro feel for if I have "chunks" of risk in one spot. In other words, I look to see if I am overweighted in a particular industry. For example, I may find that 35 percent of my portfolio is tied up in oil and gas stocks. Unless that position is based on a specific assumption, I would consider that far too much risk for any one industry. However, I also need to be aware of correlations between industries. For example, transportation stocks are frequently inversely correlated with oil and gas stocks. As the price of oil rises, the increased cost of fuels for the transportation

FIGURE 9.1   Asymptotic Chart of Risk

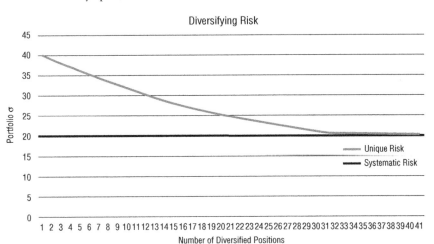

companies may reduce their profitability. Thus, my oil and gas position deltas may offset my transportation delta risks. But the two volatility risks are most likely additive, because if oil spikes and oil stocks start to fluctuate wildly it is a good bet transportation stocks will also begin to move briskly. We will speak more on assessing the risks in a bit.

But let us not lose sight of the goal in determining correlations, and that is to reduce or eliminate the unique risks from our portfolio. So, assuming we are trading diversified products, how do we know how many trades actually do the trick? Once again, statistics come to the rescue. As it turns out, it is a generally agreed upon fact that around 30 diversified positions will reduce a significant amount of unique (specific) risk from your portfolio. As can be seen in Figure 9.1, overall risk seems to "inflect" and become quite asymptotic when around 30 positions are combined. At this point, almost all risk left in the portfolio is systematic, as represented by the horizontal line.

You may be thinking, "I cannot afford to have 30 positions on at all times. And even if I could, I often cannot find 30 trades that fit my criterion for good trades." Do not despair. As we examined before, there are plenty of (already) diversified products that exist and are highly liquid that we can trade. One example we have already looked at is the SPX. As we saw in a previous graphic, its standard deviation is far below that of the average of the 500 individual stocks in its diversified portfolio. Thus, most of its unique risks have been removed and the index is subject almost entirely to systematic risks. And there are plenty of other indices and ETFs that have similar properties, such as RUT, NDX, SPY, IWM, QQQ, and DIA. Furthermore, we can expand our diversification outside of the United States equity markets by trading ETFs like EWW (Mexico), EWZ (Brazil), EWJ (Japan), ILF (Latin America), and a host of others. We can also diversify our asset classes by getting involved with fixed income (TLT), currencies (FXE for the Euro, FXY for the Yen, etc.), oil (USO), gold (GLD), silver (SLV), agricultural products (DBA), and volatility (VIX). This is but a small subset of diversified products you can trade. You certainly do not need 30 trades in these products to create diversification of your unique risks, as each product is "prediversified," if you will. By combining them, you can create a level of diversification the individual investor could never before hope to achieve. I cannot stress enough how important minimizing your unique risks can be to your overall, long-term trading profitability. I have seen more decent traders have career-ending events as a result of individual stock news (takeovers, management shake-ups, lawsuits, product issues, bankruptcies) than via any other means. There is no reason to incur this risk, despite getting paid plenty of risk premium, when you can still collect the risk premium and diversify away much of the risk.

Earlier, I stated there were two numbers that help us view the relationships between underlyings, the first of which was the correlation coefficient. The second of these is represented by the beta of the underlying. Beta is commonly used in academia as part of the Capital Asset Pricing Model (CAPM). Unlike the correlation coefficient, which is generally used to compare the movement of one asset as related to another asset, beta is typically used to compare an asset's movement to the overall market. We generally get to choose what underlying represents "the overall market." For most portfolios, I would expect the SPX or SPY to represent the overall market. But if your portfolio is heavily laden with technology stocks, you may be better off beta weighting to NDX or QQQ. And if your portfolio contains many smaller cap stocks, RUT or IWM might be your index of choice. The biggest distinction I want to make is that since we are measuring the relationship of movement between an underlying and the overall market, by definition, we are measuring the amount of systematic risk of the security! We are not measuring the unique, or specific, risk in the underlying. Thus, if we first diversify the unique risk from our portfolio, beta gives us a pretty good idea of the systematic risk left. By beta weighting our portfolio, we can view many of the risks inherent in it. More on this in a bit.

Beta is calculated by performing a regression analysis on the underlying as compared to the representation of the market against which you are beta weighting. Rather than explain the intricacies of regression analysis (which you can look up on the Internet), if you have a good trading platform, the beta of a stock should be readily available on the platform. If not, you can get the beta for a stock from many websites, such as finance.yahoo.com or morningstar.com. But once again, like correlation coefficient, different time frames can be used, yielding varied results. And choosing the most effective time frame can be a bit of an adventure. Most statisticians will use at least a five-year time horizon. But some stocks can change considerably in a five-year period. For example, five years ago, Chipotle (CMG) stock was trading for $79. Today, as of this writing, it is a $698 stock. Priceline has gone from $148 to as high as $1,379. As such, I will generally examine a five-year and a one-year beta and determine which seems most appropriate.

No matter what you beta weight to, if an underlying has a beta of one, that would mean we expect the price of that security to move similarly to the overall market. If the beta is less than one, we would expect the underlying to be less "volatile" than the overall market with respect to systematic risk. A beta greater than one implies a greater propensity for movement than the overall market, again with respect to systematic risk only. But how does knowing each underlying's beta help us manage our portfolio? Again, a good trading platform should have a feature that allows you to beta weight your positions to an index. By doing so, you will arrive at "beta weighted" deltas and gammas. These newly calculated Greeks will give you an idea of the directional risk inherent in your portfolio as compared to the overall market. In other words, the beta weighted delta shows you your systematic directional risk. For example, if you beta weighted your portfolio to SPX and found that you were short 200 deltas, that would imply you would lose approximately $200 for every point SPX rose and make $200 for every point SPX fell. Of course, this accounts only for your directional risk and is only an approximation. But it gives you quite a bit more information about how you should expect your portfolio to perform as the market moves. If your portfolio is not diversified, however, you should expect quite a bit more variance in expectations as beta weighting accounts only for systematic risk and not unique risks of each of the underlyings. If you find your portfolio is not tracking the beta weighted predictions for days on end, you may be less diversified than you think. Take note that beta weighting does not affect your theta or your vega. Decay is decay and vega is vega. If you relate an underlying to the market via beta weighting, this does not affect the rate at which the options decay nor does it affect the way a change in vega affects your options' prices. Only your deltas and gammas are affected, and therefore beta weighting helps you discern the directional bias, or risk, in your overall portfolio.

There is one other consideration with respect to betas. Though in a normal environment betas will predict how an underlying will move over time as compared to an index, when the market ceases to be "normal," this can change. When the market starts falling quickly and volatility starts to rise, one of the phenomena you should be aware of is that correlations start to rise and may even approach " + 1." In other words, everything begins to fall together with a similar magnitude (as a percentage of the stock price). This is the phase in the market where participants "throw the baby out with the bath water."

At this point, not only will the correlation go to one, but also the relative cost of options will change. Note that this is a divergence in topics from directional correlation (beta) into volatility correlation. As there are potential implications for our trading, we will look at this in more detail. Earlier, we stated that the definition of diversification is "the phenomenon whereby the average standard deviation of the parts of a portfolio is much greater than the standard deviation of the combined portfolio." In other words, we get a lot more movement (volatility) by owning the individual securities in an index than we do by owning the index. This is because the unique risks of the individual securities move the individual securities' prices in all directions, while in the diversified portfolio, the unique risks cancel. This is reflected in a security's implied volatility, and thus in its options prices. There is a professional strategy that requires a good amount of both capital and sophistication, called dispersion trading, which looks to take advantage of relative value differences in implied volatilities between an index and a basket of component stocks. This strategy typically involves short straddles in an index, against long straddles on a set of components of the index. The goal is to profit from the unique risks of the individual securities while hedging away much of the systematic risks. The trick is to determine how much extra you should pay for the individual securities' options over the index options you are selling and still profit from the extra volatility. Our goal here is not to make you a dispersion trader, but only to benefit from the lessons it can teach us for our own trading. Back in July of 2009, the CBOE began disseminating the CBOE S&P 500 Implied Correlation Index. The CBOE website states the following:

> The CBOE S&P 500 Implied Correlation Indexes are the first widely disseminated, market-based estimate of the average correlation of the stocks that comprise the S&P 500 Index (SPX). Using SPX options prices, together with the prices of options on the 50 largest stocks in the S&P 500 Index, the CBOE S&P 500 Implied Correlation Indexes offers insight into the relative cost of SPX options compared to the price of options on individual stocks that comprise the S&P 500. (Chicago Board Options Exchange, www.cboe .com/micro/impliedcorrelation/)

Part of the purpose of this index is to help dispersion traders in pricing their trades. But for us, it helps visualize what we were discussing regarding how pricing changes in times of duress. Figure 9.2 shows the SPX price with the KCJ, the implied correlation index, from back in 2011.

FIGURE 9.2 KCJ versus SPX

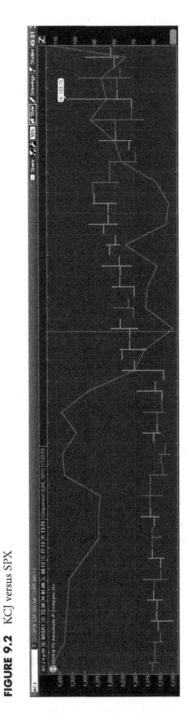

Source: TD Ameritrade.

As you can see in the center of Figure 9.2, as the price of the SPX fell, the implied correlation index started to rise. That means that the price of SPX options rises in comparison to the individual securities that make up the portfolio. Though they both rise due to a rising implied volatility, the index prices rise faster. An implied correlation of 100 means the index options are priced similarly to the individual securities. This means the options are priced as if there is no longer any unique risk and all movement is due to systematic (overall market) risk!

We said before that a great way to diversify your portfolio without making as many trades is to trade indices and ETFs. But if we have a group of index and ETF trades on our sheets and the market starts to implode, we need to be aware that the relative rise in the option prices will exceed those of a diversified portfolio of individual securities. On the other hand, once the implosion slows and eventually begins to reverse, this implied correlation will reverse fairly quickly. By selling the indices' options premium when implied correlation is high and buying the equities' options, a dispersion trader is buying the unique risk for cheap or even for free! Thus, the indices' options are far overpriced relative to the individual securities' options at that point in time. Regardless of whether we trade with a dispersion strategy, the theory behind it provides valuable information for our (less complex) strategies. We benefit from being flexible enough to trade a diversified portfolio of securities or a portfolio of diversified products (indices and ETFs), and from knowing when we get the most edge from either bundle of securities.

Identifying and Mitigating Systematic Risk

Now that we have spoken about reducing our unique risk, we need to look at how to mitigate the far more difficult systematic risk. Large moves of this sort do not occur with any frequency. Thus, it is easy to get lulled into a false sense of complacency. Yet if we believe in the statement that options markets are efficient, in normal market conditions we truly do not want to mitigate all of our risk. This is because, at least theoretically, if we do away with all our risk, we do away with all or most of our return. We make money by taking on other traders' or investors' risk. If we pass it on to someone else, we must pay them to take on our risk. Of course, if we pay less to pass on the risk than we received to accept the risk, we have a true arbitrage situation and would like to do that all day long. So, the question is, "Are there better and cheaper ways to mitigate systematic risk that you can identify in order to get a good, solid return with reduced risk?" In other words, how can we lower the risk/return ratio? I have several "go-to" methods that I like to use. Not all of them "set up" at all times, and I therefore have to be diligent and opportunistic about putting on these trades. Some of them deal with delta control, and some deal with vega control. Others just work. Let us take a look at just some of the possibilities.

First, let us look at various means of controlling our deltas. This can be a tricky topic and one that is often misunderstood. Before we begin, we need to set some ground rules and make some assumptions. We are in a chapter dedicated to portfolio management. As such, we are looking at managing the deltas of what we assume is a diversified portfolio of underlyings. Our unique risks have been diversified until they are at a minimum level, and our systematic risks are what we are trying to control. We are not managing on a trade-by-trade basis, at least until a trade hits our predefined Kelly Criterion exit level, at which time we take our profit or our loss, reassess our risks, and readjust our portfolio deltas, thetas, and vegas. One other assumption is that we are running a short premium portfolio. I have tried to hammer home the point that short premium works. It makes you the insurance company, as opposed to the insured. It makes you the casino instead of the gambler. It also makes you the risk taker as opposed to the risk-averse. And since humans are by nature risk-averse, this subject takes on far greater importance than most books give it credit for. With these assumptions as backdrop, let us dig in.

As we have discussed, by contrast, the market creeps higher and falls suddenly downward. That is, the velocity of downward movement exceeds that of upward movement. At least that is what the market gurus tell us. So, let us discover for ourselves if that is the case and, if so, how big the differential actually has been. I looked back over two time periods, the past 50 years and the past 30 years, and determined two things: what percentage of the days the SPX (as a harbinger of the overall market) moved up and down, and how much, on average, the market moved in either direction.

As can be seen in Table 9.2, the market over the past 50 years has moved up on 5.4 percent more days. Over the past 30 years, the market has moved up even more days, coming in at 7.7 percent more up days than down days. As for the velocity of the moves, true to the market gurus' claims, the down moves did have more velocity. However, the differences in velocity were miniscule. Over the past 50 years, the average down move was .04 percent larger than the average up day. And over the past 50 years, the difference was

TABLE 9.2 SPX Study of Percent Movement Up and Down

	% Up Days	% Down Days	Average Up Move	Average Down Move
30-year	53.85%	46.15%	0.74%	−0.78%
50-year	52.70%	47.30%	0.69%	−0.71%

half that, clocking in at a mere .02 percent discrepancy. So, what are we missing? Is the volatility skew that much overstated? Do we fear the downside for no reason and overcompensate with a volatility skew that is unwarranted? I dug further. I next looked at the largest day's move in either direction and found one of the reasons traders fear the downside. In the past 50 years, the largest one-day move to the upside occurred on October 13, 2008, when the SPX rallied 11.58 percent in one session. But, as we know, on October 19, 1987, as a result of the crash of 1987, the SPX closed down 20.47 percent. This largest down day is almost 77 percent greater than the largest up day. Once again, as risk-averse organisms, the Crash of 1987 sticks in our minds and guts and causes a change in our behavior. Interestingly, with the largest single day move being down, the next three largest single day moves were up. In my opinion, what I am seeing is not enough to warrant the volatility skew we trade with. But there is another consideration at which we need to look. If you have ever traded during a large correction, one of the most frustrating things is that the width of the bid/ask spread widens considerably. Furthermore, it can be virtually impossible to get filled in the middle of the bid/ask spreads. In fact, at times, due to the sheer volume that generally occurs, quotes and orders can often be slightly delayed and it may be hard to even get filled on or above the offer or at or under the bid! Let us look at a quick example. Going back to August 4, 2011, in the midst of a 4.76 percent sell-off for the day, the at the money, front month options were quoted around $5 wide. This is in sharp contrast to today, where the index is 67 percent higher and yet the at the money options are only $.30 wide. Unfortunately, it is difficult for me to show you that up moves are far more tradable, as the largest rally days we have had have been countertrend rallies in the midst of high-volatility sell-offs. But from my experience, rally days are, in fact, far more tradable than sell-offs, and I believe virtually every experienced trader will tell you the same. In my opinion, this inability to adjust your positions in the midst of a hard sell-off may be the single biggest reason the skew exists to the extent it does. The greater velocity to the downside and the Crash of 1987 contribute also, but to a lesser extent. This is my opinion only, though, and not a scientifically proven fact.

Regardless, getting back to the delta hedging, what this fear of the downside has led to is a plethora of traders who will frequently run a short delta book in combination with short premium. Traders feel they will be able to adjust their positions if the market rallies against them, but they may not always be able to adjust their positions in the midst of a sell-off. So, they "lean short" to protect the initial move down. For many years, I was a proponent of this style of hedging. Having traded through several hard sell-offs, the feeling of frustration (and helplessness if you have on the wrong position) has left an indelible impression on my psyche. But never let it be said that you cannot teach an old dog new tricks. Looking at the data, I would lose money directionally many more days than I would make money (679 more days over the past 50 years, to be exact). And, of course, 50 years ago, the SPX was trading for around $82 versus the over $2,000 it currently trades for. So, to me, short deltas seem like an expensive insurance policy that pays few benefits even if the market falls hard, as your short gamma will quickly turn your short deltas to long anyway.

And that is truly the crux of the problem. If we put on a diversified portfolio with an overall, beta weighted delta and gamma of zero, we have little directional risk. Our directional risk is created by the directional bias we have at trade entry and by the fact that we run short gammas portfolios. There are many books written on how to dynamically hedge your short and long gamma positions most effectively. Though many of those books are valuable and put out great food for thought, none have truly convinced me that there is a best way. For purposes of this book, I want to hammer home only the points that if you diversify away much of your unique directional risk, as we have discussed, you need to worry only about your systematic directional risk, and that many of your directional risks are borne of your short gamma positions. The first point we have fully discussed. The second point is a basic premise of short premium trading. As the market moves, your deltas grow in a contrary direction to the market. In other words, as the market rises, your portfolio will get shorter deltas and as the market falls, your portfolio will get longer deltas. Short premium traders hope that the decay (theta) they receive each day outweighs the directional risk they take on.

With those points as backdrop, I find there are several ways to mitigate some of the directional risk. First, and foremost, by simply risk managing individual trades that hit our Kelly Criterion exit levels, we will usually reduce our overall delta risk. Assuming the creation of our portfolio did not happen instantaneously, and that our trades are not all "centered" on a single relative market price, trades should be ready to close at different "extremes" in price movement. Let us assume the market is falling and our portfolio deltas are getting longer; if a trade hits its Kelly Criterion loss level, that particular trade is likely contributing a good deal of long deltas to the book. That is one main reason why it would hit its loss level, in fact. So, when we risk manage (by closing) that trade, our book will instantaneously get shorter overall. Though we wish that loss event did not occur, it is one way we keep control of our risk, both on a trade-by-trade basis and, ultimately, on a portfolio level.

Another way of controlling our directional risk is to continually add trades that help to balance our deltas. If the market is falling and my deltas are getting longer, I will frequently look for underlyings that have not fallen with the market, and if their volatility levels make them good trade candidates, I will look for a short delta trade that fits my normal trade criterion. In the early stages of a sell-off, I will be vigilant not to get short deltas in a stock that is at 52-week highs, unless the trade has limited risk. The reason is that if the market reverses, these "breakout stocks" will often have explosive upward movement combined with rising volatility. In that case, the benefit I might get from their short deltas is often outweighed by the risk of the trade. Any stock under the 90th percentile of its annual price range is fair game for me. The premise for shorting these underlyings that are showing strength is that, again, we are hedging systematic risk. We are protecting against large market moves where traders tend to sell everything, and everything moves down together (implied correlation approaches one). These stronger stocks are places traders and investors will look first to off-load risk, making these "catch-up underlyings" prime candidates for us. Of course, that assumes we get in before everyone else finds them. If the market continues going south and you wait too long, you will find few stragglers to trade. Furthermore, though these trades reduce your long deltas, if the market continues to fall, your long deltas keep growing (due to your short gamma) and will eventually engulf and overtake your efforts to control them by adding your typical, properly sized, short delta trades. Of course, the advantage of using these types of trades is that though they do, in fact, reduce some risk, they also add potential profitability. If the market stops falling, or even reverses, these short delta trades may still add to your profitability. That is because, in general, as the market falls, implied volatility rises and you are getting to sell calls or call spreads at a higher volatility level. If the market reverses, your short premium, short delta trade will have the benefit of falling implied volatility to offset the short deltas of the trade. An extended reversal, however, will bite you anyway, while the trades you were protecting move back to profitability.

Another means of protecting your deltas is by rolling the untested side of any strangles or iron condors you have on your sheets. Let me illustrate this with an example. Let's say a few weeks ago you sold some SPX strangles where each side of the trade had a five delta. The market has now risen considerably, and your short call now has a 22 delta while your put has a 1 delta. The short put will likely be trading for dimes while the call is trading for many dollars. Furthermore, the short 21 deltas (times however many contracts you sold), beta weighted to the SPY, for example, may be a major contributor to the short delta problems of your portfolio. If there is enough time left to expiration (at least two weeks, but preferably three or more), it may be a good risk/return trade to roll up the untested puts. I would roll them back to the original 5 delta level I was comfortable with when I first placed the trade. Though this helps only marginally, as

I am still short 17 deltas, it does help and gives me a greater credit with which to work for my Kelly Criterion. I will never be able to "flatten out" my deltas using this technique, but I can help reduce the oversized delta position while still maintaining risk parameters with which I am comfortable. If I have multiple strangles in this situation, I can potentially get my deltas back to a very comfortable level. If not, I look to add more delta offsetting trades, as we discussed.

Though, as we just discussed, a good portfolio has trades that were entered over time, with trades centered on various prices, individual trade management may not be enough to reduce your overall portfolio risk in the event of a major sell-off or rally. And since it is the systematic risk we are discussing here, there are times we need to control our deltas with futures or underlying instruments (like stocks). These instruments' deltas are not affected by gamma and do not diminish over time and movement. Of course, that can be a double-edged sword, so I use this technique sparingly and I pick my spots carefully. I also size the trades to cover a fixed percentage of my deltas that are beta weighted to the future or stock I am trading. And if the market move is reasonably controlled, if I cover a losing trade due to it hitting Kelly Criterion or because of a change in assumption, I will also reduce my hedge accordingly. As I use this method sparingly, let me explain what might cause me to enter into such a hedge. If the market is starting to fall precipitously, the S&Ps are nearing a major psychological barrier, which usually means a century mark like 1,800, 1,900, or 2,000, and my deltas are getting uncomfortably long (yet no trade is hitting an exit point), I might place a sell stop order in the futures five to seven points below the century mark. My assumption here is that if the market has broken through, many sell stops might be hit or traders may take losses, thus accelerating the sell-off. The trade in the underlying or future will give me some protection for as long as I need it. There are other times where I feel there is some buying pressure or selling pressure at some price that I want to use to scalp. In this case, if my deltas are particularly large in one direction, I will take the scalp only if it lessens my risk. That is, if my deltas are very long, I would take the scalp only if the first leg was a short delta trade. If the scalp is actually adding to my directional risk, it would be very rare that I would take that trade. I call this "scalping around my position deltas," as those deltas are truly the impetus for the trade entry.

Another means of adding offsetting deltas to my portfolio is through the use of long debit spreads. As we discussed previously, I normally buy these spreads by purchasing the one strike in the money option and selling the one strike out of the money option. Though this can help offset my deltas, it is limited in how many deltas it can add as it is a limited risk and limited profitability trade. As such, I will often trade them a bit wider and buy two strikes or even three strikes out of the money, with the short option the same distance away from the stock price. I keep them balanced so as not to pay theta on the trade. The positive theta I collect on my short premium trades is "currency" I may choose to use to help mitigate risk. But if I am going to use it, I want to use it effectively. As such, I want to use it to mitigate directional and volatility risk, not just one or the other. We will look more at this in a minute.

A final means of controlling my delta risk, assuming the market move feels like it is "growing teeth," is to take off, or reduce the size of, trades that have not moved much as of yet. Though they may be small losers, if the risk in the portfolio is growing to an uncomfortable level, sometimes reducing the size of some of your trades before they go bad can both help down the road and allow you the mental wherewithal to properly manage your positions and add new, better risk/return trades. I know that last statement may sound strange, but until you have lived through a major market move where your positions start to cause you financial "pain," you will not be aware how mentally taxing it can be. You start to panic and your mind can all but shut down. This is exactly why you need to have and follow strict, mechanical rules for exiting trades. If you follow them, you may have a bad month, but you will be around to recoup the lost money when the market normalizes. You will be off and running again. If you panic and mentally shut down, the market move may be the last one you can afford to participate in for a while!

Now that we have spoken extensively about managing deltas on a portfolio level, we will begin to look at how to manage or mitigate the volatility risk in our portfolio. Though there are other risks, such as interest rate risk, dividend risk, and early exercise risk, volatility risk and the way it affects our positions are fairly unique to options trading. We have already spoken about how implied volatility changes with market movement, but I want to quickly review the basics. We will move quickly!

- We measure our volatility risk by looking at our portfolio's vega.
- There is no effect on our vega when we beta weight our portfolio.
- Each one point move in vega will make us or cost us the dollar amount of the portfolio's vega, assuming all vegas move in concert. In the real world, however, that is normally not how it works. Different underlyings' vegas will move to their own drummers, so to speak.
- The CBOE implied correlation index gives us some idea as to how correlated the volatility movements are between underlyings.
- When the market falls quickly, several things happen. Generally, this drop will cause the implied volatility of the options to rise. It will also cause the correlations of the implied volatility levels between underlyings to rise.

- When an equity or equity index rallies, generally the implied volatility will fall. This is almost always true of indices and ETFs, and often true of equities.
- When a stock breaks out to all-time, or even 52-week, high prices, the volatility path will often invert. That means if the stock continues to rise, the implied volatility of its options will often begin to rise with it. (This may also happen if the stock is a takeover candidate.)

With this as a backdrop, remember that we are dealing with the portfolio view (a diversified portfolio) of our vega in this section. A few years ago, this was a much more difficult, uninteresting topic, with few choices as to how to proceed. But with the development of the volatility complex, there are a growing number of alternatives available to traders.

We will begin by discussing the main alternative we have had since the beginning of options trading. Though, as we have discussed, the probabilities of short option trading have an edge over long premium trading, there certainly is no reason why you cannot have some long premium in your portfolio. In fact, almost (or possibly all) professional traders have both long and short premium in their portfolios. In fact, the main strategy employed by professional options traders is called volatility arbitrage. Investopedia defines volatility arbitrage as "trading strategies that attempt to exploit differences between the forecasted future volatility of an asset and the implied volatility of options based on that asset." Though that is partly true, the definition can be expanded to include the purchase or sale of options in anticipation of a rise or fall of the implied volatility in the future. Traders who employ a volatility arbitrage strategy generally play from both the long and the short side of the volatility trade. If they believe an underlying's implied volatility is too low, either because the underlying is moving around more than implied by the options price, because of an upcoming event, or because the implied volatility is just too low for that underlying, then they will buy premium. If the option's implied volatility is too high, then they will sell premium. But most traders, most of the time, will run an overall short premium portfolio due to the edge short options give them. Turning this back to our discussion of portfolio management, what this might mean is that if the market is beginning to fall and you are worried about your volatility risk, buy some "relatively cheap volatility." We spoke before about how the implied correlation will rise in a sell-off as traders basically sell any underlying or buy any options premium that might protect their portfolio. With this foreknowledge, if something starts to seem amiss and your senses are telling you the market may see rocky roads ahead, you may wish to jump out and buy premium in an underlying whose implied volatility is very low in its 52-week percentile. If you are right, as implied correlation rises, the implied volatility of that underlying will play "catch up," giving you some needed protection. If you are wrong, since the implied volatility was so cheap in the first place, the trade may cost you some theta. But if the overall portfolio is still short gamma and long theta, you are just spending a bit of the "currency" created by the short premium trades.

Another means of controlling our volatility risk is via the newest, and ever changing, asset class in our options universe, called the volatility complex. Though there are many pieces to the complex, I will focus on the VIX options and futures. I will also discuss the structure and use of the ETFs, like VXX and UVXY. Lastly, we will look at the direction of recent growth and what it means for the future of volatility as an asset class.

The VIX is a product trademarked by the Chicago Board Options Exchange (CBOE). The futures have traded since March 2004, while the options began trading in February 2006. The VIX seeks to replicate the 30-day implied volatility of the SPX by utilizing a strip of out of the money calls and puts in the SPX options. Usually, the options utilized are a weighted average of the front two months in order to replicate the 30-day period. However, there are times during a 35-day expiration cycle where only the front month options are necessary. (The VIX technically is the square root of a variance swap, and not a volatility swap, but this means little to our trading.) As we have already discussed the volatility path for index options at some length, I will comment only that as the market falls, we generally see VIX rise. The current three-year correlation between the SPX and the VIX is − 0.7127, showing that they are strongly inversely correlated, yet not as perfectly as some traders believe.

To understand how we can use the VIX to hedge our volatility risk, we must first understand how the VIX futures work, as the options trade to the futures. Let me explain. Calendar spreads in most equity index futures trade to what is known as "a basis." That is, there is a mathematical relationship between the E-mini S&P futures prices from one quarter to the next. If we know the price of the June S&Ps, we can derive the proper price of the September S&Ps, within a small margin of error. And, therefore, all expiration cycles of SPX options prices can be driven off the front month future, or seemingly so, since they are all mathematically tied. This is not true at all in the VIX futures. Each month (and there are currently eight successive VIX futures contracts listed) trades to the market's perception of volatility for that month. In other words, there is no mathematical relationship between the futures calendar spreads. And each month's options trade to the future with the same expiration date. So, March options use the March futures as their underlying, while the May options use the May futures. Despite that, all the options and all the futures expire to the VIX cash price. That means that the price of the front month future will coincide with the price of the spot VIX (which is a derived value and not easily tradable) at the time of its expiration. So, before we can intelligently trade the VIX options or futures, we need to look at and make sense of the relationship between the various months' futures prices.

Let us begin by looking at a normal environment, where VIX is relatively low and the market is stable or rising. This describes the marketplace a vast majority of the time. During these times, the VIX futures generally form a contango pattern, where each successive, further out month has a higher price. And the spot VIX usually has the lowest price of all. Table 9.2 shows this during the trading day of September 3, 2014.

As of this date, the front month option and future expire in 13 days and will converge to the same number at that time. If the volatility of the SPX does not change, then the future will fall $1.39 to meet the VIX. Since the front month future is trading with $1.39 too much value (compared to the spot), the options are also trading to a higher-priced "underlying." When the VIX complex is in this type of contango formation, you give up a great deal of edge when you buy calls. On the other hand, puts are trading for a cheaper price than the spot would have you believe. This is an issue of "basis," and it is one that makes protecting your portfolio with outright VIX calls or VIX futures somewhat risky. On the other hand, sometimes a good insurance policy can be costly. If the market turns south, VIX can move up quickly and strongly. From the low level the VIX is at in Table 9.2, a mere 1 percent down move in the SPX could easily cause the VIX to make up the $1.39 edge you would give up if you bought VIX calls for protection. And since VIX can be quite explosive in

TABLE 9.2 VIX Contango

Symbol	Price
VIX	12.06
/VXU4	13.45
/VXV4	14.45
/VXX4	15.12
/VZU4	15.53
/VXF5	16.25
/VXG5	16.79
/VXH5	17.15
/VXJ5	17.50

a continued sell-off, the option premium you give up can be rewarded handsomely. Once again, the risk versus reward equation must be weighed instead of considering only the risk. For this reason, you will never find me short VIX calls, though I am occasionally long VIX puts due to the extra edge the basis gives me. This, of course, does not mitigate short premium risk. It is a trade in and of itself. Another consideration when trading VIX options is the implied volatility of the VIX options. Though you can view the implied volatility on a strike-by-strike basis on the options chain, the CBOE also publishes the "VIX of the VIX," as it is called, under the symbol VVIX. For the past 12 months, the VVIX has traded between roughly 60 percent and 120 percent and is currently (at the time of Table 9.2) trading a bit over 80 percent. That is some pretty lofty volatility. Yet the 20-day realized volatility of the VIX is, more times than not, greater than its implied volatility. This is one of the few underlyings I know that can claim that! There is one other consideration when trading VIX options. Because the VIX is inversely correlated with the SPX, its volatility skew is also inverse that of the SPX. This means that the volatility of the out of the money calls rises the farther out of the money they go. As such, call spreads take on a bit more attractiveness, because if you buy a call spread, you are buying a call with an implied volatility that is lower than the call you are selling. As such, the spreads trade "cheap." The downside to buying call spreads is that they have limited profit potential and therefore provide only limited protection to an unlimited risk, short premium book. They are much more effective if you have a limited risk book made up of mostly spreads.

On occasion, the term structure of the VIX futures, and synthetically its options, will give you a way of protecting your portfolio with an excellent risk versus return profile. In fact, this protective trade will often make you money even if the market does not sell off and implied volatility does not rise. If this sounds too good to be true, there is usually a reason, and in this case, the usual relationships can get a bit out of whack at times. But I find this trade works well enough that I jump in every chance I get. Remember that our goal for the trade is to protect our short premium book from a rise in volatility. So, I looked at the term structures of the VIX futures from July 1, 2008, to the present. Specifically, I tracked the spread between the first two months (second month price minus first month price) and between the second and third expiration cycles prices (third month minus second month). Specifically, I wanted to determine two pieces of information.

1. What happens to the spreads when the market sells off?
2. In a normal market, how wide does the spread usually get and where does it trade near expiration?

First, I looked at when the market falls hard. I went back and looked at the two calendar spreads on July 21, 2011, the day before the SPX began its quick descent from 1,350 to 1,100. The second month to first month calendar (we will call that the front month calendar) was trading for +1.70, while the third month to second calendar (we will call this the second month calendar) was trading for +1.20. The next day, as the market began its descent, the spreads started to collapse. By August 11, the front month spread had inverted (gone from contango to backwardation) and was trading for −7.50, while the second month calendar was trading on that date for −0.55. Clearly, when the market fell, if we were short a calendar from before the descent, we would have cleaned up. (Remember that each spread is worth $1,000 per point, so the front month spread would have netted us $9,200 minus commissions per spread, and the second month would have given us a $1,750 profit.) But, also clearly, the front month calendar had the most volatility (sensitivity) to the fall and would have been the better choice of the spreads. Thinking about this logically, we experience the same phenomenon in most other underlyings during a sell-off, particularly the equity indices. It is the sensitivity of the front month to these moves that causes it to rise much quicker than the back months, leaving us in backwardation of implied volatility. The front month runs up to meet the current historical volatility, while the back months move less, in anticipation that the volatility will burn itself out and revert to a more normal level by the time they expire. I wanted to see at least one more major data point to verify that this trend was as clear-cut as it seemed. So, I went back to the large sell-off during 2008–2009. In August 2008, before the big sell-off took place, the front month calendar was trading for around +1.40 and the second month calendar was trading for around +0.10. But by October 16, 2008, by which time the SPX had fallen from around $1,310 to around $866, the front month spread bottomed at −21.1 and the second month spread got to −10.25 a few days later. (To be clear, these are the widest the spreads have traded, so this is clearly the extreme.) Again, the spreads collapsed when the market collapsed, with the front month calendar having the largest move. So, it seems that having short calendar spreads in the VIX futures provides us with some protection against a sharp market decline. But at what level could we sell the spread and what is our cost/risk if the market does not fall precipitously? I took a two-step approach to this question. First, I wanted to know how steep the contango has gone when the market does not fall, and second, I wanted to know where the spread usually went to for expiration in normal conditions. These would be the extremes of my assessed risk. Of course, this does not mean things cannot get worse in the future than they have been in the past, but we need to set some kind of expectation to make an intelligent risk versus return assessment. Looking back at the data from the past six years, we can see that the front month spread has widened (twice) to a bit over $5. Both times it got to this extreme, the market had come off a sell-off three months prior, and the SPX implied volatility was hitting an extremely low level. With traders trying to jettison their front month volatility, the market for the spreads got particularly wide. The second month spreads widened also, but to a much lesser extent in keeping with the same pattern we saw when the spreads contracted. In looking at the dates of these extreme readings, it is interesting to note that almost all of them occurred right around expiration of the front month contract. Exclusive of expiration, since mid-June of 2008, the spread has been under $3 93.3 percent of the time. Almost every occurrence happened in one of five blocks of time. Furthermore, the spread traded for under $2 75.89 percent of the time. The front month's median spread price for this period of time was $1.15.

One point that needs to be made about the spread is that until fairly recently, there has been limited liquidity in the VIX futures. This will certainly exacerbate the volatility in the spread. Bringing the history of the spread to more relevance, I looked at the last two years of data to see how the spread has behaved. During this period of time, the spread has never closed above $3 and has closed under $2 98.61 percent of the time. In fact, the front month spread has closed below $1.50 88.49 percent of the time, and had a median price of $0.90. It should be noted that during this period the market has been upward trending most of the time with implied volatility generally under 20. (The VIX traded above 20 on only 11 days during that period.) Thus, we did not experience the rising volatility, with a narrowing of the spread, followed by a falling volatility with an out-sized expansion of the spread. But since in this section we are speaking of ways to protect our portfolio from volatility risk, I believe an awareness of the particular market conditions in which selling the spread, and from what price, generates the greatest risk to the strategy should be enough. Breaking this strategy down into a practical trading strategy, I have devised the following five rules for my own trading. Each rule will include a discussion of why the rule exists. I have traded this strategy for only the past two years and have had a 95 percent success rate, as I have made money on exactly 19 out of 20 trades. I do not have a statistically significant number of live occurrences, but the success rate is strongly supported by my back testing.

1. In general, I will not sell the spread if there is less than 15 days to expiration of the front month future. Knowing that expiration pricing can push the closing price of VIX around artificially (and therefore the

price of the front month future, since it expires to the same price as the cash index's opening print), I never want to hold these spreads on expiration day. And since I know that short-term aberrations can occur in the spread market, I want to give myself time to work out of the trade should I not need its protection services during the lifetime of the futures. This means that this protective trade is viable only a little over half the time, based on days to expiration alone.

2. The price at which I am willing to sell the front month spread is dependent on the situation. If we are in a calm market, and have been in one for some time, I will usually look to start selling the spread at $1.30. The price of the spread is less than this 76.79 percent of the time (using the shorter time frame study) and I know that if nothing happens in the market, I have a good chance (95.8 percent over the past two years) that the spread will be lower at some point before the spread expires. So, to the point, even if the spread does not get to protect my portfolio by providing profit at a time when the implied volatility is rising, it usually will make me money anyway. Instead of paying for an "insurance policy," I am getting paid to own an insurance policy! Of course, this trade setup happens in less than one out of four expiration cycles, so this protective trade with profit potential in all conditions is not something that comes around every day.

3. If I am short the calendar spread and it is five days before the front month expiration and we have not had a market sell-off, I will look to buy back the spread. I hope to pay no more than $1 for it, though with two days to expiration, if I have not had an opportunity to buy it back as of yet, I will pay up to the price I sold it for. If we are in the last trading day before the front month expires, I will buy it back and take my loss. I do not want to submit myself to the expiration markup or markdown. This has happened to me only once. This, my worst occurrence of this spread, cost me 20 cents per spread. My best trade has netted me far greater. But even if nothing happens in the market, I usually make 20 to 40 cents at a minimum on the trade.

4. If the market begins to fall and my portfolio is relatively undefended against a volatility expansion, I am willing to sell the spread at 90 cents. As I stated, this is the median price of the spread over the past two years. Even if the market falls only 4 or 5 percent, the spread is likely to fall to zero or a small negative value. Thus, the risk versus return of the trade is still good.

5. As we have seen when we looked at the extremes of the trade, it is rare that I am willing to do the trade in reverse. In other words, when the

spread is in backwardation, that may present a probabilistic opportunity to buy the front month spread in hopes the spread will move back into contango. But the risk of the spread moving much further into backwardation exists, as occurred in 2008–2009. This turns the risk versus return of the trade on its head. And since buying the contango adds to the risk of a short volatility portfolio, there is no justifiable reason from a portfolio management perspective to make the trade. However, there are two conditions in which I have been known to dabble in the long contango trade. The first is if I was able to aggressively defend my deltas and/or vega as the market fell and it feels as though the market has bottomed and is turning back upward. I now may purchase the contango to manage my risk as volatility falls and the market rises. I have also been known, on rare occasions, to trade my assumption that the market has cratered and is beginning its ascent by buying the contango exclusive of my portfolio. In either case, because of the risk in the trade, I keep it on a short leash. In other words, I will determine how much I believe I will make on the trade if I am correct and set my exit (loss) strategy so that I take my loss at half of my profit potential. A quick note to consider is that if you are correct and the market rallies, it takes only a short time for the VIX futures to return to contango. Of course, this depends from how deep in backwardation it began. But it will take a while for the contango to return to a level (like $0.90) where I will be comfortable selling it as an opening trade. As a general rule, the contango seems to get to around 45 to 65 cents, before it pauses for a week or two, when moving back into a contango pattern of a calm market. Since 2008, the front month spread has been in contango 82.9 percent of the time, and in the past two-year period, it has been in contango 96.6 percent of the time.

Assuming that we are selling the contango to defend our portfolio, how do we size the trade? That is a question that cannot be answered without using a specific portfolio example. And many assumptions will go into the decision, many of which are personal. So there is no definitive answer. That being said, since the goal is to hedge your implied volatility risk, I urge you to take a good look at the vega of your portfolio. Keep in perspective that volatility risk is a "fleeting thing." Since implied volatility affects only the extrinsic value of your options, and since the extrinsic value of your options goes to zero at expiration, you are trying to defend against short-term losses in your portfolio. Longer-term losses are supplied by stock price at expiration as compared to your short strike prices. In essence, delta is a far greater, more permanent disease for your portfolio. But until you have lived through a volatility explosion, you cannot fathom how painful it is nonetheless. And if your account is not large enough to weather the storm, you could be forced to liquidate positions at an inopportune time, leading to very permanent losses. So, mitigating your volatility risk is a wise strategy, if the costs are not too great. If I get to sell the contango on my terms, as outlined in the foregoing rules, I do the following:

1. I estimate how far I believe the front month VIX calendar spread will fall for a 5 percent down move in the market. I then multiply that amount by 1,000 to put the move into dollar terms since the spread is worth $1,000 per point.
2. I estimate how far I believe volatility will rise for that same 5 percent move.
3. I multiply my portfolio's vega by the assumed rise in volatility to arrive at an "assumed dollar loss" due to the volatility increase.
4. I next divide the "assumed dollar loss" by the estimated calendar spread gain we arrived at in Step 1. This will give us the number of calendar spreads we need to sell to cover 100 percent of our estimated vega risk. I can then determine if I want to cover all or part of my vega risk and size my trade accordingly.

One of the sticky points of managing portfolio risk is that we are managing trade risk mechanically both via the Kelly Criterion and via proper trade sizing, which we will discuss in the next section. Do we allocate the profits made in our risk mitigating trades and allocate them to the losing trades? If not, how do we view and manage the portfolio as a whole? I believe that is a bit of a personal decision. But I have a very strong (personal) answer for my own trading. I am convinced of the value of managing my trades via the Kelly Criterion. The math works. So I continue, even in tough times, to take my profits and losses according to plan. If I have risk mitigating trades on that counterbalance my risks, I have sized them according to my portfolio risk. If trades hit their exits as profit or losses, I reassess the balance of my risks in my portfolio. For example, say a short vega trade hits its Kelly Criterion loss level, but I have short calendar spreads on that are covering, partially covering, or more than covering the loss of the losing trade. I will take my loss according to plan, and then, right after I close the trade, I will take my profit on a percentage of my risk reducing trade, whose purpose it was to cover that trade's vega and/or delta risk. I continue to match the risk of my portfolio to the power of my risk reducing trades virtually on a daily basis. I do not want to end up with a position contrary to what my original intent was, unless my assumptions have changed.

Of course, the VIX is not the only product to live in the volatility asset class. Many other products have already been developed, with more hitting the market with seeming regularity. One such product is the RVX. The RVX is to the Russell 2000 what the VIX is to the SPX. Though there are options listed on the RVX, the volume as of yet is small. As such, I do not yet trade it. But if volume picks up and spreads tighten, I will use the RVX in place of the SPX when my portfolio is full of smaller capitalized stocks. After all, since the goal is to mitigate the risk in my portfolio, it is best to match the defensive trade to the risk of the offensive trade.

One of the most liquid products in the volatility asset class is VXX. A lot of attention (and volume) flows to VXX as it not only is optionable but also has a tradable underlying, unlike the VIX. Since the underlying does not expire, I know traders who hold the underlying in their portfolios to hedge their volatility risk. But unless you understand the product, I would be very careful using it to hedge volatility risk for any length of time. Let us start by looking at the description of the product from iPath's website.

> The S&P 500 VIX Short-Term Futures Index Total Return (the "Index") is designed to provide access to equity market volatility through CBOE Volatility Index futures. The Index offers exposure to a daily rolling long position in the first and second month VIX futures contracts and reflects the implied volatility of the S&P 500 at various points along the volatility forward curve. (iPath, www.ipathetn.com/us/product/vxx/)

From a practical aspect, what this description is telling us is that every day the managers of the fund are purchasing the second month VIX future and selling out some of their front month VIX futures. They do this to maintain the volatility exposure of a 30-day time frame. Since we are in a contango most of the time, the managers are purchasing a higher-priced future and selling a lower-priced future on most days. This, along with the commissions and fees involved and the bid/ask spread they must cross (or at least partially cross) on every trade, leads to a natural degradation in VXX's price. So, the product's price is basically designed to go to zero! To account for this, and to keep the product alive (and the fees rolling in), the managers will frequently declare a reverse split in the product to artificially boost the share price and keep it viable. With this as a backdrop, VXX is not a good long-term hedge against our volatility risk as the product's price "decays" on most days. The only time I use VXX to protect my portfolio is if I get caught without enough protection, the contango is not steep, or better yet is flat or in backwardation, and I want quick protection. Then, I will reach out and buy some underlying for a short-term ride. But when the market ceases its sell-off, I am quick to jettison the shares of VXX due to their natural propensity to drop.

Other volatility ETFs, like UVXY, which is a leveraged ETF (think VXX on steroids), suffer from the same price drag issues as VXX. Also, since UVXY seeks to replicate two times the daily volatility movement, it does not track our portfolio's volatility as well as other products. For these reasons, I never use this product as a portfolio hedge. If I trade it, I trade it speculatively for very short-term trades. In this way, I do not let the overnight activity of the managers, or the pricing discrepancies, affect and control the trade.

There are other volatility indices that are optionable. However, many of these are of little, or lesser, value to the typical trader looking to hedge a portfolio as the products on which they are based do not match a typical portfolio. That being said, for traders more globally focused, that statement may have less validity. There are currently volatility indices on the emerging market ETF, "EEM." It is listed under the symbol "VXEEM." "VXEWZ" is the volatility index on the Brazilian ETF, "EWZ." If you trade a portfolio of stocks that make up either of those indices, these are applicable underlyings for you. There are also volatility indices in some of the commodities. In particular, gold (GVZ) and oil (OVX) are listed and optionable. At this point, none of these products have much volume. If the volume were to pick up, I would expect a large expansion in the number of listed volatility indices.

There are currently five individual equities that have their own volatility indices listed. None of these are tradable, however, and are informational only. The stocks whose volatility indices are listed are Apple ("VXAPL"), Amazon ("VXAZN"), Goldman Sachs ("VXGS"), Google ("VXGOG"), and IBM ("VXIBM"). For more sophisticated traders, these indices contain some information about both volatility and skew, and may be worth tracking. For the rest of us, beyond showing us a general landscape of what is happening to volatility in five major stocks, there are much better ways of assessing the volatility marketplace through our trading platforms.

Trade Sizing

You may be wondering why a section called "Trade Sizing" is part of a portfolio management discussion and not part of a section about choosing your trades, or something similar. Though it truly can be placed in either type of discussion, I wanted to stress the point that much of the portfolio risk management we do should be done at trade entry via appropriate position sizing. As we saw in the previous paragraph, trade size adjustment (after the fact) can be a useful means of risk managing your portfolio. But if you get an overnight market shock, a lot of damage can occur to your account before you get to make that adjustment. For that reason, it is far more important that you size your trades properly when you first enter into it. And like everything else I do in trading, I size my trades mechanically.

I occasionally get questions from colleagues who ask, "Why do you use the Kelly Criterion for trade exits (which is a technique unique to me), yet do not use it for trade sizing (which is a technique used by many hedge funds)?" The basic premise of using Kelly Criterion for position sizing is that the better the odds of success of a trade, the more you should "bet" on a given trade. But if option markets are efficient, the risk versus return of each trade should be somewhat balanced by the options' prices. Therefore, sizing the higher probability trades to be larger than the lower probability trades should come as a natural process. By using the Kelly Criterion exit strategy, as defined in an earlier chapter as a percentage of the credit received for the sale, you are in essence following the "higher probability, bigger size" rule.

How do we size our trades then? For our probability-based trading to mathematically work as defined, we need all our trades to take on approximately the same size in terms of profits and losses and not in terms of contracts. If we do not do that, we risk the situation where our probabilities work, but our profits are negative. Here is a quick example. Let us say we trade consistent trade sizes instead of consistent risk sizes. Assume we sold five contracts for each of our trades and our trades consisted of the following 30 delta put sales, all in the same expiration cycle:

CLF 14 puts for $0.59
JCP 10 puts for $0.35
P 25 puts for $1.25
CMG 650 puts for $13.00

Suppose we make money on 75 percent of our trades. This is true to the probabilities as it is slightly higher than the 70 percent probability of profit defined by our option chain. But if the loser is CMG, even if we followed the Kelly Criterion, we will clearly have a loss.

Many traders will choose their position sizes by balancing the buying power reduction of each trade. There are again major flaws in that design, in my opinion. For example, how would you mathematically adjust for the fact that one trader could be trading in a cash account, while another is trading in a portfolio margin account? You cannot say the margin allotted is proportional as the cash account is allotted on a trade-by-trade basis, while the margin in a portfolio margin account is assigned based on an overall portfolio's risk. Thus, they can differ greatly. And it is not correct to make the argument that internally to each type of account the math works. Math is math. The same profitability cannot be achieved if the sizing differs between the accounts but the probabilities in each account are the same. So how do we go about sizing our trades? While no method is perfect, I go back to what I find to be mathematically consistent and intellectually sensible. I use the levels at which I would take losses on each trade based on my application of the Kelly Criterion. I then try to size each trade so that my loss level is the same percentage of my trading account. As usual, let us visualize this by following through with the foregoing example. First, let us define our Kelly Criterion exits. Assume our probability of profit is around 70 percent (note that it is probably a little better as we sold a 30 delta option so our breakeven is a bit better) and we wish to take our profit at 65 percent of maximum profit (which is the same as the credit received). Also, we are looking for a 10 percent edge. This would mean we would be trying to take our losses at around 100 percent of max profit, per the Kelly Criterion formula we presented earlier. Let us further assume we are trading in an account that has $250,000 of capital and that we are willing to risk only 1 percent of our portfolio on any given trade. Thus, our max loss at Kelly Criterion exit would be around $2,500. Conveniently, by using 100 percent of maximum possible profit as our loss exit, we will look to close our trades if the trade shows 100 percent loss of the capital received. Using the following table, calculating the dollar losses at exit, and dividing that amount by our $2,500 loss amount, gives us trade sizes as shown in the right-most column:

	Credit Received	Exit Price	Loss per Contract	Size for 1 Percent Loss
CLF	$0.59	$1.18	$59	42
JCP	$0.35	$0.70	$35	71
P	$1.25	$2.50	$125	20
CMG	$13.00	$26.00	$1,300	2

At first glance, the dramatic differences in trade sizes might look imbalanced. Yet this is far more balanced than what buying power reduction or any other commonly purported means of trade sizing might determine. The one risk that we need to account for is gap risk. Though we hope to take off our losing trades at a 1 percent portfolio loss, this is not always possible. Large, overnight gaps do occur. And even in a diversified portfolio, these gaps can cause a single trade to "outdistance" our projected maximum loss. It is for this very reason that I do two things:

1. I give myself an extra 10 to 15 percent edge in probabilities when defining my Kelly Criterion levels.
2. I size my trades to a lower portfolio size than most traders. One percent is far lower than many traders' risk tolerance. And using the Kelly Criterion sizing formula, it is far too low. But I prefer to take lower returns in exchange for lower risk. In this way, these outsized losses are still reasonable and absorbable. Also, it leaves me room to roll the untested side of strangles, thereby increasing my risk in the trade (since I took in more credits with which to recalculate my Kelly Criterion exits). That does not mean that you should trade that small. A maximum loss of 2 percent of your portfolio for any given trade is also very reasonable. Each trader needs to define his own levels. But I caution you that for me, much more than 2.5 percent can get painful if you have an outsized loser due to a gap. Until you have lived through one of those occurrences, you will not have a good means of assessing your tolerance. Thus, as always, I suggest you walk before you run by keeping your trade sizes a bit smaller until you get stung. Once stung, if you feel you can size up a bit, have at it. But be methodical when you do so and size all your trades consistently.

Early Exercise

One of the questions that seems to confuse traders is, "When should I exercise options early, and when should I expect to be assigned early?" Put another way, when I asked one of the couples I coach if they wanted to see a section on early exercise in this book, their response was, "When we both started out in options the *one* question that stopped us dead was 'If we are selling something, when do people come to collect?'"

In my opinion, it is early exercise that led to the demise of the OEX pit, which used to be the single largest option pit in the world, and where I spent 10 years of my career. OEX is an American option that settles into cash, as opposed to single equity options, which are American options that settle into stock, and the SPX, which is a European option that is not subject to early exercise. Institutional traders who sold covered calls against their portfolios did not want people to "come collect their cash" (meaning they got assigned) early. As such, over a period of years, the SPX became the premier institutional equity index options trading pit.

But many traders that I coach cannot afford to trade the large SPX product and trade SPY instead. This, like all listed individual equity options, is American in nature and is therefore subject to early exercise. And I see a lot of money given away needlessly in the SPY on the day the ETF goes ex-dividend, which it does quarterly.

In the low interest rate environment we have lived in during the past few years, there is a simple, shortcut rule for estimating when you should exercise early. It is all you need for now. We will get to that after we look at the entire framework for the early exercise decision. But once interest rates rise again, which they inevitably will, you can come back to this chapter to review these concepts again. We will begin with a basic understanding of the premise for early exercise.

Very simply, the owner of an in the money option exercises the option early (turns it into stock, cash, or futures, depending on the specifications of the contract being exercised) if the cost of continuing to carry the position is greater than the benefit of doing so. It really comes down to a very simple cost versus benefit comparison. This comparison, though the same in principle, is slightly different for calls versus puts. Therefore, we will break this down separately, beginning with calls.

When you exercise a call, you are giving up the calls to buy the stock at the strike price. Looking back at the relationship between stock and synthetic stock, we see the following:

Long Stock is offset, or hedged by, "short calls + long puts."

The right side of the statement (in quotes) is synthetic short stock, which balances out the long stock on the left. When we exercise calls, you are in effect selling the calls (since you will no longer have them) and getting long stock in return. But since you have not yet purchased the puts (to complete the equation), you have, in essence, synthetically sold the put. This will become important as we go on.

First, we look at the benefits of exercising our calls.

1. One of the disadvantages of owning calls instead of stock is that you do not receive any dividends that are paid. Only the stock holder receives these payments. So, the first benefit of exercising the call into stock is you receive the dividend.
2. In the money calls, depending on the price of the underlying, can trade for a significant amount of money. If you exercise the calls, you no longer have to pay the cost of carry on the call premium. As I stated before, in low interest rate environments, this generally does not amount to much. But as rates rise, this becomes a much more serious consideration.

Next, we look at the costs of exercising our calls:

1. We now have to pay carry on our stock. This is a more significant cost of carry than that of the long calls, but again, is often not very significant in low interest rate environment.

2. As we discussed before, when we exercise our call, we are synthetically selling the put of the same strike in the same expiration cycle. Thus, the current market price of the put is a cost to us because to re-create our long call position, we would need to purchase that put.

Boiling this down to a formula, we get:

If Carry on the call + Dividend received is greater than Carry on the stock + Price at which we can purchase the put, then we exercise the call. If not, we do not exercise the call. Since the dividend is the biggest benefit to exercising, under normal conditions, the day before a stock goes ex-dividend is the only day we need to worry about early exercise of calls. And back to the shortcut we spoke about earlier, since interest rates are currently so low, the costs of carry are relatively low. Thus, the decision boils down to whether the dividend you would receive is greater than the cost of the corresponding put you are synthetically selling. If so, you exercise your call. If not, you hold the position.

Looking at an example shown in Figure 9.3, SPY went ex-dividend in the amount of $0.94 on June 20, 2014. Looking at the July puts the day before (June 19, 2014), every put up to and including the 191 strike has an offer that is significantly under the amount of the dividend. The 192 strike is barely under the dividend amount and, with the cost of exercising and the nominal amounts of carry, would be a toss-up. We also need to check on all our other expiration cycle options, as this holds true for every one of them. However, if you are trading longer dated options that will receive more than one dividend, this adds to the complexity of our analysis. In this case, our analysis requires a two-step approach. First, we check our cost versus benefit analysis until expiration of the option, being careful to count all dividends the stock would receive between now and that date. If the analysis says "exercise the call," we now need to perform the same analysis, but only up until the next ex-dividend date. In this case, we account for only the one dividend and use the number of days until the next ex-dividend date. If this test also says "exercise the calls," then we exercise. If not, what the numbers are telling you is that we need to wait until the next ex-dividend date and retest for an early exercise.

Now, we turn our attention to the early exercise of puts. Looking again at our synthetic relationship, if we exercise (same as if we sell) the put and get short stock in return, we are synthetically selling the call, since short stock is balanced by long call + short put. We will be short the put (relatively, since we lose a put from our position) and short stock as a result of the exercise.

FIGURE 9.3 SPY Options Chain Showing Early Exercise

UNDERLYING

| SPY | SPY TR S&P 500 ETF TR | Last 196.46 | Net Chng -.225 | Volume 85,928,320 | Open 196.43 | High 196.60 | Low 196.48 |

OPTION CHAIN — Strikes ALL — Spread Single — Layout Impl Vol, Probability OTM, Delta

	CALLS						PUTS				
Impl Vol (29) 100	Prob OTM	Delta	Bid	Ask	Strike	Exp	Bid	Ask	Impl Vol	Prob OTM	Delta
--	0.00%	1.00	30.30	30.51	166	JUL 14	.05	.07	25.64%	98.57%	-.01
--	0.00%	1.00	29.30	29.51	167	JUL 14	.05	.07	24.62%	98.53%	-.01
--	0.00%	1.00	28.29	28.50	168	JUL 14	.05	.08	24.26%	98.40%	-.01
--	0.00%	1.00	27.29	27.50	169	JUL 14	.07	.08	23.91%	98.17%	-.02
--	0.00%	1.00	26.29	26.50	170	JUL 14	.07	.09	23.29%	98.03%	-.02
--	0.00%	1.00	25.29	25.50	171	JUL 14	.07	.09	22.65%	97.88%	-.02
--	0.00%	1.00	24.29	24.49	172	JUL 14	.08	.10	21.98%	97.73%	-.02
--	0.00%	1.00	23.28	23.49	173	JUL 14	.08	.10	21.30%	97.56%	-.02
--	0.00%	1.00	22.28	22.49	174	JUL 14	.09	.11	20.77%	97.29%	-.02
--	0.00%	1.00	21.28	21.49	175	JUL 14	.10	.11	20.21%	97.01%	-.03
--	0.00%	1.00	20.28	20.49	176	JUL 14	.11	.12	19.59%	96.72%	-.03
--	0.00%	1.00	19.28	19.49	177	JUL 14	.12	.13	18.65%	96.50%	-.03
--	0.00%	1.00	18.28	18.49	178	JUL 14	.13	.14	18.19%	96.17%	-.03
--	0.00%	1.00	17.28	17.49	179	JUL 14	.15	.15	17.73%	95.62%	-.04
--	0.00%	1.00	16.27	16.48	180	JUL 14	.15	.17	17.00%	95.24%	-.04
--	0.00%	1.00	15.27	15.48	181	JUL 14	.16	.18	16.44%	94.63%	-.05
--	0.00%	1.00	14.27	14.48	182	JUL 14	.18	.20	15.82%	93.99%	-.05
--	0.00%	1.00	13.27	13.48	183	JUL 14	.20	.22	15.22%	93.19%	-.06
--	0.00%	1.00	12.27	12.48	184	JUL 14	.23	.24	14.63%	92.25%	-.07
--	0.00%	1.00	11.27	11.48	185	JUL 14	.26	.27	13.98%	91.23%	-.08
--	0.00%	1.00	10.27	10.48	186	JUL 14	.29	.30	13.43%	89.84%	-.09
--	0.00%	1.00	9.27	9.48	187	JUL 14	.33	.35	12.84%	88.24%	-.11
--	0.00%	1.00	8.27	8.48	188	JUL 14	.36	.40	12.24%	86.32%	-.13
--	0.00%	1.00	7.27	7.48	189	JUL 14	.44	.46	11.69%	83.88%	-.15
--	0.00%	1.00	6.27	6.48	190	JUL 14	.52	.54	11.15%	80.88%	-.18
--	0.00%	1.00	5.27	5.48	191	JUL 14	.62	.64	10.59%	77.31%	-.22
--	0.00%	1.00	4.31	4.50	192	JUL 14	.74	.76	10.10%	72.77%	-.26
7.96%	29.19%	.84	3.52	3.65	193	JUL 14	.90	.93	9.59%	67.39%	-.31
8.14%	37.68%	.71	2.79	2.89	194	JUL 14	1.10	1.13	9.07%	61.00%	-.38
8.10%	46.25%	.60	2.17	2.19	195	JUL 14	1.35	1.38	8.56%	53.50%	-.45
7.80%	55.18%	.50	1.56	1.59	196	JUL 14	1.66	1.70	6.56%	44.99%	-.54
7.55%	64.40%	.39	1.08	1.09	197	JUL 14	2.06	2.12	7.83%	36.07%	-.63
7.25%	73.47%	.29	.68	.71	198	JUL 14	2.60	2.64	7.32%	26.73%	-.72

Source: TD Ameritrade.

Since we have not yet purchased the call, we are synthetically short it. This is just the flip side of the call exercise.

The two benefits to exercising the put early are as follows:

1. We no longer have to pay the carry on our long put.
2. We will end up with short stock, which, once interest rates rise, may pay you a short stock rebate. A short stock rebate is carry in reverse. Your broker pays you an interest rate (though less than the rate they charge you for long stock) for the stock you are short. If you happen to be long the stock with your long put, then the benefit is you no longer have to pay carry on your long stock. These benefits are not identical because of the differing interest rates for long and short stock.

The costs associated with exercising the put are as follows:

1. If you are short the stock, you will have to pay the dividend to whoever loaned you the stock. Again, if you were long the stock, you no longer receive the dividend. These amount to the same cost.
2. You are giving up the extrinsic value of the call, since you are creating a synthetic short call.

When the benefits are greater than the costs, you have passed the most important test. Put exercises theoretically have two more minor tests. But rather than confuse you with a lot of detail you will not use frequently, if at all, we will confine ourselves to the foregoing. With interest rates low, there is almost never a time where we want to early exercise our puts. Once interest rates rise, however, you must start paying attention.

Conclusion

Simply described, trading options is an exercise in probability theory. It is not gambling and it is truly not "high finance." Properly approached, you should be able to make money virtually every year of your trading career, regardless of whether the market is up or down. Not many trading strategies can make that claim. But the key to success is in understanding the concept and management of risk. Every time you place a trade, a risk transference occurs. If you are a seller of options, you are taking on someone else's risk. Your job as a trader is to discern whether the price you are being paid for the option warrants you taking on that risk, as this is the side of the trade that most often presents money-making opportunities.

In this book, I have laid out a map for you to follow in setting up a profitable trading business. This can be a 5- or 10-minute per day business or a full-time endeavor. I covered option theory with a light stroke, but delved into the practical side with more enthusiasm. My purpose was to provide you, the trader/investor, with the information that is frequently not presented in books. In fact, you can spend many thousands of dollars in classes and still miss some of the topics presented here.

I am confident that a mastery of each of the sections will enhance your trading returns going forward. Choosing the right broker through which to trade is far more important than most realize. Ask those who traded through MF Global or PFGBest about their experiences, and you will begin to understand why. But fear of default is not the only reason your broker matters. Most are as safe, or even safer, than your bank. But if they do not provide a full-service trading platform that helps you with your probability-based options decisions, they should quickly fall off your radar screen. Trade execution is another key area that is overlooked. Investors often worry about their commissions and fees. They will choose one broker over another for a 25-cents-per-contract difference. Yet the cheaper broker may be providing inferior trade fills that cost you $5 or more per trade than you would be receiving from a good broker. We also discussed execution skills that are somewhat independent of your broker to get the best fills possible in the best situations.

Any book on options is remiss without a clear discussion of volatility. Yet many books eschew a discussion of historical (or realized) volatility entirely, despite the fact that implied volatility is nothing more than an imperfect predictor of historical volatility. Thus, we covered both topics and how they interrelate to allow us to choose the plum trading opportunities available. We also looked at many trading strategies with an eye on which environment each is best utilized.

Lastly, we discussed trade and portfolio management with a particular emphasis on managing and controlling risk. The use of a modified Kelly Criterion exit strategy once again makes use of basic math and probability theory to aid in trade management. Our discussion of portfolio management paid particular attention to not only identifying your overall risk but also reducing both the unique and systematic risk in your portfolio.

A final word about a topic we did not cover explicitly, and that is trading psychology. There are plenty of books written on the topic, and, though I do find it important, I believe understanding risk control and trade sizing nullifies the necessity to dwell on it. If you keep control of the risk in your portfolio through the means we discussed, trading should not be overly painful when the probabilities are serving you the predicted percentage of losses. Yes, there will be losses. The probabilities say so. But they also say that, if properly utilized, the winners will dish up a healthy dose of profits that outweigh and outlast those losers.

I hope you enjoy the journey options trading provides. It is an exciting and fun endeavor that, if done properly, will provide returns greater than you are currently receiving, with less risk than you are currently taking.

About the Website

This book has a companion website, which can be found at www.wiley.com/go/tradeoptions. Enter the password: sherbin123.

The companion website provides a Kelly Criterion spreadsheet, an Excel-based correlation spreadsheet, a basic template (needing to be customized) for a trading log, and various blogs from my website that further illustrate the application of many of the topics discussed in the book.

About the Author

AL SHERBIN has been a professional options trader for more than 26 years without a single losing year. He has written trading models, risk-managed firms, run trading desks for large firms, and traded on the floor as well as over the computer.

Al is currently the managing member of Al on Options LLC, a consulting firm that utilizes his extensive background in financial markets, especially futures and options. Of note, Al:

- Has launched a coaching service to provide options trading knowledge one-on-one.
- Is fielding numerous requests for speaking engagements.
- Is teaching classes to Chinese investors preparing for the launch of options on their exchanges.

Before starting his own firm, Al was the director of research and an on-air personality for Tastytrade, Inc., an IP TV financial news network focusing on engaging self-directed investors in the science and art of options and futures trading. Al developed most of the content for the network, and in 14 months, wrote over 500 20-minute TV segments filled with technical, useable options and futures content. He was also seen on the air each week on two different shows.

Previously Al was an equity options trader at Peak6, where he built most of his own trading tools using a proprietary programming language. He was also Peak6's Special Situations Committee chair, where he scrutinized the 2,000+ companies Peak6 traders dealt in—including simple scrip dividends, mergers, Dutch tenders, rights offerings, regular tenders, and so forth—to ascertain the trade's effects on the firm's overall positions, to determine the future value of the options, and to ensure that no abnormal situations were occurring. Al was also one of two teachers who trained new classes of trader trainees how to become successful traders.

At Al's prior firm, Ideas in Motion, LLC, he was a managing member, and for 12 years he designed and implemented many of the quantitative models and trading systems he used to trade equity and equity options and to perform quantitative risk arbitrage. Al traded currencies, both as a hedge to foreign arbitrages and special situations, and as part of pairs trading and straight economic forecasting trades. Al also traded commodities as arbitrage situations against other commodities, convertible preferred stock, and currencies.

Prior to that position, Al was president of ING TT&S U.S. Securities Inc., a division of ING Bank in the Netherlands. There, Al was solely responsible for starting up a floor trading operation in the United States for the bank. He completed the task in 18 months (with a three-year "budget").

Previously, Al was president of SCMS Inc., a floor trading operation that specialized in index options arbitrage. For the six years he led the company, the firm was highly successful and grew by over 120 percent in terms of employees.

Al's trading career began at Tradelink Corp., a large floor trading operation that was represented on all three Chicago derivative floors. There he traded equity index options and futures as well as individual equity options and stock.

Al mentors traders (13 currently) and frequently speaks in front of trading groups. He is setting up a series of webinars designed to put traders on their way to profitability. These will be available through his website www.AlOnOptions.com. He is active on social media (@sherbn), where he has over 1,700 followers and has been seen frequently on the IP TV network "tastytrade." He has also recently been seen on CBOE-TV, Bloomberg, and BNN in Canada. He teaches options and futures classes both at the college and professional levels in the United States and various countries throughout the world. Of note, Al has taught risk management and options theory to Chinese and Dutch investors and derivatives classes at Carthage College and Lake Forest College, has mentored students in the master's and PhD programs in finance at Illinois Institute of Technology in volatility arbitrage and automated trading systems, and has taught new professional traders at SCMS Inc., Ideas in Motion, and Peak6 Investments.

Index

Printed and bound by CPI Group (UK) Ltd, Croydon, CR0 4YY

16/04/2025

14658522-0002